GOURMET LAB

The **Scientific Principles**

Behind Your Favorite Foods

GOURMET LAB
The Scientific Principles
Behind Your Favorite Foods

Sarah Reeves Young

NSTApress
National Science Teachers Association

Arlington, Virginia

National Science Teachers Association

Claire Reinburg, Director
Jennifer Horak, Managing Editor
Andrew Cooke, Senior Editor
Judy Cusick, Senior Editor
Wendy Rubin, Associate Editor
Amy America, Book Acquisitions Coordinator

Art and Design
Will Thomas Jr., Director, Cover and interior design
Cover and interior design by Lucio Bracamontes

Printing and Production
Catherine Lorrain, Director
Jack Parker, Electronic Prepress Technician

National Science Teachers Association
Francis Q. Eberle, PhD, Executive Director
David Beacom, Publisher

NSTA is committed to publishing material that promotes the best in inquiry-based science education. However, conditions of actual use may vary, and the safety procedures and practices described in this book are intended to serve only as a guide. Additional precautionary measures may be required. NSTA and the authors do not warrant or represent that the procedures and practices in this book meet any safety code or standard of federal, state, or local regulations. NSTA and the authors disclaim any liability for personal injury or damage to property arising out of or relating to the use of this book, including any of the recommendations, instructions, or materials contained therein.

Permissions

Library of Congress Cataloging-in-Publication Data
Young, Sarah (Sarah Reeves)
  Gourmet lab: the scientific principles behind your favorite foods / by Sarah Young.
    p. cm.
Includes bibliographical references and index.
ISBN 978-1-936137-08-4
1. Food—Analysis—Popular works. 2. Chemistry—Laboratory manuals. I. Title.
TX533.Y68 2011
664'.07—dc22
                    2011001156

eISBN 978-1-936137-48-0

CONTENTS

INTRODUCTION

Are you hungry for science? *Gourmet Lab: The Scientific Principles Behind Your Favorite Foods* takes that phrase to a whole new level as students have the opportunity to discover science concepts and learn experimental design skills through interactions with everyday foods. This collection of hands-on experiments challenges students' take on the role of both scientist and chef, as students boil, bake, and toast their way into a better understanding of science concepts from chemistry, biology, and physics. Based on cooking edible food items such as pancakes and butterscotch, students have the opportunity to learn about physical changes, states of matter, acids and bases, biochemistry, and molecular structure. Rather than recipes, students are presented with laboratory explorations that use lab equipment such as Bunsen burners, beakers, and tongs, and work with chemicals such as sodium chloride and sucrose to experience science through cooking. This collection of lab activities brings science to life through an engaging exploration of cooking that will enhance any classroom experience.

The creation of *Gourmet Lab* stems from the general definition of *science* as "the study of the world around you." Often this connection to the real world eludes teachers and students who rely on textbooks to illustrate concepts through labs that attempt to support content with activities that are contrived and narrow in their scope. As a teacher, I found that the experiments in this book encourage students to investigate science phenomena through materials that they can connect to their daily experiences in the kitchen. This connection allows students to actively engage in the science concepts, making for an enhanced learning experience that is both meaningful and memorable.

The labs are designed for secondary science instruction, targeting students in grades 7–10.

The labs can be used to illustrate individual concepts such as physical and chemical changes, or used in a series to teach a more complete picture of science concepts including molecular structure, biochemistry, and acids and bases. These topics are identified by the National Science Education Standards as integral to the education of middle school and high school students when studying chemistry, biology, physics, and more. These standards state, "The program of study in science for all students should be developmentally appropriate, interesting, and relevant to the student's lives; emphasize student understanding through inquiry; and be connected with other school subjects" (NRC 1996, p. 212). Each experiment in this book has been correlated to both content and skill standards in the National Science Education Standards, which are outlined in the table following this introduction.

Each lab is presented with both a student section and a teacher section. The student section of the lab is designed so that it can be handed out directly to students for easy implementation. Each lab begins with background information about the food and science concepts covered in the lab, and then offers a structured approach for investigating a question while building science skills. The investigations conclude with an analysis of data and with connection questions that encourage students to apply concepts from the lab to life experiences beyond the kitchen. Teachers are encouraged to remove elements of the labs such as the Data Analysis, Procedure, or Hypothesis sections to allow students the opportunity to experience the concepts through an inquiry-based model. All the elements provided allow the teacher to decide what information to use to excite students' curiosity and scaffold their investigation of each topic.

The teacher section of each experiment presents a detailed description of how to prepare for each lab, including safety highlights, a materials list that has been decoded for the grocery store, and prelab preparations for a successful experiment. This section goes on to detail demonstrations and activities to engage students, a detailed outline describing implementation of the lab, and answer keys for the students' data analysis and conclusion and connections questions. To enhance the overall learning experience, each teacher section concludes with cross-curricular suggestions for math and literacy (and technology in some cases), and suggests optional extension activities that highlight ways to make the activities engaging for middle school and high school students. The teacher sections are designed to provide teachers with a detailed approach to presenting the activity that allows you to implement it in your class the following day.

Whether you choose to implement a few of the experiments or all of them, *Gourmet Lab* is designed to improve student understanding, skills, and enthusiasm for physics, biology, and chemistry. So put on your apron, safety goggles, and chef hat and help your students start cooking up science!

REFERENCE

National Research Council (NRC). 1996. *National science education standards*. Washington, DC: National Academies Press.

NATIONAL SCIENCE EDUCATION STANDARDS: INCORPORATING *GOURMET LAB* INTO YOUR CURRICULUM

These tables are designed to help teachers identify how the experiments in this book align to the National Science Education Standards. The tables identify correlations for both middle school (grade 5–8) and high school (grade 9–12) science classrooms.

NATIONAL SCIENCE EDUCATION STANDARDS: INCORPORATING *GOURMET LAB* INTO YOUR CURRICULUM

The tables below are designed to help teachers identify how the experiments in this book align to the National Science Education Standards. The tables identify correlations for both middle school (grade 5–8) and high school (grade 9–12) science classrooms.

GRADE 5–8 NATIONAL SCIENCE EDUCATION STANDARDS

NSESS Standards	Changes in Matter					Acids and Bases			Biochemistry					Molecular Structure	
	Experiment 1: Butter Battle	Experiment 2: Exploding Corn	Experiment 3: "Melting" Apples	Experiment 4: Cold Milk	Experiment 5: Gummy Invertebrates	Experiment 6: Acidic Milk	Experiment 7: Berries and Bacteria	Experiment 8: American Mozzarella	Experiment 9: Ballpark Pretzels	Experiment 10: Cinnamon Rolls	Experiment 11: Growing a Pancake	Experiment 12: Under Pressure	Experiment 13: Regular or Diet Soda?	Experiment 14: Crystal Carbohydrates	Experiment 15: Strong Sugar Science
Science as Inquiry															
Abilities necessary to do scientific inquiry	X	X	X	X	X	X	X	X	X	X	X	X	X	X	X
Understanding about scientific inquiry	X	X	X	X	X	X	X	X	X	X	X	X	X	X	X
Physical Science															
Properties and changes of properties in matter	X	X	X	X	X	X		X	X	X	X	X	X	X	X
Motion and forces															

NATIONAL SCIENCE TEACHERS ASSOCIATION

X

Transfer of energy	X	X	X	X	X	X	X	X					X	X
Life Science														
Structure and function in living systems					X	X	X	X	X				X	X
Reproduction and heredity							X							
Regulation and behavior							X	X	X				X	X
Populations and ecosystems							X		X					
Diversity and adaptations of organisms														
Earth and Space Science														
Structure of the earth system														
Earth's history														
Earth in the solar system														
Science and Technology														
Abilities of technological design								X	X			X	X	X
Understanding about science and technology				X			X	X	X			X	X	X
Science in Personal and Social Perspectives														
Personal health	X												X	X
Populations, resources, and environments														
Natural hazards					X	X								
Risks and benefits	X			X					X			X	X	X

Category	NSESS Standards	Science and technology in society	Science as a human endeavor	Nature of science	History of science
			History and Nature of Science		
Molecular Structure	Experiment 15: Strong Sugar Science	X	X	X	
Molecular Structure	Experiment 14: Crystal Carbohydrates	X	X	X	
Biochemistry	Experiment 13: Regular or Diet Soda?	X	X	X	
Biochemistry	Experiment 12: Under Pressure	X	X	X	
Biochemistry	Experiment 11: Growing a Pancake	X	X	X	
Biochemistry	Experiment 10: Cinnamon Rolls	X	X	X	
Biochemistry	Experiment 9: Ballpark Pretzels	X	X	X	
Acids and Bases	Experiment 8: American Mozzarella	X	X	X	X
Acids and Bases	Experiment 7: Berries and Bacteria	X	X	X	
Acids and Bases	Experiment 6: Acidic Milk	X	X	X	
Changes in Matter	Experiment 5: Gummy Invertebrates	X	X	X	
Changes in Matter	Experiment 4: Cold Milk	X	X	X	
Changes in Matter	Experiment 3: "Melting" Apples	X	X	X	
Changes in Matter	Experiment 2: Exploding Corn	X	X	X	X
Changes in Matter	Experiment 1: Butter Battle	X	X	X	

GRADE 9–12 NATIONAL SCIENCE EDUCATION STANDARDS

NSES Standards	Exp 1: Butter Battle	Exp 2: Exploding Corn	Exp 3: "Melting" Applies	Exp 4: Cold Milk	Exp 5: Gummy Invertebrates	Exp 6: Acidic Milk	Exp 7: Berries and Bacteria	Exp 8: American Mozzarella	Exp 9: Ballpark Pretzels	Exp 10: Cinnamon Rolls	Exp 11: Growing a Pancake	Exp 12: Under Pressure	Exp 13: Regular or Diet Soda?	Exp 14: Crystal Carbohydrates	Exp 15: Strong Sugar Science
Category	Changes in Matter	Changes in Matter	Changes in Matter	Changes in Matter	Changes in Matter	Acids and Bases	Acids and Bases	Acids and Bases	Biochemistry	Biochemistry	Biochemistry	Biochemistry	Biochemistry	Molecular Structure	Molecular Structure
Science as Inquiry															
Abilities necessary to do scientific inquiry	X	X	X	X	X	X	X	X	X	X	X	X	X	X	X
Understanding about scientific inquiry	X	X	X	X	X	X	X	X	X	X	X	X	X	X	X
Physical Science															
Structure of atoms	X	X	X	X	X	X		X	X	X	X	X	X	X	X
Structure and properties of matter	X	X	X		X	X		X	X	X	X	X	X	X	X
Chemical reactions				X	X	X	X	X	X	X	X	X	X	X	X
Motions and forces							X								
Conservation of energy and increase in disorder	X	X		X										X	X

NSES Standards		Interactions of energy and matter	Life Science						Earth and Space Science	
			The cell	Molecular basis of heredity	Biological evolution	Interdependence of organisms	Matter, energy, and organization in living systems	Behavior of organisms	Energy in the earth system	Geochemical cycles
Molecular Structure	Experiment 15: Strong Sugar Science									
Molecular Structure	Experiment 14: Crystal Carbohydrates									
Biochemistry	Experiment 13: Regular or Diet Soda?		X			X	X			
Biochemistry	Experiment 12: Under Pressure		X			X	X			
Biochemistry	Experiment 11: Growing a Pancake		X			X	X			
Biochemistry	Experiment 10: Cinnamon Rolls		X				X			
Biochemistry	Experiment 9: Ballpark Pretzels		X				X			
Acids and Bases	Experiment 8: American Mozzarella		X							
Acids and Bases	Experiment 7: Berries and Bacteria		X			X	X			
Acids and Bases	Experiment 6: Acidic Milk									
Changes in Matter	Experiment 5: Gummy Invertebrates									
Changes in Matter	Experiment 4: Cold Milk	X								
Changes in Matter	Experiment 3: "Melting" Applies	X								
Changes in Matter	Experiment 2: Exploding Corn									
Changes in Matter	Experiment 1: Butter Battle	X					X			

NATIONAL SCIENCE TEACHERS ASSOCIATION

Standard													
Origin and evolution of the earth system													
Origin and evolution of the universe													
Science and Technology													
Abilities of technological design	X	X	X	X	X	X	X	X	X	X	X	X	X
Understanding about science and technology	X	X	X	X	X	X	X	X	X	X	X	X	X
Science in Personal and Social Perspectives													
Personal and community health	X												X
Population growth				X									
Natural resources													
Environmental quality													
Natural and human-induced hazards													
Science and technology in local, national, and global challenges	X	X	X	X	X	X	X	X	X	X	X	X	X
History and Nature of Science													
Science as a human endeavor	X	X	X	X	X	X	X	X	X	X	X	X	X
Nature of scientific knowledge	X	X	X	X	X	X	X	X	X	X	X	X	X
Historical perspectives	X	X	X	X	X	X	X	X	X	X	X	X	X

SAFETY PROTOCOL
How to Make Cooking Safe in a Laboratory

The first topic that I cover in my eighth-grade science classroom is laboratory safety. In the past, after going over rules such as "Always follow directions" and "Safety goggles are the number one fashion accessory required for lab," I always taught my students, "Food and drink are *not* allowed in the lab." When I asked them to explain why this was a rule, the students were quick to explain that food and drinks consumed in the lab may be contaminated with chemicals, and could be unsafe. It was clear, even to my eighth-grade students, that eating in a lab was not a good choice.

So I was completely taken aback when a fellow teacher shared that she was doing an "edible lab" with her class. This concept went against every lab safety poster I had ever seen in a science classroom. Eating in the laboratory was definitely not something that I would ever consider implementing with my students…or so I thought.

This teacher was nice enough to invite me to visit her class so that I could see the edible lab in action. The students were testing whether vitamin C could prevent the oxidation reaction that turned apple slices brown. Students were given food products such as tomatoes, orange juice, and lemon juice that contained different levels of vitamin C. They worked in teams to apply these solutions to the apples and measure how quickly they reached a predetermined brown color.

As I moved around the room and watched student groups, I was amazed at how engaged the students were in the experiment. Not only were students completing the experiment but they also were generating the discussion and asking questions about employing other methods for preventing oxygen from changing the color of the apples. I heard several students comment that they had asked their parents about this process, and some shared stories about how their family members approached keeping apples from turning brown. The lab engaged the students' curiosity in a context that allowed them to create personal connections.

After leaving the classroom that day, I was impressed, but still a bit skeptical. Maybe this was an honors class or there was a reward promised for good behavior, or maybe this teacher just deserved to be nominated for teacher of the year. There were many possible factors that could have created the effective learning environment. So, as a science teacher, I decided to run my own experiment. I had been approached to do a weeklong summer course for adolescent students at my school. The topic was my choice, so I decided to go with edible science. This would give me an opportunity to test the feasibility of food in the classroom with a smaller group. It would also give me an opportunity to see if edible science was really going to be as amazing in my classroom as it was in the vitamin C experiment.

I decided to start off in the most sterile science environment I could think of: a math classroom. Rather than worrying about the chemical contamination of my room, I was going to set up camp in a regular classroom. As part of being away from my regular lab-integrated classroom, I didn't have access to all of my science supplies, just some basic measurement tools. Each lab experiment was done with disposable items such as paper cups; Styrofoam bowls; and plastic knives, forks, and spoons. I started off with simple experiments such as comparing the melting time of chocolates in students' mouths to talk about thermal energy transfer, and creating solutions with different percentages of fruit drink mix. I was truly floored by the student response. The students were excited to come to the summer course, even though most of their parents had signed them up without asking their permission. I had parents e-mailing me to see if they could get copies of the experiments so they could see what prompted the enthusiasm from their kids as they talked about the class in the car ride home. I even had students join the class midweek based on word of mouth.

But again, the skeptic in me held off judgment. These were students whose parents felt they would be interested in a science summer course, so they had to already have some interest in the topic. What about doing this with a class of eighth-grade students who were required to be in the lab as opposed to making the personal choice to attend? But in order to test that question, I was going to have to make a big leap. I was going to have to start running the experiments in my science room.

I was terrified at the thought that I might inadvertently harm a student by exposing him or her to a chemical through an edible classroom lab experience. Although I mainly used household chemicals in my classroom, I was still concerned that cross-contamination was a huge possibility. So I erred on the side of caution. I was not willing to use *any* of the lab equipment that I had used previously in a science setting with other chemicals. Luckily, I was starting a new school year and would be receiving my requested lab replacement materials. This was a few beakers, a few thermometers, a few droppers, a couple of plastic bottles, and three new Bunsen burners. Rather than placing these items into the cabinets with the other supplies, I made space for my new "edible science" equipment. The equipment was placed in a sealed plastic storage container in a locked cabinet, so I could be sure that the equipment wasn't being used elsewhere in the lab with other chemicals.

Based on the few supplies I had, I started with a simple lab—Butter Battle—to introduce the topic of physical change. The lab didn't require heat and had very few chemicals and supplies. I was so nervous

about the experience; I actually had the students complete the lab in the classroom area just to make sure we weren't exposing the food products to chemicals in the lab environment. I watched students work in pairs to create butter, and I was amazed again by their interest, engagement, and overall excitement. I had students asking for containers or cups so they could take their butter home to share with friends and family. Upon leaving class, one student who at the beginning of the year had openly told me he had never liked science said, "That was great. What are we making tomorrow?"

From that initial classroom experiment, I have slowly grown to incorporate more and more edible labs into my curriculum. With each lab, I consider safety the number one priority, and have learned many ways to make food in the lab a safe activity. With the help of books like *Inquiring Safely: A Guide for Middle School Teachers* by Terry Kwan and Juliana Texley, resources from Flinn Scientific, and cautious methods learned from working with chemicals as a high school and college student, I have been able to bring science to life for my middle school students.

GENERAL SAFETY GUIDELINES

It is recommended that all of these lab activities be carried out in a consumer science laboratory or home economics kitchen that has been designed and operated for the safe use of food products that can be eaten when health and safety protocols are followed. The following is a list of general safety guidelines that should be followed by any teacher planning to implement any of the labs in this book. Please read these guidelines before completing any of the experiments with your students.

- Use only special glassware and equipment, stored away from all sources of laboratory chemical contamination and reserved only for food experiments. (Using laboratory equipment that has been used in other laboratory experiments is *not* recommended; even after cleaning and sterilizing, it is not guaranteed that the materials will be free from all chemical residue.)

- Wear indirectly vented chemical-splash goggles in the laboratory at all times.
- Sanitize personal protective equipment such as goggles before and after use.
- Wear proper lab attire for edible science labs, such as long pants, closed-toe shoes, and long-sleeved shirts, when working with hot liquids or chemicals that may splatter.
- Remove all jewelry and baggy clothing.
- Pull back long hair to keep out of the face before entering the lab area.
- Use nitrile-type gloves when working with acids.
- Wash your hands thoroughly at the end of all labs.
- Have 10-second access to an eyewash station and acid shower.
- Review material safety data sheets (MSDS) with students prior to using hazardous chemicals.

SAFETY GUIDELINES FOR CLEANING AND STORAGE

- If an experiment was performed in a classroom (outside the laboratory), clean all work surfaces to be sure they are free from laboratory chemicals. After cleaning work surfaces, cover all work areas with aluminum foil or a food-grade paper covering.
- Clean all glassware and apparatus to be sure they are free from laboratory chemicals, and label them FOOD ONLY.
- Store all chemicals and food-grade materials separately from other lab chemicals. This includes having a separate labeled cabinet and refrigerator for cold materials.

SAFETY GUIDELINES FOR BUNSEN BURNERS

- Model the appropriate procedures for students when using hazardous equipment such as Bunsen burners.
- Remove all flammable and combustible materials from the lab bench and surrounding work area when Bunsen burners will be used. Do *not* use a Bunsen burner in any lab when working with flammable liquids or solvents.
- Review the basic construction of a Bunsen burner and inspect the burner, attached tubing, and gas valve before use. Check for holes or cracks in the tubing and replace the tubing if necessary. (*Note*: Use only American Gas Association–approved Bunsen tubing connectors. Do not use only latex tubing.)
- Use only heat-resistant, borosilicate glassware when using a Bunsen burner. Check the glassware for scratches, nicks, or cracks before use and discard defective glassware, which may shatter without warning when heated.
- Never reach over an exposed flame.
- Never leave a lit burner unattended. Always turn off the gas at the gas source when finished using the burner.
- Do not place a hot apparatus directly on the laboratory desk or bench. Always use an insulating pad, and allow plenty of time for the apparatus to cool before touching it.
- Never look into a container that is being heated. When heating a test tube, make sure that the mouth of the tube is not pointing at anybody (including yourself).
- Use matches as a checkpoint with all student groups. Matches are specifically not handed out as a part of the materials list for any of the labs. All student groups must come and get matches from me. Before I distribute matches, I will check off that students have properly set up their

Bunsen burner and ring stand, they have the proper equipment and materials ready, and they are wearing the appropriate safety gear. I often ask the students to articulate who is in charge of the Bunsen burner at all times, so that they are clear on who is watching the burner, and who is available to talk to other lab groups, get additional supplies, or come to me for help.

SAFETY GUIDELINES FOR HOT PLATES

- To reduce heat stress, allow hot glassware or equipment to cool slowly before removing the object from the hot plate. Remember that hot objects remain hot for a long time, so use tongs, heat-protective gloves, or hot vessel–gripping devices as needed.
- Turn off the hot plate when not in use. The surface of the plate stays hot for quite some time and looks exactly the same as a "cold" hot plate. Place a laminated "HOT" caution sign in front of the hot plate immediately after use.
- Use only heat-resistant, borosilicate glassware and check for cracks before heating on a hot plate. Do not place thick-walled glassware such as filter flasks, or soft-glass bottles and jars, on a hot plate. The hot plate surface should be larger than the vessel being heated.
- Do not use the hot plate in the presence of flammable or combustible materials because fire or explosion may result. The device contains components that may ignite such material.
- Place boiling stones in liquids being heated to facilitate even heating and boiling. Do not evaporate all of the solvent or otherwise heat a mixture to dryness on a hot plate—the glass may crack unexpectedly when heated directly on a hot plate.
- Use a medium to medium-high setting of the hot plate to heat most liquids, including water.

Do not use the high setting to heat low-boiling liquids. The hot plate surface can reach a maximum temperature of 540°C.
- Do not place metal foil or metal containers on the hot plate—the top of the hot plate can be damaged and a shock hazard may result.
- Use only Ground Fault Circuit Interruption (GFCI) protected wall receptacles for a power source.

SAFETY GUIDELINES FOR STUDENT ALLERGIES

- Many students have food allergies that often are not shared with teachers but exist in their school files. As part of my class, I specifically ask parents to document any food allergies on the lab safety acknowledgment form I ask students and parents to sign at the beginning of the year. This helps me know if there are materials or lab activities I need to avoid, so I can plan my approach effectively.
- Allergies exist in many forms, from peanuts to fruit, dairy, and wheat. Take every student allergy seriously, and know the steps and procedures to follow in the event that a student is exposed to a product he or she is allergic to. In some cases, this means having access to epinephrine injection devices. Know where these injectors are kept so that you don't find yourself searching the school for them when they are needed most.

Aside from the suggestions offered here, please note that many schools and districts have their own rules and guidelines for laboratory safety. Many times this includes rules about having food in the classroom. Check with your school administration to ensure that giving out edible products in the class-room is allowed. Also, most teachers as employees are required to be working in laboratories under the Occupational Safety & Health Administration (OSHA) laboratory standards and best professional practices. (See the NSTA position statement *Safety and School Science Instruction* for more information.)

If you feel that you cannot meet all the expectations outlined here for the safe implementation of edible laboratory activities, then you should not use these activities in your classroom with the purpose of having students taste or consume the edible materials. The experiments can be implemented without students consuming the products with modifications to the questions and presentation.

The most important rule of all is to be safe. Your students will not love science if they get hurt learning about it. Always be cautious, and when in doubt, seek out additional resources to clarify questions before taking on a new lab. Suggested resources include the following:

- OSHA's Laboratory Standard or Hazard Communication Standard outlines safety expectations for a laboratory environment.
- Local and state health codes require specific environments, free from hazardous microorganisms and hazardous chemicals for food preparation.
- Books on best practices, such as *Investigating Safely* and *Inquiring Safely* published by NSTA, have content that addresses food safety in the science classroom.

Gourmet Lab Reminders

Following is a list of general reminders for teachers implementing any of the experiments in this book.

All science lab supplies need to be used exclusively for *Gourmet Lab* experiments. Cleaning and sterilization of other supplies does not guarantee that all chemical residues have been removed from previous experiments.

Gourmet Lab materials, such as beakers and glass rods, need to be cleaned and sterilized before being used to create food that will be consumed by the students. Please see the Safety Protocol section at the beginning of the book for specific instructions about safely cleaning your lab equipment.

Label each of the ingredients with their chemical name and appropriate hazard warning. You can place the ingredients in separate lab containers such as beakers and flasks and then have students try to identify the common name through observation such as taste, smell, or appearance, or you can place the labels directly on the store-bought containers so students can compare the chemical names with the ingredients listed on the package.

Remind students to practice the ABC policy—Always Be Cleaning— at the outset of the lab.

PART ONE: CHANGES IN MATTER

The activities in this section are designed to help introduce and reinforce the idea of changes in matter. Experiment 1: Butter Battle highlights the differences between physical and chemical changes in the creation of butter. Experiment 2: Exploding Corn highlights how water can change state from liquid to gas in the popping of corn. These changes are measured by mass and volume, and the experiment highlights the differences in these measurements. Experiment 3: "Melting" Apples pushes students' understanding of phase changes further to show that these changes are a result of thermal energy changes in molecules. Students use graphing skills to see how temperature relates to the phases of matter. Experiment 4: Cold Milk highlights how temperature change can come from places other than Bunsen burners, and introduces students to the concepts of endothermic reactions and exothermic reactions. Finally, Experiment 5: Gummy Invertebrates challenges students to look at how phase changes can be initiated by the introduction of new chemical elements such as gelatin. The experiment also introduces the concept of independent variables, and how changing a variable in a recipe can impact the final outcome. These activities are designed to introduce students to basic concepts in changes in matter with a progression that starts with basic concepts and builds to a discussion of molecular energy and chemical interactions. Each activity highlights different fundamental science skills in measurement, graphing, and experimental design.

EXPERIMENT 1:
Butter Battle: Student Pages

PHYSICAL CHANGES VERSUS CHEMICAL CHANGES

BACKGROUND

When passing hot rolls around the dinner table, buying popcorn at a movie theater, or making cookies, it is there: butter. The average American eats 5 pounds of butter a year. At this rate, you will have eaten close to 100 pounds of butter by the time you graduate high school. If the adage "You are what you eat" is true, then the composition of butter is worth investigating.

Butter is created from warm cream through a process known as churning. Our current understanding states that when air is mixed into the cream, foam is formed. Within that foam, fat globules collect in the bubble walls. If you begin with cream that is chilled and stop when the foam is formed, then you end up with a final product of whipped cream. If you begin with warm cream, then the fat globules liquefy to some degree. Further agitation through churning breaks down the protective membrane around the fat globules and causes them to congregate into a solid mass. The liquefied fat helps to cement the exposed fat droplets together into butter. The final product is about 80% milk fat, 18% water, and 2% milk solids. The remaining liquid is buttermilk. With the majority of butter composed of fat, it is no wonder that it tastes so good.

This experiment will give you an opportunity to create your own butter for consumption while calculating the calories created in your butter contrasted with the calories expended in making the butter. While creating your "fat and foam," consider whether the creation of butter is a *physical change* or *chemical change*. What is the difference between these two changes, and which is taking place in the churning of butter?

HYPOTHESIS

For this experiment, you will be generating the energy necessary to create butter. Make a hypothesis stating "Do you think it will take more calories to create the butter than the calories you will get from eating the butter?"

MATERIALS NEEDED PER PAIR OF STUDENTS

- 50 ml of emulsified colloid of liquid butterfat in H_2O (heavy cream)
- 0.25 g of sodium chloride, NaCl (salt)
- 500 ml chilled dihydrogen monoxide, H_2O (ice water)
- Starch and a piece of *Cinnamomum verum* (cinnamon bread), one piece per student
- Graduated cylinder, 100 ml
- Balance
- Filter paper
- One plastic jar with lid, or test tube with stopper
- Plastic knife or spreader
- Indirectly vented chemical-splash goggles
- Aprons

Optional:
- Bunsen burner or toaster oven
- Tongs

PROCEDURE

1. Read through the entire Procedure section before beginning.

2. Put on your safety goggles and apron, and gather all your materials at your lab station. If you notice any of the materials are dirty or discolored, notify your teacher.

3. Using the balance, find the mass of your container without the lid and record the mass in your data table.

4. Measure 50 ml of emulsified colloid of liquid butterfat in H_2O in the 100 ml graduated cylinder.

5. Pour the 50 ml of emulsified colloid of liquid butterfat in H_2O into your container (plastic jar or test tube with stopper).

6. Cap the container with the lid and seal it tight.

7. Before you begin shaking, record the time you begin in the data table.

8. Shake the container about 20 times. Open the top slightly to relieve the pressure, and then reseal.

9. Continue to shake the container until all the liquid appears to have solidified. Once you have a complete solid, record the time in the data table.

10. Open the container and inspect the contents. Use the edge of your knife or your finger to taste a small amount of the contents. Describe the taste and texture of the contents in the data table.

11. Close your container tightly and continue to shake until lumps of solid fat form surrounded by a thin and opaque liquid. The liquid is known as buttermilk. Record the time in the data table when you reach this phase.

12. Open the container and taste the liquid buttermilk. Record your observations in the data table.

13. Pour the liquid buttermilk out of the container, being careful not to lose any of the solidified fat.

14. Add fresh, cold water until the container is about one-third full. Replace the lid and shake about five times. Pour off the wash water and repeat the washing until the water pours off clean. Record the number of rinses you completed.

15. Once the water pours off clean, use the balance to record the mass of the container with the butter and record this in your data table. Complete the calculations necessary to determine the mass of the butter you created.

16. Place the butter on starch and a piece of *Cinnamomum verum*.

17. Clean your lab area and answer the Data Analysis and Conclusion and Connections questions that follow.

DATA AND OBSERVATIONS

Balance Measurements	
	Mass (g)
Mass of container without lid	
Mass of container with butter	
Mass of butter created	

Time and Taste Observations		
Phase	Time (hours and minutes)	Observations
Agitation of container start time		
Initial solidification of liquid		Taste of solid
Secondary solidification and liquefaction of buttermilk		Taste of liquid Number of rinse cycles

DATA ANALYSIS

For each of the following questions, be sure to explain using detail and complete sentences. If the question requires you to complete calculations, show all of your work.

1. How much time did it take you to transform your cream into butter? Use the recorded times in your data table.

2. If butter contains 1,628 kilocalories per cup (227 g), then how many calories are in a single gram of butter?

3. How many grams of butter did you transform from the original cream? How many kilocalories are in that butter?

4. If the average person burns 135 kilocalories while shaking for 30 minutes, how many calories did you burn while making the butter?

CONCLUSION AND CONNECTIONS

1. Was your hypothesis correct or incorrect? Explain using data to support your answer.

2. Is creating butter a physical change or chemical change? Explain.

3. Name three other examples of this kind of change in the kitchen that are different from those already discussed in class.

EXPERIMENT 1:
Butter Battle: Teacher Pages

PHYSICAL CHANGES VERSUS CHEMICAL CHANGES

Creating butter in a bottle helps students see how a physical change can be more drastic than an ice cube melting. This experiment provides an opportunity for students to use observation skills to investigate how a liquid heavy cream can undergo a physical change to become butter. This lab also can be used for study of the creation and utilization of calories, and of comparing and contrasting physical and chemical changes.

STANDARDS ADDRESSED

National Science Education Standards: Grades 5–8

Content Standard A: Science as Inquiry
- Abilities necessary to do scientific inquiry
- Understanding about scientific inquiry

Content Standard B: Physical Science
- Properties and changes of properties in matter

Content Standard F: Science in Personal and Social Perspectives
- Personal health
- Risks and benefits
- Science and technology in society

Content Standard G: History and Nature of Science
- Science as a human endeavor
- Nature of science

National Science Education Standards: Grades 9–12

Content Standard A: Science as Inquiry
- Abilities necessary to do scientific inquiry
- Understanding about scientific inquiry

Content Standard B: Physical Science
- Structure of atoms
- Structure and properties of matter
- Conservation of energy and increase in disorder
- Interactions of energy and matter

Content Standard C: Life Science
- Matter, energy, and organization in living systems

Content Standard E: Science and Technology
- Abilities of technological design
- Understanding about science and technology

Content Standard F: Science in Personal and Social Perspectives
- Personal and community health
- Science and technology in local, national, and global challenges

Content Standard G: History and Nature of Science
- Science as a human endeavor
- Nature of scientific knowledge
- Historical perspectives

VOCABULARY

Chemical change: Any process where there is change in the atomic and molecular composition and structure of the substances. (Princeton University 2006).

Physical change: A change from one state (solid or liquid or gas) to another without a change in chemical composition. (Princeton University 2006).

MATERIALS NEEDED, DECODED FOR THE GROCERY STORE

50 ml of emulsified colloid of liquid butterfat in H_2O (heavy cream)
- A quart of heavy cream contains about 950 ml, so enough for almost 20 student lab groups.

0.25 g of sodium chloride, NaCl (salt)
- Each student uses a pinch of salt for their butter, so a single saltshaker will be more than enough for a class.

Chilled dihydrogen monoxide, H_2O (ice water)
- Each student lab group will need about 500 ml of chilled water.

Starch and a piece of *Cinnamomum verum* (cinnamon bread)
- Each student will need one piece of bread.

SAFETY HIGHLIGHTS

- Sterilize the churning containers prior to and after student use. (This includes the stopper or cap.)
- Sterilize the fresh or distilled water containers prior to student use.
- Sterilize the spreading utensils or use plastic knives that are specific for edible science labs.

Note that these safety highlights are in addition to the safety information detailed in the Safety Protocol section at the beginning of this book. Please refer to that section for additional information about safety when implementing this or any lab in this book.

PREPARATION

1. It is important that the cream is at room temperature, around 16.6°C (62°F). If the cream is too cold, students will end up with whipped cream rather than butter. Depending on the day, set out the cream 20–30 minutes before the lab is to begin. Only set out sealed containers, as open containers are more likely to spoil.

2. Place water into plastic bottles and place in a refrigerator to cool. Wash bottles or dropper bottles work well, and keep the science equipment theme of the lab, but you can use any container that is available. I do not recommend placing these in a freezer, as the ice can expand and potentially damage the containers.

3. Students can use test tubes and stoppers, plastic jars with lids, or baby food jars to create the butter. Have one container available for each group.

PROCEDURE

I recommend having the students work in pairs for this experiment. Although the procedure is relatively simple and straightforward and can be done by students individually, I have found that allowing students to work with a partner in the creation of butter allows them to make observations and clean more effectively. The amount of butter made is more than enough for two students to enjoy.

1. Begin by reading the Background section. Encourage students to share their favorite food that involves butter, because making that connection will help them become more invested in the lab.

2. The final paragraph in the Background section introduces the concepts of physical change and chemical change. Allow students the opportunity to create a web of examples of each type of change on the board in a brainstorm. If students are unfamiliar with the concepts, you can give the examples listed below. Based on the examples, create a list of specifications of what characterizes a chemical versus physical change. If students feel confident, you can ask them to create a definition based on the characteristics. If the information is new, then create a definition after students have completed the lab as part of the postlab conclusion and connections discussion. Use the information on the board as a reference to help guide students' inquiry and questions during their lab experience.

Physical Change	Chemical Change
Examples: melting chocolate, mixing salt and sugar, boiling water, breaking a salt block into smaller pieces	Examples: frying an egg, mixing vinegar and baking soda, baking bread
Characteristics of a physical change: Changes the state of matter (solid, liquid, gas). Does *not* change the chemical makeup (e.g., if you melt chocolate from a solid to a liquid, it is still chocolate). You can reverse the process to get back your original materials (e.g., you can refreeze the water to get another ice cube).	Characteristics of a chemical change: Creates a new chemical substance. The new chemical substance often has different physical properties when compared with the original substance. The process cannot be reversed to gain back original materials.
Definition of *physical change*: A change from one state (solid or liquid or gas) to another without a change in chemical composition. (Princeton University 2006)	Definition of *chemical change*: Any process where there is change in the atomic and molecular composition and structure of the substances. (Princeton University 2006)

3. After reading the Background section, have students complete their hypothesis. I ask students to use an "If…Then…Because…" format to make sure they address the cause-and-effect relationship in the experiment.

4. For timing, you can have students use stopwatches or the clock on the wall. The entire process takes 15–20 minutes from cream to butter depending on the speed of shaking, so I use the wall clock.

5. When students release the pressure, often some of the cream will spray out, which is usually surprising and exciting for the students. As they continue to shake the container, facilitate a discussion about other liquids that gain pressure when shaken (such as carbonated sodas).

6. The release of pressure and cream can make the jars difficult to reopen. Paper towels make it easier, as does soap and water so that students can wash their hands to get a better grip.

7. It will take students about 10 minutes of shaking to reach the first solidification stage. I encourage them to trade off shaking with their partner, as it can be a tiring process.

8. Provide soap to clean all the equipment thoroughly after the lab.

DATA ANALYSIS ANSWER KEY

All the data analysis for this lab is math based and involves solving for a simplified base unit such as calories/minute or calories/gram from students' individual data. If students are struggling with the calculations, I recommend using a sample data set and going through the calculations as a class on the board. Then they can use the same skills and apply them directly to their data.

1. *How much time did it take you to transform your cream into butter? Use the recorded times in your data table.*

    On average, it takes students 15–20 minutes total to go from the heavy cream to the butter. This number depends on the speed of their agitation, and the starting temperature of their butter.

2. *If butter contains 1,628 kilocalories per cup (227 g), then how many calories are in a single gram of butter?*

    1,628 calories (227 g) = 7.172 kilocalories/g
    Note that this question asks about kilocalories. Many students are familiar with the term *calorie* and will ask what the difference is between a calorie and

kilocalorie. A calorie is a unit of energy: The energy it takes to raise one gram of water by one degree Celsius. When the word *calories* is used to describe food in the United States, it is actually referring to kilocalories (1,000 calories = 1 kilocalorie). It is supposed to be represented by writing *Calorie* with a capital C, but is often not. In an effort to be correct in our use of the metric system in science we will refer to kilocalories or kcal to prevent confusion.

3. *How many grams of butter did you transform from the original cream? How many kilocalories are in that butter?*

The amount of butter created will depend on the students, but averages around 30–35 g of butter. To find the calories in the butter they created, students need to multiply the mass of butter by 7.172 cal/g. For example, a student who made 30 g of butter would have the following calculations: 30 g × 7.172 cal/g = 215 cal.

4. *If the average person burns 135 cal for shaking for 30 minutes, how many calories did you burn while making the butter?*

135 cal ÷ 30 minutes = 4.5 cal/minute

Students' answers will vary based on the time it took them to create butter, which was calculated in Data Analysis question 1. A student group that took 18 minutes to create its butter would have the following calculations:

18 minutes × 4.5 kilocalories/minute = 81 kilocalories burned

CONCLUSION AND CONNECTIONS ANSWER KEY

This section of the lab offers a great opportunity to engage the entire class in discussion to clarify the main ideas of the lab and allow students to make their own connections between science and cooking. I ask that students answer the Data Analysis questions and attempt to answer the Conclusion and Connections questions, with the understanding that we will spend time the next day discussing the Conclusion and Connections section.

1. *Was your hypothesis correct or incorrect? Explaining using data to support your answer.*

Unless the students end up with very little butter, then all student groups should find that they create more butter calories then they expend in the process. They can use the data in their Data Analysis questions 3 and 4 to support their answer.

2. *Is creating butter a physical change or chemical change? Explain.*

   Physical change is defined as "a change from one state (solid, liquid, or gas) to another without a change in chemical composition." The fat globules exist in the cream at the outset of the experiment, and are only being rearranged through the agitation process. This information is available in the Background section in the student handout. Therefore, the chemical composition remains the same, and the creation of butter is a physical change.

   Another way to look at physical change versus chemical change is by asking students if it is possible to reverse the process. If you can reverse the process, then it is a physical change in state rather than a chemical change in composition. You can use an ice cube to demonstrate this. If you melt an ice cube, you can refreeze the water back into an ice cube. If you take buttermilk and add it to the butter and stir slowly, you can reincorporate the liquid back to form cream. This is a good demonstration that allows students to arrive at an understanding that creating butter is a physical reaction not a chemical reaction.

   Many students will automatically jump to the conclusion that it must be a chemical reaction because of the discussion of chemical composition in the background information. It is important to note that the components themselves are not changing, just being rearranged.

3. *Name three other examples of this kind of change in the kitchen that are different from those already discussed in class.*

   - Mixing any type of dry ingredient such as flour and salt. The salt is still salt and the flour is still flour.
   - Melting items such as butter or chocolate. Changing the state of an object is a physical change.
   - Boiling water. Again this is a state change from liquid to gas.
   - Creating salad dressing by mixing oil and water. The molecules of each liquid stay together and will separate back into their original volumes if given time.

CROSS-CURRICULAR NOTE: MATH

This lab provides an ideal opportunity to work with the math teacher on skills such as simplifying and cancelling units.

CROSS-CURRICULAR NOTE: LITERACY

This lab provides an ideal opportunity to work with the English teacher to have students compose a creative story. Ask students to write a story about what they would have to do to burn off all the calories in the butter. As a part of this, students could research how completing certain exercises and tasks could burn a set number of calories. This is also a great connection to student health classes and making healthy life choices.

OPTIONAL EXTENSIONS

Middle School

1. This investigation can use student inquiry to direct the questions and experiment. After presenting the background information, allow students to brainstorm questions they have about making butter. I often ask students, "What variables might impact the creation of butter?" (Potential examples include temperature, agitation time, fat percentage in cream, and container for butter formation.) After allowing them to brainstorm on the board, have students narrow down the selections to self-select a variable to test in the creation of butter. After writing a hypothesis, provide them with a sample materials list and then allow them to write a procedure and test the impact of changing a variable on the creation of butter.

2. Students can compare the physical change of the butter with the chemical change that occurs when toasting the cinnamon bread. This can be accomplished in the lab with a simple toaster or toaster oven. It is also possible to allow students to toast the bread over an open Bunsen burner flame using tongs to hold the bread (two sets of tongs are better if you have fresh bread). If you use Bunsen burners, it is important that they have been cleaned of all chemicals inside and out. I have separate Bunsen burners that I use only for toasting.

3. Students can compare the butter to margarine and answer the following questions: What are the differences in the ingredients? Is there a major taste difference? What about the difference in calories?

High School

1. A chemical change changes the chemical composition of the item. Ask students to research and identify the chemical equations of some of the chemical reactions identified in a kitchen. Ask, "How do those equations compare

to items that go through a physical change? Can you identify the type of change occurring based on the chemical equation?"

2. Students can compare the difference in the chemical composition of butter to the chemical composition of margarine. Ask, "How does the change in chemical composition impact the digestion of each food in humans?"

3. Students can test the calories present in foods with a lot of butter when compared with foods with little butter using a calorimeter.

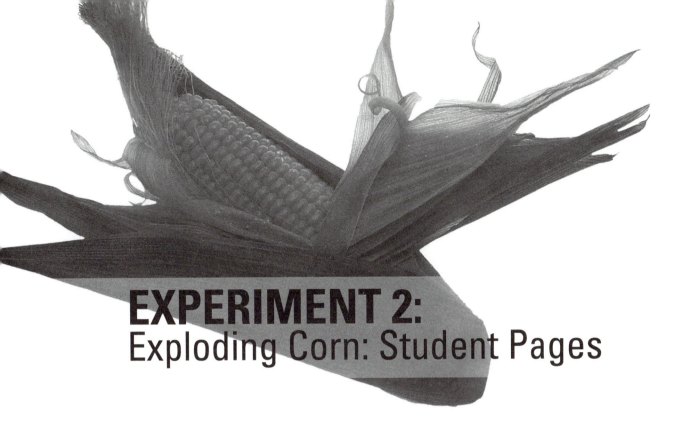

EXPERIMENT 2:
Exploding Corn: Student Pages

DIFFERENCE BEWEEN MASS AND VOLUME CHANGES WITH POPCORN

BACKGROUND

According to The Popcorn Board, Americans today consume 17 billion quarts of popped popcorn each year (see www.popcorn.org). The average American eats about 52 quarts of popcorn per year. Think about that the next time you sit down for a movie with a big bowl of popcorn.

The science behind corn popping is as simple as boiling water. Each popcorn kernel contains starch and water. The kernel needs to have a moisture content around 14% in order to have the fuel to pop. The starch grains of the popcorn are enclosed in a pericarp, or seed, covering (see Figure 2.1, p. 20). When the kernel is heated, the starch grains gelatinize in a gooey substance and the water begins to boil inside the pericarp and starchy endosperm. As the water temperature reaches the boiling point of water, the water vaporizes and expands rapidly in volume. The hard starch matrix holds until the pressure becomes too great at 135 pounds per square inch, at which point the kernel bursts open and the endosperm expands in volume because of the pressure difference. The water evaporates and the cooked starch granules are dried out, making the endosperm light and crisp. If the moisture cannot escape, it gets reabsorbed by the popped corn making it chewy and tough.

Pressure, explosions, and phase changes—who knew that popping corn was so intense? This experiment will give you a chance to watch the action occur in front of your eyes while you consider the overall energy and mass of the popcorn. Does the mass stay the same, increase, or decrease as it goes from kernel to popcorn? How can you measure this throughout the experiment?

Figure 2.1: Anatomy of a corn kernel.

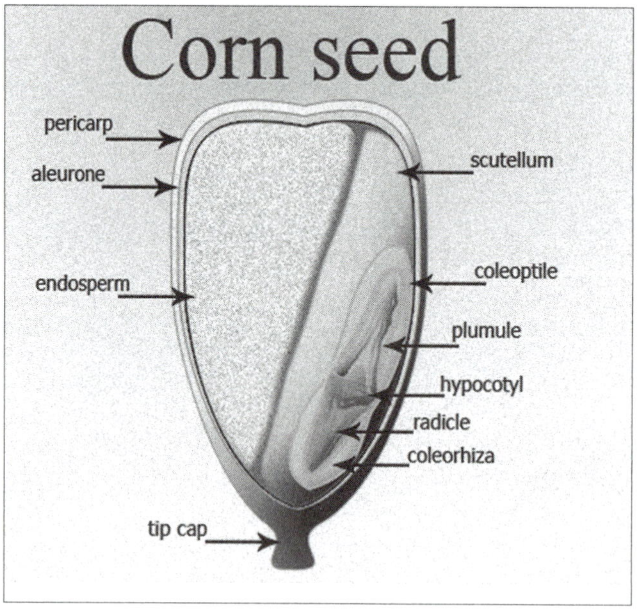

HYPOTHESIS

For this experiment, you will be measuring the overall mass of the corn as it goes from kernel to popcorn. What do you predict will happen to the mass during the experiment? Make a hypothesis stating how the mass will change, with an explanation of why you think that change will occur.

Next, consider how you think the volume will change. Make a hypothesis stating how the volume will change, with an explanation of why you think that change will occur.

MATERIALS NEEDED PER GROUP

- 30 *Zea mays everta* in pericarp covering (popcorn kernels)
- 5 ml of liquid vegetable lipids (vegetable oil)
- 0.25 g of sodium chloride, NaCl (salt)
- Erlenmeyer flask, 250 ml
- Beaker, 250 ml
- Graduated cylinders
- Aluminum foil, 10 cm × 10 cm square
- Toothpick
- Paper towel
- Bunsen burner
- Ring stand with wire mesh
- Pair of flask tongs
- Balance
- Indirectly vented chemical-splash goggles
- Aprons

PROCEDURE

1. Read through the entire Procedure section before beginning.

2. Put on your safety goggles and apron, and gather all your materials at your lab station. If you notice that any of the materials are dirty or discolored, notify your teacher.

3. Take the 250 ml Erlenmeyer flask. Make a cover for the opening of the flask using a small square of aluminum foil. (*Safety note:* Do not use a stopper when heating the flask.)

4. Poke three or four small holes in the top of the aluminum foil with a toothpick.

5. Using the balance, find the mass of your flask with the foil lid and record the mass in your data table for balance measurements.

6. Add 5 ml of liquid vegetable lipids to the flask.

7. Using the balance, find the mass of the flask, liquid vegetable lipids, and cover and record in your data table for balance measurements under "My Results."

8. Place 30 kernels of *Zea mays everta* in a small graduated cylinder. Record the approximate volume of the kernels in your data table for volume measurements.

Figure 2.2: Bunsen burner and ring stand.

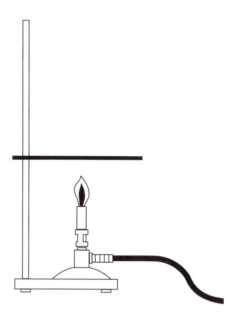

9. Carefully remove the cover from the flask and add the 30 kernels to the flask.

10. Using the balance, find the mass of the flask, foil cover, liquid vegetable lipids, and *Zea mays everta* and record that mass in your data table for balance measurements.

11. Set up a Bunsen burner and ring stand with wire mesh on the iron ring. Make sure your Bunsen burner gas intake tube is securely connected to the gas nozzle and that the ring is set about 3 in. above the barrel of the burner (see Figure 2.2). Light the Bunsen burner to create a flame that is no more than 3 in. high.

12. Using the tongs, move the flask across the flame to evenly heat the *Zea mays everta*.

13. As the *Zea mays everta* burst, remove the flask from the heat and then heat only gently to pop the remaining kernels. Some kernels may not pop, so take care not to burn the popcorn. What do you observe inside the flask as the kernels are popping? Record your observations here:

14. Allow the flask to cool to room temperature. Use the balance to find the mass of the flask, lid, and contents and record in your data table for balance measurements.

15. Transfer the *Zea mays everta* to the 250 ml beaker. Record the approximate volume and appearance of the popped corn in your data table for volume measurements.

16. Compare your results with another lab group in the class. Record the other data on balance measurements and volume measurements in the data table column listed "Results From Other Scientists" for analysis.

17. Pour your popped *Zea mays everta* onto a paper towel. Sprinkle with sodium chloride for taste, and then feel free to eat your final lab product.

18. Clean your lab table and answer the Data Analysis and Conclusion and Connections questions below.

DATA AND OBSERVATIONS

Balance Measurements		
	My Results (g)	Results From Other Scientists (g)
Mass of flask and cover (step 5)		
Mass of oil, flask, and cover (step 7)		
Mass of flask, cover, oil, and *Zea mays everta* in pericarp (step 10)		
Mass of flask, cover, oil, and *Zea mays everta* after heat expansion (step 14)		

Volume Measurements		
	My Results (ml)	Results From Other Scientists (ml)
Volume of *Zea mays everta* in pericarp (step 8)		
Volume of popped *Zea mays everta* after heat expansion (step 15)		

DATA ANALYSIS

For each of the following questions, be sure to explain using detail and complete sentences. If the question requires you to complete calculations, show all of your work.

1. What was the overall mass of oil used for your experiment? Calculate this using your measurements from the Balance Measurements data table.

2. What was the mass of the *Zea mays everta* used in the experiment? Use your measurements from the Balance Measurements data table, and your answer to Data Analysis question 1 to help you solve for this value.

3. What was the mass of the *Zea mays everta* once it was popped? Use your measurements from the Balance Measurements data table to help you solve for this value.

4. What was the change in volume of the *Zea mays everta* from kernel to when it popped? Use your measurements from the Volume Measurements data table to help you solve for this value.

CONCLUSION AND CONNECTIONS

1. How are volume and mass different? How are they similar? Use the Venn diagram below to describe mass and volume. Use the intersection of the two circles to explain how they are similar.

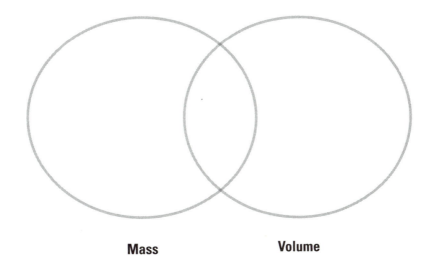

Mass   **Volume**

2. How do your results compare between the two trials and with other groups in the class? Explain any potential differences in the data.

3. Why do we use oil instead of water to heat the *Zea mays everta*?

4. Why do you think that some of the *Zea mays everta* did not pop?

EXPERIMENT 2:
Exploding Corn: Teacher Pages

DIFFERENCES BETWEEN MASS AND VOLUME CHANGES WITH POPCORN

The physical change in popcorn allows students a tangible experiment to see how mass and volume are two different measurements of matter. This procedure gives you an opportunity to use student measurements of mass and volume to see how volume can change while the overall mass of the system remains constant. The experiment can also initiate a discussion on the laws of conservation of mass and energy, allowing students to consider how mass can remain the same even after the substance has undergone a physical change, such as going from kernels to popcorn.

STANDARDS ADDRESSED

National Science Education Standards: Grades 5–8

Content Standard A: Science as Inquiry
- Abilities necessary to do scientific inquiry
- Understanding about scientific inquiry

Content Standard B: Physical Science
- Properties and changes of properties in matter
- Transfer of energy

Content Standard F: Science in Personal and Social Perspectives
- Science and technology in society

Content Standard G: History and Nature of Science
- Science as a human endeavor
- Nature of science
- History of science

National Science Education Standards: Grades 9–12

Content Standard A: Science as Inquiry
- Abilities necessary to do scientific inquiry
- Understanding about scientific inquiry

Content Standard B: Physical Science
- Structure of atoms
- Structure and properties of matter
- Conservation of energy and increase in disorder

Content Standard E: Science and Technology
- Abilities of technological design
- Understanding about science and technology

Content Standard F: Science in Personal and Social Perspectives
- Science and technology in local, national, and global challenges

Content Standard G: History and Nature of Science
- Science as a human endeavor
- Nature of scientific knowledge
- Historical perspectives

VOCABULARY

Mass: The property of a body that causes it to have weight in a gravitational field (Princeton University 2006); or the amount of "stuff" that makes up a defined body of matter.

Volume: The amount of three-dimensional space occupied by an object (Princeton University 2006)

Law of conservation of energy: In a chemical or physical process, energy is neither created nor destroyed.

Law of conservation of mass: In any physical change or chemical reaction, mass is conserved; mass can be neither created nor destroyed.

MATERIALS NEEDED, DECODED FOR THE GROCERY STORE

30 *Zea mays everta* in pericarp covering (popcorn kernels)

- A bag of popcorn kernels contains over 1,000 kernels. A single bag can be used for more than 100 students. If you are planning on using the same popcorn kernels year after year, make sure they are placed in an airtight container so they can maintain their correct moisture content. Otherwise, they may dry out and not pop.

Liquid vegetable lipids (vegetable oil)

- Each student group uses 5 ml of vegetable oil. A regular container at the store contains 950 ml and will be more than enough for 100 students.

Sodium chloride, NaCl (salt)

- Each student uses a pinch of salt for his or her popcorn, so a single saltshaker will be more than enough for a class.

Aluminum foil, 10 cm × 10 cm square

- This is a small square of aluminum foil to cover the Erlenmeyer flask when heating the popcorn. I tell my students it is about the size of their closed fist if I do not want them to spend the time measuring because of class time constraints. One roll of 30 yards of aluminum foil will be more than enough for 100 students.

Paper towel

- Each student group will need one paper towel to pour its popcorn out onto before eating. This step makes it easier for students to salt their popcorn and divide it among their group. It is possible for each group to eat the popcorn straight out of the beaker, but I have found that this can lead to more broken glassware. A single roll of paper towels will meet the needs of more than 100 students.

Dish soap

- This is necessary for cleanup, especially because of the presence of vegetable oil in the lab. I ask students to use an amount about the size of a quarter for each glass container, and I have one bottle available for every four lab groups to share.

SAFETY HIGHLIGHTS

- Because the popcorn often spills onto the table when being transferred from the Erlenmeyer flask to a beaker, it is a good idea to sterilize the lab tabletops by covering the tables with a food-safe material, such as waxed paper, to prevent contamination.
- The Bunsen burners and ring stands present the potential for students to accidentally burn themselves if used incorrectly. Make sure that students have had Bunsen burner safety training before allowing them to participate in this lab. As a teacher, you also need to be prepared with burn treatment options, such as running the burned area under cold water, if a student gets hurt.

Note that these safety highlights are in addition to the safety information detailed in the Safety Protocol section at the beginning of this book. Please refer to that section for additional information about safety when implementing this or any lab in this book.

PREPARATION

1. It is important that the popcorn maintains the proper moisture content. If the popcorn has been stored in a container that is not airtight, it is better to purchase a new bag. Otherwise the popcorn kernels will not pop, leaving you with unhappy students and with Erlenmeyer flasks that have permanent scorch marks at the base.

2. You may consider giving the students precut squares of aluminum foil. This will decrease the time needed for each group to gather materials. If your class period is less than 45 minutes, I recommend this for completing the lab experience in a single period.

PROCEDURE

The entire process of popping takes between about 20 minutes from making measurements to popping. Cleaning for this lab takes another 5–10 minutes. I often break this lab into three 45-minute periods. In the first period, I read the Background section and introduce mass and volume. I ask students to complete the Hypothesis section and then read the Procedure section with their lab group. In the second period, students complete the experiment, making popcorn and measurements. In the third period, we go over the data and analysis, and the Conclusion and Connections questions. This schedule can be adjusted based on your time constraints.

I recommend having students work in pairs for this experiment. Because of the presence of the Bunsen burner, it is helpful to have at least two students in a lab group to help with lighting the burner and keeping it attended throughout the experiment. If you create student groups of more than two, keep in mind each student will get less popcorn. You can increase the number of kernels in the beaker, but I would not recommend going over 50 kernels. More than 50 kernels would need a larger size Erlenmeyer flask and increase the risk of burning the kernels.

1. Begin by reading the Background section. Encourage students to share their favorite event where they eat popcorn (such as at the movies, at sporting events, or at home). These connections will help students see the real-world application of the science they are considering, as well as how science can be seen in their daily lives.

2. The lab requires measurement in both mass and volume. Allow students the opportunity to explain the difference between mass and volume. A great visual demonstration for this can be done using cotton balls and a clear container, such as a beaker. Ask a student to fill the container with cotton balls. Ask students, "What is the volume of cotton in this container?" This can be measured using the volume measurements on the side of the beaker, or you can ask a student to come up and measure them in a graduated cylinder, depending on the precision of measurement that you are trying to teach. Record this information on the board with correct units, for example:

    Volume of cotton = 250 ml

    Then ask the class, "What is the mass of cotton in this container?" This can be measured using a balance (electronic balance or triple-beam balance, depending on your supplies). This is a great moment to point out that you only want the mass of the cotton, so you need to remove it from the container, or measure the mass of the cotton and container together and then measure the mass of the container empty and subtract to find the final mass of cotton. This sets up the students for solving for the mass of popcorn that is required in the Data Analysis section of the lab. Record this information on the board with correct units, for example:

    Mass of cotton = 30.6 g

    If students are unfamiliar with the concepts, you also might consider writing the tools used to measure these two different ways of quantifying matter. Use the information on the board as a reference to help guide their inquiry and questions during their lab experience.

3. After reading the background information, have students complete their hypothesis. I ask students to use an "If…Then…Because…" format to make sure they address their thinking behind why the mass will change in that way. This is an ideal moment to grasp students' background knowledge of mass and volume. Most students know from previous experience that the volume will increase because the popcorn gets larger. Many students also assume the mass goes up because they consider both mass and volume synonymous. It often helps students to write their hypothesis with their lab group so they can verbally discuss their thoughts with another person before writing it down. Have them make a second hypothesis for the change in volume. These hypotheses help you clearly see student preconceptions and can help you guide the lab.

4. For the experiment, it is best that the students gather all materials at their lab station before they begin. Especially with the presence of a Bunsen burner, it is better to have all students remain at their lab stations to attend to the flame, rather than running back and forth to the supply table.

5. When students begin their measurements, it is important that they record the proper measurements in the correct cell of the data table. There are two data tables to keep the mass and volume measurements separate to help students see them as different types of measurement. If students get confused about where to record their data, I use the cotton ball demonstration data on the board to help them remember the difference in measuring mass and volume.

6. Note that students should not use rubber stoppers in this experiment because they can create a projectile hazard.

7. When students begin to heat the Erlenmeyer flasks, they need to move the flask gently over the flames so they don't overheat one area. This should be a slow circular movement; there is no need to shake the flasks.

8. It will take the kernels approximately three minutes over heat before they begin to pop. Once the popping begins, students can remove the flask from the direct heat. It is important to remind your students it is OK if every kernel does not pop; student groups often will leave their popcorn on the heat for one last kernel, burning the rest of the popcorn in the process.

9. Soap is necessary to clean all the equipment thoroughly after this lab. If the popcorn burns the bottom of the beaker, soaking the beaker with dish soap for 30 minutes before scrubbing can be helpful.

DATA ANALYSIS ANSWER KEY

All the data analysis for this lab is math based and involves solving for mass and volume from students' individual data. If students are struggling with the calculations, I recommend using a sample data set and going through the calculations as a class on the board. Then they can use the same skills and apply them directly to their data.

1. *What was the overall mass of oil used for your experiment? Calculate this using your measurements from the Balance Measurements data table.*

   The overall mass of the oil should be a little less than 5 g. Although the density of oil is less than water, the ml to g ratio is very close to one. Students can calculate this by taking their second balance measurement of the mass of the flask, cover, and oil and subtracting their first balance measurement of the mass of the flask and cover. This answer gives you as a teacher a clear indication of how precise students' measurements were for the experiment. If the mass is above 7 g or below 3 g, the students most likely made an error in their measurements, which will impact their answers for the rest of the data analysis. If you catch this mistake, you might encourage the students to use the second set of data they obtained from another student group for the rest of their lab analysis.

2. *What was the mass of the* Zea mays everta *used in the experiment? Use your measurements from the Balance Measurements data table, and your answer to Data Analysis question 1 to help you solve for this value.*

   This value will depend on the individual popcorn kernels, but should be in the range of about 3 g. To achieve this value, students must take the mass of the flask, cover, oil, and *Zea mays everta* and subtract the mass of the flask, cover, and oil. A sample student calculation may look like this:

131.45 g Mass of flask, cover, oil, and Zea mays everta	–	128.55 g Mass of flask, cover, and oil	=	2.9 g Total mass of Zea mays everta

3. *What was the mass of the* Zea mays everta *once it was popped? Use your measurements from the Balance Measurements data table to help you solve for this value.*

   Again, this data will depend on a couple of factors. First, the value should be close to the first value of the mass of the kernels, and be around 3 g. This value should be close to show a conservation of mass in the system. If a student has a value that is more than half of a gram lower, it is most likely because he or she allowed water vapor to escape from the flask before massing it. For this reason, students are asked to have two sets of data so they can use a second group's data if they struggled with this portion of the lab. A sample student calculation is as follows:

131.25 g		128.55 g		2.7 g
Mass of flask,	–	Mass of flask,	=	Total mass
cover, oil, and		cover, and oil		of *Zea mays everta*
Zea mays everta				after heat expansion
after heat expansion				

Note: A common error for students is to use the mass of the flask, cover, oil, and *Zea mays everta* after heat expansion and subtract the mass of the flask, cover, oil, and *Zea mays everta* in pericarp. This will give them a negative value, and solves for the amount of mass lost from the system during popping, not the mass of the popped popcorn.

4. **What was the change in volume of the Zea mays everta *from kernel to when it popped? Use your measurements from the Volume Measurements data table to help you solve for this value.***

This value has a wide range depending on the initial student measurements and the precision of the measuring devices. Using beakers, these values can range from 50 ml to 75 ml. For this question, evaluate if students use correct units, and use their data from the volume data table. A sample student calculation looks like this:

62 ml		4 ml		58 ml
Volume of	–	Volume of	=	Change in volume
Zea mays everta		*Zea mays everta*		of *Zea mays everta*
after heat expansion		as kernels		when popped

CONCLUSION AND CONNECTIONS ANSWER KEY

This section of the lab offers a great opportunity to engage the entire class in discussion to clarify the main ideas of the lab and allow students to make their own connections between science and cooking. I ask that students complete the Data Analysis questions and attempt to answer the Conclusion and Connections questions, with the understanding that we will spend time the next day discussing the Conclusion and Connections section.

1. *How are volume and mass different? How are they similar? Use the Venn diagram below to describe mass and volume. Use the intersection of the two circles to explain how they are similar.*

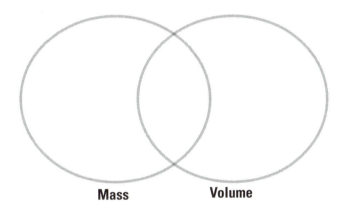

Mass   **Volume**

This question allows your visual students an opportunity to use a graphic organizer to present their knowledge. I encourage teachers to draw this diagram on the board, and allow students to come up and fill in characteristics to create a class answer. Possible characteristics can include the following:

Mass	Mass and Volume	Volume
Can be used to measure the amount of matter an object has. Measured with a balance. Measured using grams. Stays the same when popcorn is popped.	Both can be used to measure matter. Both can be measured using metric units. Both are quantitative observations, or measured with numbers.	Can be used to measure the amount of space an object takes up. Measured with a graduated cylinder. Measured using liters. Changes when corn is popped.

2. *How do your results compare between the two trials and with other groups in the class? Explain any potential differences in the data.*

Students may note differences in their results. The difference in mass can be affected by how tight the lid was on the flask, as well as the accuracy of students' measurements. The volume tends to differ greatly because of the odd shape of the popcorn and the large amounts of space between the kernels when measuring volume.

3. *Why do we use oil instead of water to heat the Zea mays everta?*

This question allows students to make another connection between boiling oil and water. The answers can vary a great deal from "We don't want the popcorn to get wet," to "The water doesn't taste as good." The true reason is that the boiling point of water is too low to adequately heat the kernels to the temperature required for popping (this information is provided to students in the background section of the lab). The water would all boil away, causing the kernels to be heated directly. This causes uneven heating and could lead to a lot of burnt popcorn and uncooked kernels. If you want your students to take their answers to this level, encourage them to use the Background section for support.

4. *Why do you think that some of the Zea mays everta did not pop?*

There are many reasons that the kernels may not pop, including the following:

- The kernels did not get hot enough.
- The kernels did not contain the right moisture content.
- The kernels were not close enough to the flame.
- The pericarp on the kernels was too thick.

In this case, students have provided a reason from the background information that links back to an understanding of why the kernels pop.

CROSS-CURRICULAR NOTE: MATH

This is a great opportunity to use absolute value notation from math to show that we refer to change in a positive value no matter which volume you choose to start with.

CROSS-CURRICULAR NOTE: LITERACY

Read *The Popcorn Book* by Tomie dePaola to your students. This picture book incorporates both science and historical facts about popcorn in a way that is accessible for young students. Ask your class, "How does the author make the scientific facts in this book accessible to young children?" After reading the book, have your students make a small picture book about popcorn to share their experiment with students in kindergarten through second grade. If possible, allow them to visit a classroom of young students to read their stories aloud.

OPTIONAL EXTENSIONS
Middle School

1. This investigation can use student inquiry to direct the questions and experiment. After presenting the background information, allow the students to brainstorm questions they have about measurement. I often ask students, "What are different ways that we can measure these cotton balls?" (Potential answers include temperature, volume, number, mass, and weight.) After allowing them to brainstorm on the board, you can have students narrow the selections to self-select a variable to test during the popping of the kernels. After writing a hypothesis, provide them with a sample materials list and procedure, and then allow them to choose the points in the procedure when they want to take measurements. I would help guide these decisions by letting them know that I would like them to share data about the change in their variable for the entire experiment setup, as well as the change in just the popcorn kernels. I ask them to write in the measurement steps directly on the procedure, and have them approved before beginning the experiment. Once their procedures are approved, I also ask students to contribute their data on a large class table on the board. You can use the table as a springboard to discuss the different ways you can measure matter.

2. It is possible to have students test how different liquids impact the popping of popcorn to follow up on question 3 in the Conclusion and Connections section. You need to ensure that the liquids are edible and that there are no student allergies to materials such as peanut oil. Even vapors

or cross-contaminated equipment can be enough to cause an allergic reaction, so be mindful of the materials you allow for testing based on your student population.

3. Students can investigate if the pericarp plays a role in the popping of corn. Have students remove the pericarp from the corn to see if the popcorn still pops.

High School

1. You can use this experiment to discuss the law of conservation of mass by adding the following questions to the Conclusion and Connections section of the lab:

    (a) The law of conservation of mass: In any physical change or chemical reaction, mass is conserved; mass can be neither created nor destroyed. With that law in mind, explain how the volume of popcorn was able to change.

    (b) If we had not used an aluminum cover, the mass of the flask would have decreased after the *Zea mays everta* had popped. Why would the mass have gone down? Does this disprove the law of conservation of mass?

    Although it is necessary to let some steam escape so the foil top doesn't pop off the Erlenmeyer flask, the majority of mass is contained and students should find that the mass of the entire beaker, oil, cover, and kernels before and after popping is almost exactly the same. This leads students to a discussion of how the contents of a system can change, but the overall mass can stay constant. This is an ideal starter activity to begin the discussion of mass conservation because the lab reviews the vocabulary and measuring devices associated with mass.

2. Ask students to measure the change in density of the corn as it goes from unpopped kernel to popped kernel. Ask, "How does the density change, and do changes in density denote a change in overall mass? Why or why not?"

3. Ask students, "Is it really the moisture that is causing the kernel to pop?" Have students create a control set that tests how moisture level impacts the popping of the corn.

EXPERIMENT 3:
"Melting" Apples: Student Pages

USING A TEMPERATURE GRAPH TO SHOW PHASE CHANGES IN APPLESAUCE

BACKGROUND

Have you heard the old saying "An apple a day keeps the doctor away?" Apples are popular fruit that have been cultivated in North America for several centuries, beginning with the Native Americans. These early trees produced "crab apples," which are a small, hard, sour fruit. The English colonists brought over other varieties of apples, along with honeybees for pollination purposes. The apple trees spread west with settlers, thanks in part to John Chapman. Known more widely as "Johnny Appleseed," Chapman distributed apple seeds from cider mills to settlers who were headed west. Apples continue to be a popular fruit today among farmers and consumers, with the average American eating 18 pounds of fresh apples a year.

Apples, scientifically named *Malus domestica*, are one of the most popular fruits sold in the world today. They are used to make everything from apple juice to apple pie. One of the reasons they are so widely used is because of their high water content. Apples are made up of 85% water and 10% sugar. With all that water, it gives us as scientists the opportunity to test how temperature and time can be used to create a "sauce" or liquid version of apples.

Matter appears in many phases including solids and liquids. The difference in phases is due to different amounts of energy and the arrangement of molecules and atoms (see Figure 3.1). Solids have atoms that are tightly bound and vibrate because of their packed nature and lower energy. Liquids have atoms that can move freely around each other and have a higher energy state when compared with atoms in solids.

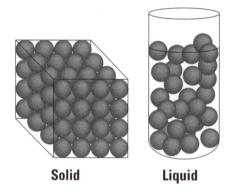

Solid   **Liquid**

Figure 3.1: Molecule arrangements for a solid and a liquid.

In this experiment we will look at how much energy is required to change a solid apple to liquid applesauce to create a delicious final product.

HYPOTHESIS

Based on your knowledge of heat and water, what temperature will the apples "melt" at? In other words, when will the apples change from a solid to a liquid? Make a hypothesis stating an exact temperature the apples will change from liquid to solid, with an explanation of why you think that change will occur.

MATERIALS NEEDED PER GROUP

- Two *Malus domestica* (apples) halved and cored
- 90 ml of dihydrogen monoxide, H_2O (water)
- 30 ml of sucrose, $C_{12}H_{22}O_{11}$ (sugar)

- Beaker, 400 ml
- Tongs
- Glass stir rod
- Bunsen burner and ring stand, or hot plate
- Plastic knives, one for each student
- Plastic or metal fork
- Metal scoop
- Paper towels
- Paper cups, one per student
- Graduated cylinder, 100 ml
- Thermometer (nonmercury)
- Clock/timer
- Indirectly vented chemical-splash goggles
- Aprons

PROCEDURE

1. Read through the entire Procedure section before beginning.

2. Put on your safety goggles and apron, and gather all your materials at your lab station. If you notice any of the materials are dirty or discolored, notify your teacher.

3. Begin by washing your *Malus domestica* in the sink with cold water, cleaning off any excess dirt.

4. Place the *Malus domestica* on a dry paper towel, and begin the process of removing the outer layer of skin. This can be achieved using the plastic knife or metal scoop. Push down gently on the *Malus domestica* with your chosen tool and scrape off the skin. Make sure you are scraping away from your body and all appendages (such as other fingers).

5. Discard the skin. Using the same paper towel, begin the process of chopping your *Malus domestica* into small pieces. The pieces should be no larger than the size of a dime, about 2 cm × 2 cm.

6. Place all the *Malus domestica* pieces into a 400 ml beaker.

7. Measure 30 ml of sucrose into a graduated cylinder and add it to the 400 ml beaker with *Malus domestica*.

8. Measure 90 ml of H_2O in a graduated cylinder and add it to the 400 ml beaker with the *Malus domestica* and sucrose.

9. Set up a Bunsen burner and ring stand with wire mesh on the iron ring. Make

sure your Bunsen burner gas intake tube is securely connected to the gas nozzle, and that the ring is set about 3 in. above the barrel of the burner (see Figure 3.2). Light the Bunsen burner to create a flame that is no more than 3 in. high. (It should not be touching the wire mesh.)

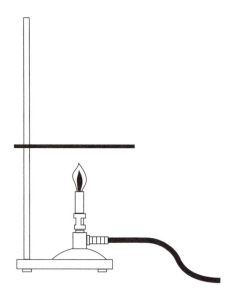

Figure 3.2: Bunsen burner and ring stand.

10. Using the tongs, place the beaker onto the ring stand. Note the time that you begin heating.

11. Slowly stir the mixture in the beaker. Make sure you stir with a glass stir rod and not the thermometer or plastic knife. This keeps the mixture heating evenly so nothing burns.

12. After one minute, measure the amount of thermal energy present within the molecules in the beaker. Carefully place the thermometer in the mixture and record the temperature in degrees Celsius in your Energy Data Table. Repeat this step every minute until 20 minutes have passed.

13. After 20 minutes, use the tongs to remove the beaker from the heat and allow it to cool for three minutes. You can begin to clean your lab station during this time.

14. After three minutes, mash the remaining *Malus domestica* with a fork.

15. Pour the liquid into paper cups for the group and feel free to eat your final lab product.

16. Clean your lab table and answer the Data Analysis and Conclusion and Connections questions.

DATA AND OBSERVATIONS

Energy Data Table		
Time (minutes)	Temperature (Celsius)	Observations (sight and smell)
1		
2		
3		
4		
5		
6		
7		
8		
9		
10		
11		
12		
13		
14		
15		
16		
17		
18		
19		
20		

DATA ANALYSIS

For each of the following questions, be sure to explain using detail and complete sentences. If the question requires you to complete calculations, show all of your work.

1. Draw a line graph of your temperature data obtained while heating the apple pieces. Remember to include all elements of a scientific graph (title, labeled axes, units, etc.).

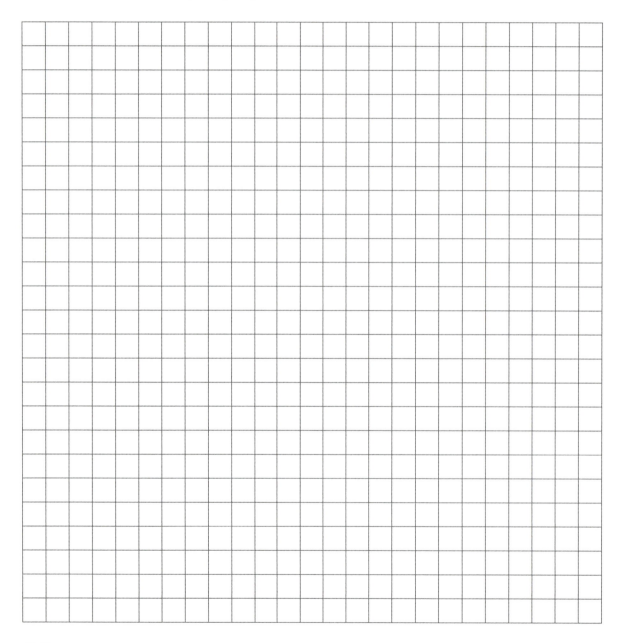

2. What is the total amount of energy that you gained in the *Malus domestica* mixture from the start of the experiment until the end?

3. What was the average energy gain per minute for the *Malus domestica* mixture over the course of this experiment?

CONCLUSION AND CONNECTIONS

1. In the table below give three characteristics of a solid and three characteristics of a liquid.

Solid	Liquid
1.	1.
2.	2.
3.	3.

2. As the *Malus domestica* mixture gained energy, it turned into a liquid. Explain why atoms with more energy would be a liquid rather than a solid. Feel free to use pictures or diagrams to explain your answer.

3. During one point in the experiment the thermal energy of the mixture did not increase or decrease. (There is a horizontal line on your graph that shows the energy was not changing.) Why did the energy stay the same if you were continuing to add heat?

4. Why do you think it is necessary to remove the skin or peel from the *Malus domestica* before heating it?

5. Sketch what you predict your graph would look like if you did not remove this part of the apple before heating. Label the axes on your graph.

EXPERIMENT 3:
"Melting" Apples: Teacher Pages

USING A TEMPERATURE GRAPH TO SHOW PHASE CHANGES IN APPLESAUCE

This experiment allows students to study a phase change in a way that is accessible and edible. The experiment models a physical change from solid to liquid through the release of sugars and water from the apples. Building on the ideas of physical and chemical changes introduced in Experiment 1: Butter Battle, students measure the amount of thermal energy that occurs during a phase change and link that change back to atomic structure and phases of matter. This experiment is a great alternative to melting an ice cube into water, and gets students asking questions about how temperature and energy relate to states of matter. The content is reinforced through graphing and math equations to provide a lab that integrates data analysis skills and scientific knowledge.

STANDARDS ADDRESSED
National Science Education Standards: Grades 5–8
Content Standard A: Science as Inquiry
- Abilities necessary to do scientific inquiry
- Understanding about scientific inquiry

Content Standard B: Physical Science
- Properties and changes of properties in matter
- Transfer of energy

Content Standard F: Science in Personal and Social Perspectives
- Science and technology in society

Content Standard G: History and Nature of Science
- Science as a human endeavor
- Nature of science

National Science Education Standards: Grades 9–12

Content Standard A: Science as Inquiry
- Abilities necessary to do scientific inquiry
- Understanding about scientific inquiry

Content Standard B: Physical Science
- Structure of atoms
- Structure and properties of matter
- Interactions of energy and matter

Content Standard E: Science and Technology
- Abilities of technological design
- Understanding about science and technology

Content Standard F: Science in Personal and Social Perspectives
- Science and technology in local, national, and global challenges

Content Standard G: History and Nature of Science
- Science as a human endeavor
- Nature of scientific knowledge
- Historical perspectives

VOCABULARY

States of matter: One of the four principal conditions in which *matter* exists: solid, liquid, gas, and plasma (The American Heritage Science Dictionary 2005).

Solid: A substance having a definite shape and volume; one that is neither liquid nor gaseous. A substance where the atomic molecules are closely packed together and vibrate (*The American Heritage Science Dictionary* 2005).

Liquid: One of four main states of matter, composed of molecules that can move about in a substance but are bound loosely together by intermolecular forces. Unlike a solid, a liquid has no fixed shape, but instead has a characteristic readiness to flow and therefore takes on the shape of any container. Because pressure transmitted at one point is passed on to other points, a liquid usually has a volume

that remains constant or changes only slightly under pressure, unlike a gas (*The American Heritage Science Dictionary* 2005).

Energy: The capacity or power to do work, such as the capacity to move an object (of a given mass) by the application of force. Energy can exist in a variety of forms, such as electrical, mechanical, chemical, thermal, or nuclear, and can be transformed from one form to another. It is measured by the amount of work done, usually in joules or watts (*The American Heritage Science Dictionary* 2005).

Heat: Internal energy that is transferred to a physical system from outside the system because of a difference in temperature and does not result in work done by the system on its surroundings. Absorption of energy by a system as heat takes the form of increased kinetic energy of its molecules, thus resulting in an increase in temperature of the system. Heat is transferred from one system to another in the direction of higher to lower temperature (*The American Heritage Science Dictionary* 2005).

MATERIALS NEEDED, DECODED FOR THE GROCERY STORE

Two *Malus domestica* (apples) halved and cored
- You will need two apples for each lab group to complete the experiment. Multiply the number of lab groups you have by two, and that will give you the quantity of apples necessary. It is often more cost-effective to purchase the apples that are already bagged in quantities of 10 or more rather than purchasing apples individually and paying by total weight.
- The variety of apples you choose is up to you. It's best to choose softer apples, so McIntosh or Red Delicious are good options. It's not recommended that you use Granny Smith apples, as they can be tart in the final applesauce, unless that is the taste you are trying to achieve.

90 ml of dihydrogen monoxide, H_2O (water)
- This will be about a liter of water for every 10 student groups. If you have access to a sink or drinking fountain, this is a material you can get at school.

30 ml of sucrose, $C_{12}H_{22}O_{11}$ (sugar)
- Sugar is sold in 5 lb. bags. This will give you enough sugar for about 70 lab groups for this experiment.

Plastic knife

- I recommend having enough knives for each student in the group to have one. This helps speed up the peeling procedure for the apples and keeps all students involved. The knives can be cleaned and used for the next class, so buy as many as you'll need for your largest single class, plus a few extras in case there is breakage. Plastic knives are sold individually in boxes of 30–50.

Plastic or metal fork

- Plastic forks are ideal because they give students a device for mashing the apples and a device for eating the applesauce. If you are letting students use them only as a tool, they can be used as a class set. If you are allowing students to eat off of them as well, they can either be disposed of, or washed with dish soap before being used by another student. Purchase according to the size of your class and student groups.

Paper towel

- Each student group will need one paper towel to use while peeling and dicing their apples. This step makes it easier for students to keep all their apple pieces on the table. I encourage students to use the same sheet of paper towel for both peeling and dicing, keeping in mind that some paper towels will rip and need to be replaced. A single roll of paper towels will meet the needs of more than 100 students.

Paper cups

- The cups are used for dividing the final product of applesauce. Having enough cups for each student to have his or her own allows for the final amount to be divided equally, and students can drink the applesauce without using additional utensils. Paper cups are sold in packages of 200 to 1,000 depending on your needs.

Dish soap

- This is necessary for cleanup. I ask students to use an amount about the size of a quarter for each glass container, and I have one bottle available for every four lab groups to share.

SAFETY HIGHLIGHTS

- Unless students are using plastic knives and forks that are disposable, it is necessary to sterilize the metal utensils before allowing them to be used in the experiment.
- The Bunsen burners and ring stands present a potential for students to burn themselves if used incorrectly. Please make sure students have had Bunsen burner safety training before allowing them to participate in this lab. As a teacher, you also need to be prepared with burn treatment options, such as running the burned area under cold water, if a student gets hurt.
- If a glass stir rod breaks, you should dispose of the entire mixture in the beaker. Even if the break is minor, you may have shards of glass in the mixture that are not visible.

Note that these safety highlights are in addition to the safety information detailed in the Safety Protocol section at the beginning of this book. Please refer to that section for additional information about safety when implementing this or any lab in this book.

PREPARATION

1. Using a sharp metal knife, cut all the apples in half. I highly recommend cutting and coring the apples before giving them to students. The plastic knives are not sharp enough for students to adequately cut through the apple and remove the core, so this step needs to be completed prior to the lab.

2. If you are feeling particularly helpful, you can also peel the apples for the students ahead of time. This is a good idea if you have younger students and there are concerns about them handling a knife or sharp object. There are also apple-peeling devices that can be purchased for the students to use that reduces the safety risks of them removing the peel themselves. Most students enjoy removing the peel.

3. I recommend placing the paper towels at each lab station prior to the start of the lab. Many students tend to take too many, so if they have a set quantity to work with, this step can cut down on waste.

PROCEDURE

I recommend having the students work in a pairs or groups of three for this experiment. Because of the peeling of the apples, as well as the constant temperature taking, timing, and stirring required in this experiment, there are enough tasks to keep two or three students focused and engaged throughout the experiment.

1. Begin by reading the Background section. Ask students to name their favorite foods that include apples, or why they think, "An apple a day keeps the doctor away," as making that connection will help them become more invested in the lab.

2. The Background section introduces the idea of phases of matter. Ask students to brainstorm qualities or characteristics that distinguish a solid and liquid and write them on the whiteboard. Set out markers and ask each student to write at least one characteristic or quality that defines a substance as a solid or a liquid. I ask that each student contributes at least one idea to one of the two phases, and give them a few minutes to offer their answers. Another approach would be to assign individual student groups a specific phase, such as solids, and ask them to come up with a list of qualities that define a solid. Once the class is finished adding information, ask students to take a moment to look at the ideas and see if there is anything that they want to add, because reading the ideas often helps spark more ideas and thoughts.

Characteristics of Solids	Characteristics of Liquids
1. Definite shape	1. Changes to fit the shape of the container
2. Definite volume	
3. The atomic particles are packed closely together.	2. The atomic particles are able to move around each other, and have more energy than particles in a solid.
4. The atomic particles vibrate.	
5. Not easily compressed, little free space between the particles	3. Not easily compressed, little free space between the particles

3. Once students have an idea of the characteristics of each phase, you can ask how energy plays a role in each of these phases. I often show a rock and a glass of water and ask, "Which do you think has more energy? Why?" This allows students the opportunity to look at how objects in different phases have different amounts of energy in their molecules.

4. A great demonstration is to hold an ice cube in your hand. You can also ask a couple of student volunteers to do this as well, or give one to each lab group. Ask, "What phase is the ice cube in? As it sits in your hand, what phase is it changing to? Why does the ice cube make that change?" Most students are familiar with the melting of ice and will be able to say it is melting because it is heating up from the heat from your hand. Ask them how this relates back to changing energy.

5. This leads students to their hypothesis. Ask, "At what point will the energy be great enough to change apples from a solid to a liquid?" This is a great opportunity to let students talk it out within their lab groups. You can ask each student to make his or her own hypothesis, or ask the group to come up with a consensus verbally before writing anything. Circulate among the groups to see who understands the link between phase change and heat energy, and who is still unclear. When students try to describe why they believe this, I often remind students of the background information that states the apple is 85% water. Ask students what they know about water that would help them make a good hypothesis.

6. While students are cutting, you can ask each group, "Why is it necessary to cut the apple pieces so small?" The answer is to increase the surface area to improve energy transfer, which encourages the students to be thoughtful about their cutting.

7. The lab process takes about 10 minutes for students to peel, and another 20 minutes for the apples to heat and liquefy. Students can use the clock on the wall or timers to keep track of time and take data at the appropriate moments.

8. Students can use Bunsen burners or hot plates to achieve this phase change. If you have younger students, I recommend hot plates on medium heat. The older students may use the Bunsen burners, but depending on the size of your group, hot plates may be the safer choice.

9. Students are asked to measure out the sugar first. This is to prevent the sugar from sticking to the inside of the graduated cylinders. Make sure students obtain the sugar first in dry cylinders to prevent a sticky mess.

10. Remind students to continually stir their mixture. If the heat is too high, the apples and sugar can burn, which makes it nearly impossible to clean the beaker. Many students will want to stir with the thermometer. This is not a good idea because they are designed as measuring tools, not for the utility of stirring. If there are three students, I often ask them to take on the following roles:

- Timekeeper—This person is in charge of watching the timer or the clock on the wall and letting his or her group know when to take temperature readings.
- Energy monitor—This person is in charge of measuring the temperature and recording the data in the data table.
- Chef—This person is in charge of monitoring and stirring the mixture consistently throughout the experiment.

These roles help students use the tools appropriately and stay engaged in the entire lab.

11. Soap is necessary to clean all the equipment thoroughly after this lab.

DATA ANALYSIS ANSWER KEY

All the data analyses for this lab are math based. If students are struggling with the calculations, I recommend using a sample data set and going through the calculations as a class on the board. Then they can use the same skills and apply them directly to their data.

1. *Draw a line graph of your temperature data obtained while heating the apple pieces. Remember to include all elements of a scientific graph (title, labeled axes, units, etc.).*

Each student's graph will be slightly different based on actual temperatures achieved in the experiments. This is a great opportunity for students to use the graphing standards of their math classes. An example student graph is on page 55:

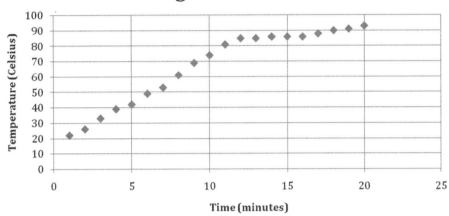

Energy change found in *Malus domestica* when heating more than 20 minutes

2. *What is the total amount of energy that you gained in the* Malus domestica *mixture from the start of the experiment until the end?*

Answers to this question will range based on the students' individual data but should be fairly consistent based on the initial room temperature for all students and the final heating temperature of the apple mixture. Students can solve for the answer by taking their final temperature reading and subtracting their initial temperature reading. A sample student calculation could look like this:

91°C	–	22°C	=	69°C
Final temperature reading		Initial temperature reading		

3. *What was the average energy gain per minute for the* Malus domestica *mixture over the course of this experiment?*

Again, individual student data will vary slightly based on their methods and specific data. Students can solve this problem by taking the total temperature change (their answer to Data Analysis question 2) and dividing it by the 20-minute time over which the mixture was heated. A sample student calculation could look like this:

69°C total temperature change ÷ 20 minutes = 3.45°C change per minute

CONCLUSION AND CONNECTIONS ANSWER KEY

This section of the lab offers a great opportunity to engage the entire class in discussion to clarify the main ideas of the lab and allow students to make their own connections between science and cooking. I ask that students complete the Data Analysis questions and attempt to answer the Conclusion and Connections questions with the understanding that we will spend time the next day discussing the Conclusion and Connections section.

1. *In the table below give three characteristics of a solid and three characteristics of a liquid.*

    For this answer, students should be able to use the brainstorm from the board in their answer. If students did not start with characteristics and provide only examples, this is a good moment to discuss what characteristics are shared by all the items and put together a class list.

Solid	Liquid
1. Definite shape	1. Changes to fit the shape of the container
2. Definite volume	
3. The atomic particles are packed closely together.	2. The atomic particles are able to move around each other, and have more energy than particles in a solid.
4. The atomic particles vibrate.	
5. Not easily compressed, little free space between the particles	3. Not easily compressed, little free space between the particles

2. *As the Malus domestica mixture gained energy, it turned into a liquid. Explain why atoms with more energy would be a liquid rather than a solid. Feel free to use pictures or diagrams to explain your answer.*

    Atoms with more energy are going to be more likely to move around each other, and that movement is seen in liquids, which change their shape to fit their container. It is often helpful to have students draw a picture of the molecules in a solid and liquid to explain the difference. Use the applesauce example to explain how the atoms were gaining energy from the flame and are to change into a liquid.

3. *During one point in the experiment the thermal energy of the mixture did not increase or decrease. (There is a horizontal line on your graph that shows the energy was not changing.) Why did the energy stay the same if you were continuing to add heat?*

This occurs when the mixture contains both solids and liquids. The temperature remains constant because it is trying to excite all the atoms to a state in which they can all be liquid. The energy is being directed at getting all atoms throughout the mixture to the same temperature, which keeps the temperature constant.

4. *Why do you think it is necessary to remove the skin or peel from the Malus domestica before heating it?*

The skin or peel of the apple works as human skin does: to help keep moisture in. Placing a whole unpeeled apple on the table next to an apple that has been peeled can clearly show this to students. The whole apple will retain its moisture, while the apple without a skin slowly begins to dry up. Many students have seen this and can be led to this answer by asking them what happens to sliced apples when they are left out on the table for a long time. If the skin was left on during heating, it prevents the loss of water, making it more difficult to heat the apples in the time provided. The applesauce would remain chunky and uneven because of the skin preventing water from escaping from the fruit.

5. *Sketch what you predict your graph would look like if you did not remove this part of the apple before heating. Label the axes on your graph.*

Students generally take one of two approaches to this question. Some may think that because the apple is being prevented from losing water, it may take more heat and therefore have a higher final boiling temperature. On the other hand, students might assume that it takes longer for the heat to achieve a fully liquid phase and therefore have a line that shows a longer time where the temperature does not change. Either answer shows that students are thinking about how the peel impacts energy and phase changes in apples, so both are acceptable for this conclusion.

CROSS-CURRICULAR NOTE: TECHNOLOGY

This is an ideal opportunity to use technology in the classroom by asking the students to create their graphs on computers using software such as Microsoft Excel.

CROSS-CURRICULAR NOTE: MATH

This is an ideal opportunity for students to work with a direct application of solving for averages and rates.

CROSS-CURRICULAR NOTE: LITERACY

Johnny Appleseed is a historical figure that is highlighted in many poems and songs. Have students research a poem about Johnny Appleseed, or give them one as a class. Ask students to write their own haiku (a three-line poem with five syllables in the first line, seven syllables in the second line, and five syllables in the third line) about their favorite fruit.

OPTIONAL EXTENSIONS
Middle School

1. Another option for increasing the complexity of the lab is to allow students to choose different varieties of apples, or vary the size of the apple pieces to see if it affects the temperature required for the apples to change phase. Students can pool data from several groups and graph all the data sets on a single plot to compare.

2. To use this lab with more student inquiry, encourage students to develop their own recipe for making applesauce. Use the demonstration with the ice cube melting to prompt them to consider how to "melt" an apple into sauce. Allow them to create the materials list and procedure, and make changes and adjustments based on the quality of the final applesauce.

3. Encourage students to test what would happen to the temperature required for the melting of the apples when the peel is left on. Relate the impact on temperature to the roll of the peel to maintain moisture within the fruit.

High School

1. Students can consider how the percentage of water content affects the melting temperature of different fruits. Allow students to bring in their own fruits, make predictions about melting points based on water content, and test the creation of peach sauce, banana sauce, and so on.

2. Have students investigate the chemical makeup of an apple and how the arrangement of molecules affects the temperature that allows it to move from a liquid to a solid. Students can test different materials, such as chocolate and butter, to compare the temperature at which the phase transition from solid to liquid occurs. Challenge students to predict the melting temperature of an object based on its chemical structure.

EXPERIMENT 4:
Cold Milk: Student Pages

MEASURING ENERGY TRANSFER IN THE CREATION OF ICE CREAM

BACKGROUND

I scream, you scream, we all scream for ice cream! This popular children's rhyme highlights one of America's favorite desserts: ice cream. People have been craving ice desserts for centuries, dating back to the Roman emperor Nero. He would send his attendants up mountains to gather ice to combine with fruit to create iced desserts. Now that's what I call a craving!

The first step in the creation of ice cream is the cream. Cream is a dairy product with a high amount of butterfat. The high amounts of fat when combined with bacteria, in this case rennet, changes the chemical structure of cream. This change prevents large ice crystals from forming within the cream when it changes from a liquid phase to a solid phase. This makes for smoother ice cream texture.

The second step is the creation of the "ice" in the ice cream. Although there are many methods for reducing the thermal energy of the cream, we are going to be using an *endothermic* reaction in this lab (see Figure 4.1). This causes the cream to cool and solidify into a solid to create ice cream.

For this experiment, you be measuring the temperature changes of the cream and the ice, looking at what happens to the two during an endothermic reaction.

Figure 4.1: Endothermic—a reaction in which heat is absorbed.

HYPOTHESIS

At the end of this experiment you will have ice cream that is solid. When the cream reaches a solid phase, do you think the temperature of the ice will be the same as the temperature of the cream, higher than the temperature of the cream, or lower than the temperature of the cream? Make a hypothesis stating what you predict the temperature will be in relation to the temperature of the cream at the conclusion of making ice cream, with an explanation of why you believe this to be true.

MATERIALS NEEDED PER GROUP

- 30 ml of sucrose, $C_{12}H_{22}O_{11}$ (sugar)
- 250 ml of emulsified colloid of liquid butterfat in H_2O (whole milk)
- 2.5 ml of *Vanilla planifola* liquid (vanilla extract)
- 180 ml of coarse sodium chloride, NaCl (coarse table salt)
- One half tablet of rennet bacteria

- 1,000 ml of solid dihydrogen monoxide, H_2O (ice)
- One pint-size plastic food storage bag or small plastic thermos
- One gallon-size plastic food storage bag
- Rubber band
- Two thermometers, nonmercury
- Graduated cylinder or beaker for measuring
- Plastic spoons, one for each student
- Paper cups, one for each student
- Indirectly vented chemical-splash goggles
- Aprons

PROCEDURE

1. Read through the entire Procedure section before beginning.

2. Put on your safety goggles and apron, and gather all your materials at your lab station. If you notice any of the materials are dirty or discolored, notify your teacher.

3. Take the half tablet of rennet bacteria and dissolve it in 15 ml of cold water. Pour the rennet bacteria mixture into the small plastic bag.

4. Measure 30 ml of sucrose using a beaker or graduated cylinder and place it in the small plastic bag with the bacteria.

5. Measure 250 ml of emulsified colloid of liquid butterfat in H_2O using a beaker or graduated cylinder and place it in the small plastic bag with the sucrose and bacteria.

6. Measure 2.5 ml of *Vanilla planifola* liquid using a small graduated cylinder and pour it into the small plastic bag mixture.

7. Place a thermometer in the small plastic bag. Seal the bag closed, using a rubber band if necessary, to keep the liquid from spilling out.

8. Take the larger plastic bag and fill it with 1,000 ml of solid dihydrogen monoxide. *Safety note*: Immediately wipe up any melted or spilled water on the floor to prevent a slip-and-fall hazard.

9. Add 180 ml of coarse sodium chloride to the large bag with solid dihydrogen monoxide.

10. Carefully place the second thermometer in the larger plastic bag. It's fragile, so it can break. Take a thermal energy reading for both the large plastic bag

with the solid water and the small plastic bag with the cream mixture. Record the readings in your thermal energy data table.

11. Place the smaller plastic bag in the larger bag, and seal the larger bag.

12. Gently rock the bag from side to side holding the top seal. Take temperature measurements of both bags every 30 seconds and record them in your Thermal Energy Data Table.

13. Once the cream has solidified, discontinue your measurements and remove the small plastic bag.

14. Using a plastic spoon, scoop out some of the frozen cream and place it in a paper cup.

15. Feel free to enjoy your final product while cleaning your lab area. Then answer the Data Analysis and Conclusion and Connections questions.

DATA AND OBSERVATIONS

Thermal Energy Data Table		
Time (minutes)	Thermal Energy of the Solid Water (°C)	Thermal Energy of the Cream (°C)
Initial (0 min)		

DATA ANALYSIS

For each of the following questions, be sure to explain using detail and complete sentences. If the question requires you to complete calculations, show all of your work.

1. Draw a line graph of your temperature data obtained from the ice over the course of this reaction. Draw a second line of the temperature data of the cream. Remember to include all elements of a scientific graph (title, labeled axes, units, legend, etc.).

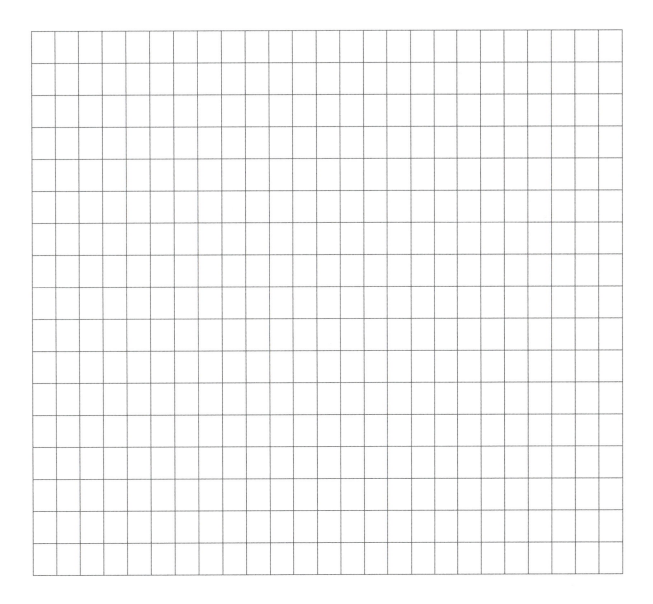

2. What is the total amount of energy that you lost from the cream mixture from the start of the experiment until it solidified?

3. What was the average energy loss per minute for the cream mixture over the entire experiment?

CONCLUSION AND CONNECTIONS

1. Was your initial hypothesis correct? Explain why or why not, citing specific data from your experiment.

2. Why do we add salt to the ice? How does this impact the thermal energy in the reaction?

3. Why is salt used on highways after winter snowstorms?

4. Can you think of other endothermic reactions that occur in our daily lives? Give two examples and explain why they are endothermic.

EXPERIMENT 4:
Cold Milk: Teacher Pages

MEASURING ENERGY TRANSFER IN THE CREATION OF ICE CREAM

This experiment demonstrates endothermic reactions in a way that creates a learning experience that connects science with the popular dessert ice cream. Students are introduced to the concept of endothermic reactions, and how a change in thermal energy can create a phase change. The experiment is a hands-on activity that incorporates knowledge from chemistry and physics, leaving students with a concrete example of endothermic reactions in the classroom.

STANDARDS ADDRESSED
National Science Education Standards: Grades 5–8

Content Standard A: Science as Inquiry
- Abilities necessary to do scientific inquiry
- Understanding about scientific inquiry

Content Standard B: Physical Science
- Properties and changes of properties in matter
- Transfer of energy

Content Standard F: Science in Personal and Social Perspectives
- Science and technology in society

Content Standard G: History and Nature of Science
- Science as a human endeavor
- Nature of science

National Science Education Standards: Grades 9–12

Content Standard A: Science as Inquiry
- Abilities necessary to do scientific inquiry
- Understanding about scientific inquiry

Content Standard B: Physical Science
- Structure of atoms
- Chemical reactions
- Conservation of energy and increase in disorder
- Interactions of energy and matter

Content Standard E: Science and Technology
- Abilities of technological design
- Understanding about science and technology

Content Standard F: Science in Personal and Social Perspectives
- Science and technology in local, national, and global challenges

Content Standard G: History and Nature of Science
- Science as a human endeavor
- Nature of scientific knowledge
- Historical perspectives

VOCABULARY

Heat: Internal energy that is transferred to a physical system from outside the system because of a difference in temperature and does not result in work done by the system on its surroundings. Absorption of energy by a system as heat takes the form of increased kinetic energy of its molecules, thus resulting in an increase in temperature of the system. Heat is transferred from one system to another in the direction of higher to lower temperature (*The American Heritage Science Dictionary* 2005).

Endothermic reaction: A reaction that occurs when heat is absorbed.

Exothermic reaction: A reaction that occurs when heat is released.

MATERIALS NEEDED, DECODED FOR THE GROCERY STORE

30 ml of sucrose, $C_{12}H_{22}O_{11}$ (sugar)
- Sugar is sold in 5 lb. bags and goes up in quantity from there. A 5 lb. bag will give you enough sugar for about 90 lab groups for this experiment.

250 ml of emulsified colloid of liquid butterfat in H_2O (whole milk)
- Each student group will need 250 ml of whole milk. A gallon of whole milk will be enough for 14 lab groups.
- It is possible to complete the lab using 2% milk as well, but the ice cream will not be as thick and creamy.

2.5 ml of *Vanilla planifola* liquid (vanilla extract)
- Vanilla extract can be purchased in the spice section of the grocery store. I recommend using vanilla extract instead of vanilla flavoring, but that is just a personal preference. A 2 oz. bottle contains almost 60 ml, which is enough for 24 lab groups.

180 ml of coarse sodium chloride, NaCl (coarse table salt)
- Rock salt is best purchased at a hardware store, where it is sold in bulk to be used for salting driveways and sidewalks in the winter. Depending on your climate, the rock salt will also be sold in grocery stores during the cold months of the year. A 50 lb. bag runs between $5 and $10 and will last for more than 100 lab groups. You can certainly use regular table salt, but it is more expensive, which is why rock salt is suggested.

One half tablet of rennet bacteria
- This is probably the most difficult ingredient to locate. Most stores don't know what rennet is and will suggest you go to a cheese-making store. That is not necessary. Rennet bacteria tablets are sold under the product name of Junket, which is sold in tablet form in boxes that are usually kept with the gelatin or pudding. The tablets go far, and you only need half a tablet for every group. Each box contains eight tablets, so one box can be used for 16 lab groups.

1,000 ml of solid dihydrogen monoxide (ice)
- You will need lots of ice for this activity, and it can't be reused from class to class very effectively. I use a cooler and purchase two large ice bags per class from the grocery store. If your school has an ice machine, I recommend storing the ice in a cooler and using that to eliminate the cost and the need

for transportation of the large ice bags. If you use a school ice machine, let the owner or primary user know ahead of time that you are planning on using it.

One pint-size plastic food storage bag or small plastic thermos
- The pint-size plastic bags can be any brand as long as they have a seal. Make sure the bags are clear so your students can read the thermometers. You will need one bag for each lab group.
- If this is a lab that you plan on doing year after year, I recommend buying small plastic thermos bottles and poking a hole in the top to fit the thermometer. This is much cheaper in the long run than purchasing plastic bags each year. Just make sure the thermos bottles are clear so you can read the thermometers if they are side view.

One gallon-size plastic food storage bag
- The gallon-size bags can be any brand as long as you are confident in the seal. Make sure they are clear, and purchase one for each lab group. These can be reused from class to class, although they can wear out if they are aggitated aggressively by the students. I usually purchase enough for a single class with three or four extras in case a few break.

Rubber band
- Each group will need one rubber band to seal the inner plastic bag around the thermometer.

Plastic spoons
- The plastic spoons are great because they can be used to remove the ice cream from the plastic bag and used for eating. If students eat with the spoons, they can either be disposed of, or they need to be washed with dish soap before being used by another student. Purchase according to the number of students in your class.

Paper cups
- The cups are used for dividing the final product of ice cream. This may seem like an additional material that could be eliminated if you allowed the students to eat directly from the bag, but that could lead to widespread illness. Having enough cups for each student to have their own ice cream allows them to split the final amount equally and not share germs by eating from the same container. Paper cups are sold in packages of 200 to 1,000 depending on your needs.

Dish soap
- This is necessary for cleanup. I ask students to use an amount about the size of a quarter for each glass container, and I have one bottle available for every four lab groups to share.

SAFETY HIGHLIGHTS
- If a thermometer breaks, you should dispose of the entire mixture in the bag. Even if the break is minor, you may have shards of glass in the mixture that are not visible.
- Students need to hold the top of the plastic bag when gently shaking the cream and ice. The lower part of the bag will be cold and could cause freezer burn.

Note that these safety highlights are in addition to the safety information detailed in the Safety Protocol section at the beginning of this book. Please refer to that section for additional information about safety when implementing this or any lab in this book.

PREPARATION
- The milk should be refrigerated until it is used.
- I recommend having a separate labeled trash can for this experiment. The milk in the plastic bags can lead to a smelly lab if all the trash is not thrown away in a timely manner. I make a "TRASH HERE" sign and take all the other trash cans out of the classroom so that I can dispose of the trash at the end of the school day.

PROCEDURE
I recommend that students work in groups of two for this experiment. The ice cream tends to be a popular end product, and large groups can make students upset about sharing the small quantity of dessert. The work and data collection is also simple enough that two students are ideal for this experiment.

1. To introduce the lab and endothermic reaction, you can do a teacher demonstration to engage your students. This endothermic reaction involves mixing two solid chemicals, ammonium nitrate and barium hydroxide octahydrate. You need to wear goggles, an apron, and gloves and practice extreme caution under a fume hood, because this experiment can cause frostbite. This is a teacher demonstration. Do not involve the students aside from being observers. *Safety note*: Ammonium nitrate and barium hydroxide octahydrate are dangerous chemicals and are not recommended for use at the middle school

level. At the high school level, these chemicals may only be used if approved by the chemical hygiene official.

(a) Take 32 g of barium hydroxide octahydrate, 17 g ammonium nitrate (or ammonium chloride), and a 125 ml flask. You will also want a small spray bottle and a block of wood or piece of cardboard. (Chemicals can be obtained through a science supply store or a friendly high school chemistry teacher who is willing to share for one demonstration.)

(b) Wearing indirect, vented chemical-splash goggles, an apron, and gloves, show the students the two solids. Ask them what they think will happen when the two solids are combined. Have them record a prediction and then share the prediction with a partner or with the entire class.

(c) Mix the two solids together in the 125 ml flask by swirling them together. As the two solids interact, they will form a slushy mixture. Spray some water on the wood block or cardboard and place the flask on top of it. After a minute or two, the beaker will freeze to the block, allowing you to pick it up and show the students.

(d) After the demonstration is completed, the contents of the flask can be washed down the drain with water. Do not drink the contents of the flask. Avoid skin contact. If you get any solution on your skin, rinse the area with water.

What if you cannot access these chemicals or have younger students? Not to worry; a similar endothermic reaction can be accomplished using 25 ml of citric acid solution and 15 g of baking soda in a Styrofoam cup. This reaction is appropriate for both middle school and high school classrooms. The reaction is not as drastic, but can be clearly measured by the students. You can also use the internet to show a video of the demonstration outlined here. There are many video examples of endothermic reactions available online.

2. This demonstration begs the question, "What is happening here?" Students are quick to question where the "cold" comes from. It is important to address that this reaction involves a movement of heat. Cold is the absence of heat and does not correctly describe what is going on in the experiment. This demonstration can be used to introduce the vocabulary *endothermic* and *exothermic* by sharing the definitions on the board or in a handout.

3. This leads the students to read the Background section about ice cream. When they finish reading, ask students to make a hypothesis about the final temperature of the cream when compared with the ice. Most students will expect that the ice will be warmer than the ice cream because all the cold went to the cream. This is a common misconception about thermal energy that can be addressed during the experiment.

4. As students begin the Procedure section, make sure that they are only using one-half of the rennet tablet for every group. I have only two groups at each lab area, but if you have more, it may be helpful to assign which two groups are sharing rennet before the students begin the lab.

5. When salt is added to the ice bag, it is a great opportunity to ask the students why it is necessary to add salt: "What is the role of the salt in this experiment if it isn't used for taste?" To help students arrive at an answer, you can share that salt is often used on icy sidewalks and streets to make them safer in the winter. How does that application help you understand the role of salt in this experiment?

6. It is helpful to have smaller thermometers that fit completely within the small plastic bag. This allows the bag to be sealed completely so that no cream leaks out during the agitation. If you have only the larger thermometers, have students use rubber bands to seal the bag as tightly as possible around the thermometer.

7. It is also best if the thermometers are metal. If the students go overboard on the agitation process, a glass thermometer might break, causing the final product to be ruined.

8. Students need to gently shake the plastic bags by holding onto the top of the bag by the seal. This prevents the students from getting freezer burn.

9. Students can take observations every 30 seconds or every minute depending on the time you find it takes to make the ice cream. I like to have them record every 30 seconds because it keeps both students involved.

10. Soap is necessary to clean all the equipment thoroughly after this lab.

DATA ANALYSIS ANSWER KEY

All the data analysis for this lab is math based. If students are struggling with the graph and calculations, I recommend using a sample data set and going through the calculations as a class on the board. Then they can use the same skills and apply them directly to their data.

1. *Draw a line graph of your temperature data obtained from the ice over the course of this reaction. Draw a second line of the temperature data of the cream. Remember to include all elements of a scientific graph (title, labeled axes, units, legend, etc.).*

Each student will get different measurements but the general trend of the graph should be as follows:

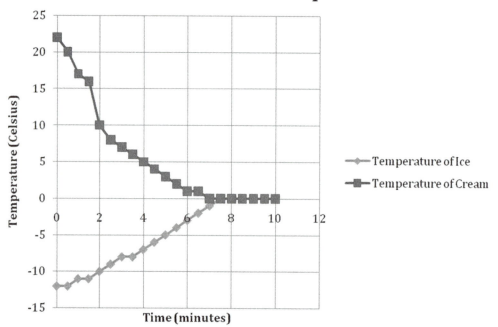

The thermal energy change of salt and ice when shaken with liquid cream

2. *What is the total amount of energy that you lost from the cream mixture from the start of the experiment until it solidified?*

   Again, students will have slight variations in their data, but should have a general temperature change around 20°C. Students can obtain this answer by subtracting their final temperature data point for the cream from their initial temperature reading. A sample student calculation could look like this:

22°C Initial temperature reading	–	0°C Final temperature reading	=	22°C Total temperature change reading

3. *What was the average energy loss per minute for the cream mixture over the entire experiment?*

Again, students' data will vary based on their methods and specific data. Students can solve this problem by taking the total temperature change (their answer to Data Analysis question 2) and dividing it by the time it took to complete the reaction. Students should calculate their answer using the time when the temperature became consistent. A sample student calculation could look like this:

22°C total temperature change ÷ 7.5 minutes = 2.93°C per minute

CONCLUSION AND CONNECTIONS KEY

This section of the lab offers a great opportunity to engage the entire class in discussion to clarify the main ideas of the lab and allow the students to make their own connections between science and cooking. I ask that students answer the Data Analysis questions and attempt to answer the Conclusion and Connections questions, with the understanding that we will spend time the next day discussing the Conclusions and Connections section.

1. *Was your initial hypothesis correct? Explain why or why not, citing specific data from your experiment.*

   Students' initial hypotheses will vary, but the data should support that the temperature of the cream at the conclusion of the experiment is the same temperature as the ice cubes and salt. Students should reference their graph or data table to support their conclusion with specific data.

2. *Why do we add salt to the ice? How does this impact the thermal energy in the reaction?*

   Salt is added to the ice to reduce the temperature at which the ice freezes. This reduction in melting temperature contributed to the thermal energy being pulled away from the cream and into the ice and salt to achieve a balance in temperature. With the temperature difference being greater, heat energy was pulled away from the cream at a faster rate. This sped up the reaction time allowing the cream to freeze faster.

3. *Why is salt used on highways after winter snowstorms?*

   This is an application of the knowledge gained in this lab experience. Salt can be used to lower the melting temperature of water, allowing it to remain liquid at lower temperatures. This is helpful on roads to prevent them from icing over in cold conditions, and can cause ice that has formed to return to liquid water. If the conditions get very cold though, salt is not going to be used because it doesn't work when the temperature drops below –15°C.

4. *Can you think of other endothermic reactions that occur in our daily lives? Give two examples and explain why they are endothermic.*

   Water provides many experiences with endothermic reactions. Ice melting, evaporation, melting, and boiling are all examples of endothermic reactions in which heat is absorbed and the phase of water changes.

CROSS-CURRICULAR NOTE: MATH

This lab provides an excellent opportunity to work with the math teacher on skills associated with graphing, such as identifying variables, predicting trends and data points using extrapolation (predicting a data point beyond the given data), and interpolation (predicting a data point between two known points on the graph).

CROSS-CURRICULAR NOTE: LITERACY

Reactions occur every day, and not just in science. Write a reaction statement on the board such as "I can't believe you did that!" Have students write a short story that explains what led to that reaction. Or, ask students to write a conversation between two individuals with opposing views who finally agree on a conclusion. How does their conversation model the trend in temperature from this experiment?

OPTIONAL EXTENSIONS
Middle School

1. Make a batch of the ice cream with the rennet, and then a second batch of ice cream without the rennet. Ask students to compare the texture of the two batches, using the microscope to investigate differences in the composition of the different recipes.

2. Students can investigate the properties of salt and the two ions Na^+ and Cl^- and how those two ions interact with water to reduce its freezing point.

3. Make the lab more inquiry based by asking students to begin by researching

how the initial demonstration was able to take place. This research should introduce the vocabulary, allowing you to prompt students to use that understanding to design a procedure for creating ice cream without a freezer.

High School

1. Encourage students to test this experiment using different types of salt. Ask, "How does the purity and crystallization of the salt impact the speed of making ice cream?"

2. Demonstrate how this same experiment can be done using dry ice. Ask, "Why does the process occur faster when dry ice is used as compared to rock salt?" Students should explain their answers using their understanding of thermal energy.

3. A change in thermal energy can cause a change in structure as well. Look at the expansion that occurs in water as thermal energy decreases and water goes from liquid to solid. Have students measure the change in area between liquid and solid water and explain how that change relates back to the polar water molecule.

EXPERIMENT 5:
Gummy Invertebrates: Student Pages

CHANGING INDEPENDENT VARIABLES IN GELATIN RECIPES

BACKGROUND

When you walk into a candy store you see lollipops, chocolate bars, peppermints, and demineralized bone. Wait, WHAT? That is correct; between the taffy and licorice you can find a variety of candies that contain gelatin. Gelatin, a product most often associated with JELL-O, is made from animal products that contain collagen. Gelatin can be obtained from pigskin, cow bones, and connective tissues, and can be used in the creation of everything from strawberry jelly to your favorite gummy creatures.

So how does animal skin end up in your favorite gummy worm? Gelatin is obtained from the breakdown of collagen proteins. The proteins exist in large helical structures kind of like jump ropes that have been braided together (see Figure 5.1, p. 80). When the gelatin is heated, these ropes break down, allowing water to seep in between them. As they cool, they reform the braid, trapping the water between the proteins. This is what allows the gummy worms to be squishy and chewy. These proteins, when combined with water, have a melting temperature that is below normal body temperature (less than 35°C). This allows gelatin candies such as gummy worms to go from solid to liquid when placed in your mouth. Other thickening chemicals that come from plants such as starch or pectin do not have the melt-in-your-mouth properties of gelatin.

Figure 5.1: The structure of collagen in a triple helix.

There are two variables that affect the outcome of the gummy worm: temperature and the amount of gelatin. For this experiment you will be working with your classmates to create the ultimate gummy worm. What temperature makes the best worm? How much gelatin is necessary to create that perfect melt-in-your-mouth candy? The questions are endless as you begin your study of gummy invertebrates.

SETUP

You will be determining the values that you would like to test for your *independent variable*. You need to come up with three values to test. For example, if you were testing the amount of Jell-O included, you could choose 10 g, 20 g, and 30 g. For your independent variable, list the three values that you will be testing. Have your values checked and initialed by the teacher before making your hypothesis.

My independent variable will be _____,
and I will test the following
      1. _____
      2. _____
      3. _____
      Teacher Initials: _____

Once your three values are approved, record them in your data table in column 1: independent variable. Make sure to include units for your variable as well.

We will also need to be able to measure what makes the best gummy invertebrate. Although preferences vary from student to student, we are going to be measuring one aspect of the worm: how far it can stretch. This is our *dependent variable*, or the variable we will use to determine which gummy worm is best. The gummy worm that stretches the farthest without breaking will be awarded the title of Best Gummy Invertebrate.

HYPOTHESIS

Based on your decision for your independent variable, what will be the ideal value for making the best gummy worms? In other words, what temperature or amount of gelatin will make the best stretching worm? Make a hypothesis stating an exact value, with an explanation of why you think that value is best.

MATERIALS NEEDED PER GROUP
- 4.5 packages of collagen protein (gelatin powder)
- 15 g of flavored gelatin and sucrose mixture (flavored gelatin mix)
- 7 g of fruit flavoring with citric acid and sucrose (fruit drink mix)
- 60 ml of near solid dihydrogen monoxide, H_2O (cold water)
- Beaker, 200 ml
- Glass stir rod
- Graduated cylinder, 100 ml

- Filter paper
- Balance
- Ruler
- Bunsen burner and ring stand, or hot plate
- Tongs
- Plastic mold, ice cube tray, or Tupperware container
- Plastic knives, one for each student
- Freezer or cooler filled with ice
- Indirectly vented chemical-splash goggles
- Aprons

PROCEDURE FOR TEMPERATURE INDEPENDENT VARIABLE

1. Read through the entire Procedure section before beginning.

2. Put on your safety goggles and apron, and gather all your materials at your lab station. If you notice any of the materials are dirty or discolored, notify your teacher.

3. Measure out 10.5 g of collagen protein on a piece of filter paper using the balance. Pour this powder into your 200 ml beaker.

4. Measure out 15 g of flavored gelatin and sucrose mixture on the same piece of filter paper using the balance. Pour this powder into your 200 ml beaker.

5. Measure out 7 grams of fruit flavoring with citric acid and sucrose on filter paper using the balance and pour it into the 200 ml beaker.

6. Mix all the powders together with a glass stir rod.

7. Pour 60 ml of near solid dihydrogen monoxide (H_2O) into the 200 ml beaker with the powders and stir with the glass stir rod for three minutes.

8. After three minutes, allow the mixture to set for seven minutes until it reaches a liquid–solid transition phase. While the mixture is setting, set up your Bunsen burner.

9. Set up a Bunsen burner and ring stand with wire mesh on the iron ring. Make sure your Bunsen burner gas intake tube is securely connected to the gas nozzle and that the ring is set about 3 in. above the barrel of the burner (see Figure 5.2). Light the Bunsen burner to create a flame that is no more than 3 in. high. (It should not be touching the wire mesh.)

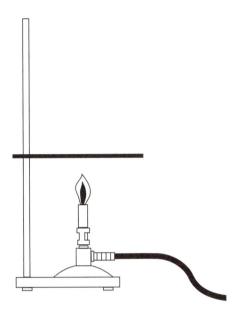

Figure 5.2: Bunsen burner and ring stand.

10. Using the tongs, place the beaker onto the ring stand.

11. Continue to stir the mixture until it reaches the temperature you determined to be your first independent variable. Measure the energy of the mixture using the thermometer.

12. Once the mixture reaches your desired temperature, use the tongs to remove the beaker from heat and turn off your Bunsen burner. Allow the mixture to sit for two minutes.

13. After two minutes of resting, pour the liquid into the plastic container and immediately place it in an environment with low thermal energy. Make sure the plastic container is level so your gummy invertebrates form correctly. Let the container cool for 10–12 minutes while you clean your lab area.

14. Once 10–12 minutes have passed, remove the plastic container from the low thermal energy environment.

15. Place a paper towel on your lab table. Use your fingers to separate the edges of the gummy from the plastic container. Flip over the plastic container and pull out the gummy.

16. Now it's time to test the gummy. Using the plastic knife, cut a 5 cm × 1 cm gummy rectangle. Place the gummy rectangle next to a ruler. Grasping the

ends of the gummy rectangle, stretch the gummy as long as possible until it breaks or snaps. Record in your data table the final distance it reached.

17. Taste the broken pieces of your gummy. Record in your data table any observations about taste, texture, or melting time in your mouth.

18. Repeat the procedure, changing the independent variable (the final temperature) until you have tested each of your independent variables.

19. Clean your lab table and answer the Data Analysis and Conclusions and Connections questions.

PROCEDURE FOR GELATIN INDEPENDENT VARIABLE

1. Read through the entire procedure before beginning.

2. Put on your safety goggles and apron, and gather all your materials at your lab station. If you notice any of the materials are dirty or discolored, notify your teacher.

3. Measure out the value of collagen protein you selected for your independent variable using the balance and a piece of filter paper.

4. Mix the collagen protein with 15 g of flavored gelatin and sucrose mixture, and 7 g of fruit flavoring with citric acid and sucrose in a 200 ml glass beaker. Mix all the powders together with a glass stir rod.

5. Pour 60 ml of near solid H_2O into the 200 ml glass beaker with the powders and stir with the glass stir rod for three minutes.

6. After three minutes, allow the mixture to set for seven minutes until it reaches a liquid–solid transition phase. While the mixture is setting, set up your Bunsen burner.

7. Set up a Bunsen burner and ring stand with wire mesh on the iron ring. Make sure your Bunsen burner gas intake tube is securely connected to the gas nozzle and that the ring is set about 3 in. above the barrel of the burner (see Figure 5.3). Light the Bunsen burner to create a flame that is no more than 3 in. high. (It should not be touching the wire mesh.)

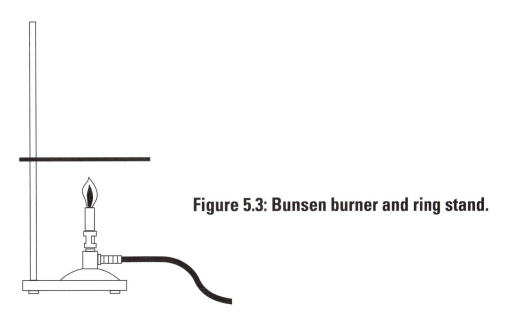

Figure 5.3: Bunsen burner and ring stand.

8. Using the tongs, place the beaker onto the ring stand.

9. Continue to stir the mixture on low heat until it reaches a full liquid state with no lumps.

10. Once the mixture reaches the full liquid state, use the tongs to remove the beaker from heat and turn off your Bunsen burner.

11. Pour the liquid into the plastic container and place immediately in an environment with low thermal energy. Make sure the plastic container is level so your gummy invertebrates form correctly. Cool for 10–12 minutes while you clean your lab area.

12. Once 10–12 minutes have passed, remove the plastic container from the low thermal energy environment.

13. Place a paper towel on your lab table. Use your fingers to separate the edges of the gummy from the plastic container. Flip over the plastic container and pull out the gummy.

14. Now it's time to test the gummy. Using the plastic knife, cut a 5 cm × 1 cm gummy rectangle. Place the gummy rectangle next to a ruler. Grasping the ends of the gummy rectangle, stretch the gummy as long as possible until it breaks or snaps. Record the final distance it reached in your data table.

15. Taste the broken pieces of your gummy. Record any observations about taste, texture, or melting time in your mouth in your data table.

16. Repeat the procedure again, changing the independent variable (the amount of gelatin) until you have tested each of your independent variables.

17. Clean your lab table and answer the Data Analysis and Conclusion and Connections questions.

Data and Observations		
Independent variable	Stretch distance (in cm)	Observations about taste, texture, and melt time
1.		
2.		
3.		

DATA ANALYSIS

For each of the following questions, be sure to explain using detail and complete sentences. If the question requires you to complete calculations, show all of your work.

1. According to the stretch data in your table, which of the three variables you tested makes the best gummy invertebrate? Explain using data to support your answer.

2. Based on your observations, which of the three variables led to the best tasting gummy? Explain using data to support your answer.

3. Was the variable you chose for Data Analysis question 1 the same as question 2? Why or why not?

4. Talk with another group that tested a different independent variable. Based on that group's data, how would you go about making the best gummy invertebrate? Give exact values for both gelatin and temperature.

CONCLUSION AND CONNECTIONS

1. Whether you chose temperature or gelatin for your independent variable, there were other items in the experiment such as amount of water that remained constant for both procedures. Explain why it was necessary to have similar procedures and measurements for both tests.

2. Name two other ways you could measure the quality of your gummy worm besides measuring how far it was able to stretch.

3. Do you think that gelatin would work to form a solid when combined with other liquids besides water? Explain why or why not.

4. Gelatin is found in the skin and connective tissue of animals, including humans. Give two qualities of this compound that are useful for skin and connective tissue in humans.

EXPERIMENT 5:
Gummy Invertebrates: Teacher Pages

CHANGING INDEPENDENT VARIABLES IN GELATIN RECIPES

This hands-on experiment allows students to witness a clear phase change from solid to liquid, while learning key vocabulary about variables and implementing the scientific method. The lab focuses on giving students the opportunity to select the independent variables they are going to be testing to create the ultimate gummy invertebrate. Using the enticement of creating your own candy, students learn how to create a controlled experiment and combine data to create a synthesized conclusion. The lab uses background knowledge of water and metric measurements to help students determine how to make the ultimate gummy worm.

Note: This experiment uses the words *independent variable* and *dependent variable*. These words are synonymous with *experimental variable* and *responding variable*. You should check with your state curriculum to see which words are expected of your students, and use that vocabulary throughout the lab.

STANDARDS ADDRESSED

National Science Education Standards: Grades 5–8

Content Standard A: Science as Inquiry
- Abilities necessary to do scientific inquiry
- Understanding about scientific inquiry

Content Standard B: Physical Science
- Properties and changes of properties in matter
- Transfer of energy

Content Standard E: Science and Technology
- Understanding about science and technology

Content Standard F: Science in Personal and Social Perspectives
- Risks and benefits
- Science and technology in society

Content Standard G: History and Nature of Science
- Science as a human endeavor
- Nature of science
- History of science

National Science Education Standards: Grades 9–12

Content Standard A: Science as Inquiry
- Abilities necessary to do scientific inquiry
- Understanding about scientific inquiry

Content Standard B: Physical Science
- Structure of atoms
- Structure and properties of matter
- Chemical reactions

Content Standard E: Science and Technology
- Abilities of technological design
- Understanding about science and technology

Content Standard F: Science in Personal and Social Perspectives
- Science and technology in local, national, and global challenges

Content Standard G: History and Nature of Science
- Science as a human endeavor
- Nature of scientific knowledge
- Historical perspectives

VOCABULARY

Variable: A factor that can change or influence an outcome.

Independent variable: The factor or variable that is being tested, or the variable that scientists choose to change in the experiment. This can also be called the *experimental variable* or *manipulated variable*.

Dependent variable: The variable that describes what happens as a result of changing the independent variable. This is the variable that is being measured to find changes that occur when the independent variable is changed. This can also be called the *responding variable*.

Controlled variables: These are factors that are not being tested and therefore are held constant throughout the experiment.

Controlled experiment: An experiment in which only one factor is being changed (the independent variable), and the other variables are being held constant to create a control group to create a standard to measure the change.

MATERIALS NEEDED, DECODED FOR THE GROCERY STORE

Collagen protein (gelatin powder)
- Each student group will need around one and a half packages of unflavored gelatin for *each trial*, which means each group will need about four and a half packages total to complete the experiment. For a class of 25 with groups of four to six students, you will need 25 packages of gelatin for the class.
- The unflavored gelatin can be found in the grocery store aisle with the regular flavored gelatin.
- This is the most expensive cost of the lab. If you prepare ahead of time, it is often worthwhile to purchase the unflavored gelatin in bulk containers from the internet. You can get a pound for around $15 to $20, which will equal 64 packages or about two and a half classes of 25 students.

15 g of flavored gelatin and sucrose mixture (flavored gelatin mix)
- This is traditional JELL-O. You can buy whatever flavor looks appealing or is on sale. Each box is usually less than a $1. Each box will have about 3 oz. or enough for between five and six trials. With each group doing three trials, one box will cover every two lab groups.
- Make sure you purchase the gelatin with sugar. There are sugar-free flavors, but they do not work as well for making gummy mixtures.

7 g of fruit flavoring with citric acid and sucrose (fruit drink mix)
- You can buy Kool-Aid, Gatorade, Crystal Light or any generic alternative. One large container of drink mix can supply more than 100 students. I try to buy flavors that are similar to the flavors of gelatin purchased. If you do not want to worry about combining flavors, you can always use white sugar instead. The recipe will be the same; the final candies will just have fewer preservatives and have a shorter shelf life.

60 ml of near solid dihydrogen monoxide, H_2O (cold water)
- You can use clean and refilled milk containers or soda liter bottles in the refrigerator to have a large quantity available to the students. If your room does not have quick access to a refrigerator, you can use ice coolers to keep the containers cold during the lab.

Plastic mold, ice cube tray, or Tupperware container
- This container can be anything from a plastic candy mold (which can be found in the baking department near the cake mix) to ice cube trays to plastic Tupperware containers. I like to use Tupperware containers because they make a nice skinny worm that is easy to cut to look like a gummy worm. All of these containers are reusable, so you need only one per group and can reuse them from class to class.

Plastic knife
- I recommend having enough knives for each student in the group to have one. This helps speed up the cutting of gummy worms and keeps all students involved. The knives can be cleaned and used for the next class, so buy as many as the number of students in your largest class, plus a couple of extras in case some break. Plastic knives are sold individually in boxes of 30–50.

Freezer or cooler filled with ice
- It is best if you have access to a freezer to freeze the gummy worms for 10–12 minutes. However, if this is not something that is available to your class, you can use plastic coolers filled with ice. I often borrow the large water coolers from the athletic department used for sporting events. If you use a cooler, have some pieces of cardboard handy so you can stack the plastic containers or molds and fit more into a single cooler.

Dish soap
- This is necessary for cleanup. I ask students to use an amount about the size of a quarter for each glass container, and I have one bottle available for every four lab groups to share.

SAFETY HIGHLIGHTS
- Unless students are using plastic knives and forks that are disposable, it is necessary to sterilize the metal utensils before allowing them to be used in the experiment.

- The Bunsen burners and ring stands present a potential for students to burn themselves if used incorrectly. Please make sure students have had Bunsen burner safety training before allowing them to participate in this lab. As a teacher, you also need to be prepared with burn treatment options, such as running the burned area under cold water, if a student gets hurt.
- If a glass stir rod breaks, you should dispose of the entire mixture in the beaker. Even if the break is minor, you may have shards of glass in the mixture that are not visible.

Note that these safety highlights are in addition to the safety information detailed in the Safety Protocol section at the beginning of this book. Please refer to that section for additional information about safety when implementing this or any lab in this book.

PREPARATION

1. I recommend dividing the lab space with signs and a large strip of masking tape. Label one side "Collagen Protein" and the other "Temperature." It is helpful to separate these two groups physically during the lab because they have different lab procedures, and you do not want students to be following the procedure for the wrong independent variable.

2. Fill empty milk gallons or soda bottles with water and place in the refrigerator. Do not place in the freezer, as the contents could explode and break the containers. If you decide to use ice coolers, add the water at the beginning of the class period.

3. Label either the freezer or coolers with a sign that says "Low Thermal Energy Environment." This allows students to make the connection between heat and energy that was presented in Experiment 3: "Melting" Apples.

4. I recommend placing the paper towels at each lab station prior to the start of the lab. Many students tend to take too many, so if they have a set quantity to work with, this step can cut down on waste.

PROCEDURE

I recommend having students work in a pairs for this experiment. However, I recommend that three pairs join together to create one group. Because each student group is going to be testing three different independent variables, it is possible to have students work with a lab partner but also work within a larger group so each student pair has to run only one trial. This is an effective way to speed up the lab to fit into one lab session, and to cut down on the amount of supplies that are necessary for the lab.

I often let students self-select their variable of choice, and then I divide them into pairs and then testing groups of three pairs. You can also assign students a variable to test, although you may find that students are less invested in testing a variable they did not get to select themselves.

1. Begin by placing gummy worms on the table and asking, "Who wants to eat a gummy worm?" (It's not hard to get volunteers for this demonstration.) Call up one or two students and give them a gummy worm. Ask them if they are *sure* they want to eat the worm. This often causes some hesitation from the students, at which point reassure them that the worms have not been tampered with. If one student decides not to eat a worm, there is always another student who is willing to take a chance and take part in the presentation. When students finish eating, ask them, "Was the candy good? Would you be interested in eating another? Why do you think I am asking these questions?" Most students assume there is something wrong with the candy. Again, assure them it is exactly what they buy in the stores, but they might be surprised about what is used to make these candies. Use this as a hook to get them interested to read more about gummy worms.

2. Then have students read the Background section. When students arrive at the part about bones and skin, most of them will have a negative reaction about eating collagen. This is a good point to ask students, "How many of you have eaten gummy candies before? How many have you eaten? How much skin do you think that is equal to?" Making that personal connection will help them become more invested in the lab.

3. It is often helpful to provide a visual with jump ropes once the students get to the part that describes the helical nature of gelatin in the Background section. Using three jump ropes, ask a student volunteer to braid them. Once braided, you can show how the helical rope still has a lot of flexibility. Make waves by moving one end of the braid up and down. When students arrive at the description of how the ropes break down and have water molecules seep in between the strands, place small-inflated balloons between the ropes. This can either take some fancy braiding, or you can use masking tape to hold them in place. Next try to recreate the wave with the rope and ask students to observe what is different. Have them share their observations that the rope wave is smaller (depending on the number of balloons, it might not exist at all). Explain that this is the process gelatin goes through to become gummy material.

4. Introduce the word *variable* by writing a definition on the board. You also can ask your students to define the word *variable* and have them use examples to

try to generate their own definition depending on their prior experience with the term.

5. Once students have a clear understanding of the word, ask them what variables might affect the quality of the gummy they can produce. Once they have a list, read the last paragraph in the Background section as a class.

6. For the experiment setup, have students identify what their independent variable is going to be. This is a good opportunity to introduce the term independent variable as the variable that you are choosing to change. Have them meet with their experimental group (group of three pairs) to determine what values they want to test. Once they have their three values, they will present them to you for confirmation.

   (a) For temperature, encourage students to choose temperatures that are less than boiling water (75°C to 90°C). This is a good reference point, linking back to the idea that students need to break down the helical structure of the gelatin so the water can incorporate without boiling away.

   (b) For gelatin, encourage students to go for a range between 0 g and 20 g. One approach would be to use the ingredients on the side of the flavored gelatin box to come up with a suggested amount or ratio. This is a great way for students to use math to back up their initial hypothesis. You can also allow them to do internet research to find suggested values.

   (c) As you approve students' values, have them record each value in their data table so they are ready for recording data during the creation of their gummy worms.

   (d) It is also a good idea to have students star the variable they are going to be testing. Especially if they are working in experimental groups of six students (three pairs), it's helpful to make this determination before moving into the procedure.

7. Once you approve students' values, you can move into a discussion about the dependent variable. Again, you can give them a definition or allow them to construct their own definition using examples and prior knowledge.

8. This will lead students into creating a hypothesis. Encourage them to use background knowledge or experience to support their hypothesis and explain their reasoning.

9. Hand out the two different Procedure sections to the separate testing groups. It is better if the students only have their variable specific procedure. Giving them both procedures often leads to confusion as to which set of steps they should follow.

10. As students begin the procedure, have them use the filter paper to measure out the powders on the balance. They can reuse the same piece of filter paper by placing their measured amount of powder directly in their 200 ml beakers.

11. While they are waiting for their mixture to set, ask students about the appearance of their mixture: "How would you describe it? Is it liquid or solid? How can you tell?" This is a great way to tie in the lessons about phases from Experiment 3: "Melting" Apples.

12. Students can use Bunsen burners or hot plates to achieve the heating step of breaking down the gelatin. If you have younger students, I recommend hot plates on medium heat. Older students may use Bunsen burners, but depending of the size of your group, hot plates may be the safer choice.

13. Remind students to continually stir their mixture. If the heat is too high, the sugar can burn, which makes it nearly impossible to clean the beaker. Many students will want to stir with the thermometer. This is not a good idea because they are designed as measuring tools, not for the utility of stirring. It takes about 5–10 minutes to heat the gelatin to a full liquid consistency depending on the flame.

14. Have students wait two minutes before pouring the mixture. This is important, especially for the temperature groups if the temperature of the liquid is high. Otherwise you could potentially melt the plastic container in which you are placing the gelatin. If the plastic melts, the gelatin is inedible and needs to be discarded.

15. Use cardboard to stack the plastic containers on top of each other in your freezer or cooler. This allows you to fit more containers in a single area.

16. The gelatin should pull out fairly easily for students. I tend to check that the gelatin is fully cooled and settled before allowing them to pull it out.

17. If you are working with testing groups of three pairs, after one round of testing, the experiment is finished. Make sure each student has the opportunity to eat a sample of each variable. This is important for the amount of detail they can produce in the data analysis questions. If you are having each student test three different variables, then they should use the same procedure to test their other two independent variables.

18. Soap is necessary to clean all the equipment thoroughly after this lab.

19. The gummy worms will have a shelf life of about 24 hours. After that they begin to dry out and aren't as appealing. I share this with students and encourage them to eat the worms within that class period.

DATA ANALYSIS ANSWER KEY

All the data analysis for this lab is math based and involves using students' individual data. If students are struggling with the calculations, I recommend using a sample data set and going through the calculations as a class on the board. Then they can use the same skills and apply them directly to their data.

1. *According to the stretch data in your table, which of the three variables you tested makes the best gummy invertebrate? Explain using data to support your answer.*

    Student answers will depend on their chosen variable as well as their stretch data. For the temperature independent variable, most students will find that the higher the temperature, the more stretch of the gummy. This is because more gelatin helixes are broken down, allowing more water to be incorporated into the gummy. There is a maximum value of about 105°C, at which point the sugar begins to crystallize and form a matrix that hardens the mixture and prevents stretch.

    For the gelatin independent variable, students should find that a value around 20 g is best. Less than that and students will end up with a gummy worm that is more like flavored gelatin and breaks quickly. More than 20 g, the gummy becomes hard and is difficult to stretch.

    Student answers should refer directly back to their data table, citing specific independent variable values with stretch measurements.

2. *Based on your observations, which of the three variables led to the best tasting gummy? Explain using data to support your answer.*

    Again, this answer will depend on individual student qualitative observations. What one student finds to be tasty, another student might dislike. Similar to Data Analysis question 1, students should refer directly back to their data table, citing specific independent variable values with stretch measurements.

3. *Was the variable you chose for question 1 the same as question 2? Why or why not?*

    Students will either find that they had the same independent variable for their answers to questions 1 and 2, or not. If their answers are the same, students can argue that stretchy gummy worms make for the best tasting gummy worms. This means that their quantitative data is the same as their qualitative data and that stretch was a good way to measure which gummy worm was best. If their answers are different, students can argue that stretchy gummy worms do not make the best gummy worms, because being stretchy often makes the candy too tough.

This is an ideal answer to discuss as a class. Find out how many groups found that their variable was the same for questions 1 and 2, and how many found it was different. This sets up a great introduction for talking about the difference between qualitative and quantitative observations.

4. *Talk with another group that tested a different independent variable. Based on that group's data, how would you go about making the best gummy invertebrate? Give exact values for both gelatin and temperature.*

For this answer, evaluate if students can synthesize data from two student groups into one collective conclusion. An effective way to approach this is to have all the students groups post their data in a visual way around the classroom, such as using large adhesive notes, or post their data on a chalkboard, whiteboard, or smartboard. This makes all the data available for students to consider. If this is too overwhelming, students can pair with another pair who tested different independent variables and swap information to have a smaller data set to consider. Values should be around 20 g for gelatin and 85–90°C for temperature.

CONCLUSION AND CONNECTIONS ANSWER KEY

This section of the lab offers a great opportunity to engage the entire class in discussion to clarify the main ideas of the lab and allow the students an opportunity to make their own connections between science and cooking. I ask that students answer the Data Analysis questions and attempt to answer the Conclusion and Connections questions, with the understanding that we will spend time the next day discussing the Conclusion and Connections section.

1. *Whether you chose temperature or gelatin for your independent variable, there were other items in the experiment such as amount of water that remained constant for both procedures. Explain why it was necessary to have similar procedures and measurements for both tests.*

Here is where students can use their prior knowledge about controlled variables. If students have not been introduced to the idea of controlled variables, it is important to use this question as a way to introduce the term and talk about what would happen if you were changing temperature and gelatin and water values. Would you ever be able to come up with the perfect gummy worm? How long would that take you?

By isolating the variable that is being tested and keeping all others the same, you can attribute the change in stretch to your independent variable. Otherwise, it could be any of the factors that caused the change in stretch.

2. *Name two other ways you could measure the quality of your gummy worm besides measuring how far it was able to stretch.*

Students can get very creative with different ways to measure the quality of the gummy worm. The key word is *measure*. Their answer needs to be something that can be measured, or a quantitative observation. Aside from distance of stretch, other ideas include how quickly it can dissolve in your mouth, or how many times you have to chew it before you can swallow it.

3. *Do you think that gelatin would work to form a solid when combined with other liquids besides water? Explain why or why not.*

In this answer, students should use the background discussion about the gelatin helix to support their answer. Gelatin can be used to thicken other liquids that do not contain water, but I allow students to answer either yes or no as long as they use a statement that refers back to the helical nature of gelatin in their response.

4. *Gelatin is found in the skin and connective tissue of animals, including humans. Give two qualities of this compound that are useful for skin and connective tissue in humans.*

The stretch and give of skin is important. It allows us to move our joints and muscles. If our skin were not flexible, it would limit our movement. Look at the joints of the knee and elbow, where humans have extra skin to allow for increased mobility.

Gelatin also allows us to have a membrane that is still solid. You want the skin to be solid so nothing is breaking or leaking out of the body. The solid nature of the gelatin helix allows our body system to be contained in a solid skin structure.

Students can use outside resources such as textbooks and the internet to answer this question if they are struggling with making connections with the skin.

CROSS-CURRICULAR NOTE: MATH

Ask students to identify how the independent variable is represented in math. Normally, it is represented as the variable x. How does that correspond to creating a graph? Students can take graphs from math and write potential experiments that would yield that data.

CROSS-CURRICULAR NOTE: LITERACY

In this experiment, students work with a gelatin, a substance that has many different uses. In one case, it is in skin for elasticity, in another case it is in a candy that is edible. Although the substance has the same properties, the uses are different. There are words that are like this in the English language called *homonyms*; these are words that are spelled the same and are pronounced the same, but have different meanings. Ask students to look at a list of homonyms (a sample list is given below) and talk about how word choice can change the meaning of a sentence. How does this compare with the role of gelatin in our daily lives?

Sample homonyms:

stalk (part of a plant) and *stalk* (follow/harass a person)
left (opposite of right) and *left* (past tense of leave)
rose (a flower) and *rose* (got up from a seat)

OPTIONAL EXTENSIONS
Middle School

1. Encourage students to come up with the dependent variable on their own and explore how they can measure which gummy worm is best in a quantitative way. Aside from distance of stretch, other ideas include how quickly it can dissolve in your mouth, and how many times you have to chew it before you can swallow it. Students should focus on using quantitative observations that can be measured rather than something that is qualitative like taste.

2. To make this lab more inquiry based, have students come up with the entire procedure to test different variables. Use the jump rope demonstration of the gelatin helix to provide background information, and then allow students to design a procedure for creating their own gummy worms and test which one is best.

3. Gelatin also can be used to make marshmallows and some yogurts. Ask students to consider what other candies could be made using gelatin and other

water-based foods. Have a candy creation contest, allowing students to make gelatin-based candies out of other household ingredients and have a stretch, melt, or taste competition.

High School

1. Gelatin molecules draw in water and hold it in place. Students can explore what parts of the gelatin molecule attract water, and why. This experiment can be related back to a discussion on polarity between molecules and atoms.

2. Gelatin is also found in cosmetics creams. Students can explore if gelatin really helps the collagen of human skin by designing an experiment to test whether gelatin affects the appearance of skin.

3. Have students design a control set for this experiment that removes the presence of gelatin. Ask, "What happens to the gummy worms? How does having a control set inform you about the role of gelatin in this process?"

PART TWO: ACIDS AND BASES

This section of experiments highlights how acidity plays a vital role in the creation of some everyday foods. Experiment 6: Acidic Milk uses lemon juice to prompt the creation of basic soft cheese. The experiment introduces students to the concepts of acid and base, and how they can be measured by pH. Experiment 7: Berries and Bacteria explores how acids can be used to prevent the growth of microorganisms in the creation of jam. This experiment shows students how acids can change the environment enough to preserve foods and stop them from spoiling, while teaching students about growing cultures of bacteria. Experiment 8: American Mozzarella asks students to make mozzarella cheese using a biological compound to change the pH of milk rather than a direct application of acid. The rate of the pH change is measured so students can compare and contrast the reaction rate that occurs in the complicated creation of mozzarella cheese with that of the cheese created in Experiment 6. The experiments in this section introduce students to skills such as measuring pH, growing bacteria cultures, and measuring chemical reaction rates.

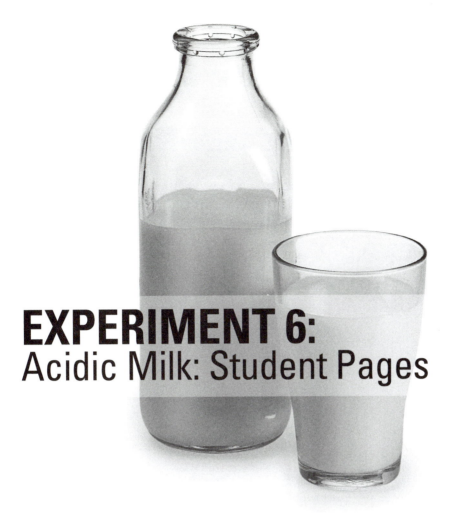

EXPERIMENT 6:
Acidic Milk: Student Pages

MEASURING PH CHANGES WHEN ACID IS INTRODUCED IN CHEESE MAKING

BACKGROUND

Most people are not quick to associate the word *cheese* with the word *acid*. But the process of making cheese actually begins by raising the acidity of a liquid to cause proteins to curdle to make sour milk. That's right; acid is used to make sour milk. That grilled cheese you ate last week doesn't sound so appetizing now, does it?

The word *acid* brings to mind liquids burning through metals as they all bubble and smoke. But not all acids are the kind used by villains in action movies. So what is an acid? An acid is any chemical compound that will increase the amount of hydrogen ions (H^+) in a substance or solution. Why does this make milk curdle and secret agents cringe? Hydrogen ions are highly reactive and can cause changes in chemical bonding and compounds. It would be like a famous movie star walking into the school cafeteria. Everyone would want to sit with him or her, which would cause total chaos in the lunchroom. The same happens when an acid is introduced, except the hydrogen ion is the movie star. The molecules and atoms want to be with the hydrogen ions, which causes the chemicals to break down and chaos to occur.

Cheese making consists of three steps: the precipitation of casein into curds, the concentration of the curds, and the ripening or aging of the curds. Milk contains several proteins and about 80% of those proteins are casein. These protein chains form small globs called *micelles* (see Figure 6.1). When acid is introduced, the micelles break open to allow fat to enter into the glob. This makes the globs larger and more visible, so that now they are called *curds*. These curds are strained out and pressed together to create the complex known as cheese.

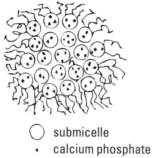

○ submicelle
· calcium phosphate
⌒ k-casein peptide chain

Figure 6.1: Casein micelle.

How much acid is necessary to make this change occur? That is the question we are going to investigate in this experiment. We will need to measure the amount of acid in our solution by measuring the pH of the milk. pH is a scale that measures the amount of hydrogen ions present in a solution on a scale of 0–14 (see Figure 6.2). Anything that we would consider an acid has a pH value of 0–6.9. We will be using pH to help us measure the acidity of the milk and looking at how the amount of acid used in the milk relates back to the amount of cheese that is produced.

SETUP

For this experiment, each student group will be testing a different amount of acid in the creation of cheese. Each group is responsible for sharing its results with the entire class for the final conclusion. Your group will be assigned a volume of acid to use in your cheese creation; fill in this measurement below.

For this experiment, my independent variable will be _____ml of citric acid.

Take a moment to circle or highlight this value in your data table so you know where to record your observations.

Figure 6.2: A pH scale with examples of acidic and basic items.

Concentration of Hydrogen ions compared to distilled water

Examples of solutions at this pH

10,000,000	pH = 0	Battery acid, strong hydrofluoric acid
1,000,000	pH = 1	Hydrochloric acid secreted by stomach lining
100.000	pH = 2	Lemon juice, gastic acid, vinegar
10.000	pH = 3	Grapefruit, organge juice, soda
1.000	pH = 4	Tomato juice, acid rain
100	pH = 5	Soft drinking water, black coffee
10	pH = 6	Urine, saliva
1	pH = 7	"Pure" water
1/10	pH = 8	Sea Water
1/100	pH = 9	Baking Soda
1/1,000	pH = 10	Great salt lake, milk of magnesia
1/10,000	pH = 11	Ammonia solution
1/100,000	pH = 12	Soapy water
1/1,000,000	pH = 13	Bleaches oven cleaner
1/10,000,000	pH = 14	Liquid drain cleaner

HYPOTHESIS

Instead of predicting an exact value, for this experiment we will be predicting a relationship. In other words, what is going to be the trend of the data that we are about to collect?

For this experiment, what do you think will happen to the amount of cheese as we increase the amount of acid used? Will it increase or decrease? Make a hypothesis stating whether you think the amount of cheese will increase or decrease as we use more acid to make our cheese. Make sure your hypothesis includes an explanation of *why* you think this will occur.

MATERIALS NEEDED PER GROUP
- 200 ml of emulsified colloid of liquid butterfat in H_2O (whole milk)
- 10 ml of citric acid (lemon juice)
- Sodium chloride, NaCl (table salt)
- Beaker, 400 ml
- Thermometer, 100°C and nonmercury
- Stirring rod
- Plastic forks, one per student
- Large funnel
- Gauze cloth
- Beaker tongs
- Bunsen burner and ring stand
- Filter paper
- Balance
- Carbohydrates for tasting the cheese (crackers or bread)
- pH paper
- Indirectly vented chemical-splash goggles
- Aprons
- Gloves

PROCEDURE

1. Read through the entire Procedure section before beginning.

2. Put on your safety goggles, apron, and gloves, and gather all your materials at your lab station. If you notice any of the materials are dirty or discolored, notify your teacher.

3. Place 200 ml of emulsified colloid containing 80% casein in H_2O in the 400 ml beaker.

4. Set up a Bunsen burner and ring stand with wire mesh on the iron ring. Make sure your Bunsen burner gas intake tube is securely connected to the gas nozzle and that the ring is set about 3 in. above the barrel of the burner (see Figure 6.3). Light the Bunsen burner to create a flame that is no more than 3 in. high. (It should not be touching the wire mesh.)

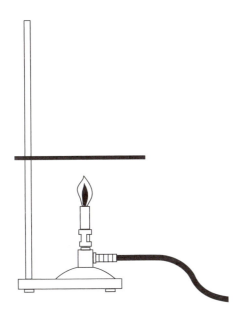

Figure 6.3: Bunsen burner and ring stand.

5. Using the tongs, place the beaker onto the ring stand.

6. Constantly stir the emulsified colloid with the glass stir rod while monitoring the temperature. You want to heat the mixture to 74°C. Do not stir with the thermometer because it can break and ruin your final product.

7. Record in the Data and Observation section any observed changes in the emulsified colloid while heating. While you are waiting for the emulsified

colloid to heat, one of the people in your group can go and measure out your assigned volume of citric acid.

8. When the emulsified colloid reaches a temperature of 74°C, remove the beaker from the heat using the tongs.

9. Add the citric acid to the beaker and stir to mix. Record any observed changes in the emulsified colloid in the Data and Observations section.

10. Use the pH paper to measure the pH of the mixture. Dip a small piece of the paper into your liquid and allow it to dry. Once dry, compare the color to the chart on the box to determine the pH. Record this information in your data table.

11. Allow the mixture to stand for 10 minutes. At this point you can clean your ring stand, thermometer, and stir rod.

12. Line a large funnel with a double layer of gauze cloth. Pour the mixture through the gauze cloth, allowing the liquid to go into the sink. *It is very important that you get all of the cheese curds into the gauze cloth.* The class data is dependent on your efforts. If there are curds stuck in the beaker you can add 20 ml of warm water to the beaker to remove them. Allow the funnel, gauze, and cheese curds to stand for five minutes.

13. Pick up the gauze cloth by the corners. Squeeze off all the remaining liquid.

14. Use a plastic fork to scrape the cheese curds off the gauze cloth and onto a piece of filter paper. Dispose of the gauze cloth.

15. Measure the mass of a piece of clean filter paper using the balance. Record that mass in the Data and Observations section.

16. Measure the mass of the filter paper and cheese using a balance. Subtract the mass of the clean piece of filter paper. This is the mass of cheese you created. Record this amount of cheese in your data table.

17. Your final product can now be eaten. It is recommended that you add a small amount of salt to the cheese for flavor. The cheese can be spread on carbohydrates and eaten.

18. Clean your lab table.

19. Once your teacher has approved your lab table as clean, you need to post your data on the large class data table. You then need to record the data of your classmates to help you complete the lab questions.

DATA AND OBSERVATIONS

Observations From Heating Milk

Observations From Adding the Citric Acid

CALCULATIONS

Mass of Clean Filter Paper:	_____ g
Mass of Filter Paper and Cheese:	_____ g

Amount of Citric Acid Used	Amount of Cheese Created (g)	Taste of Cheese
6 ml		
7 ml		
8 ml		
9 ml		
10 ml		
11 ml		
12 ml		
13 ml		
14 ml		

DATA ANALYSIS

For each of the following questions, be sure to explain using detail and complete sentences. If the question requires you to complete calculations, show all of your work.

1. Draw a graph of the relationship between the amount of citric acid used (your independent variable) and the amount of cheese that was created (your dependent variable). Remember to include all elements of a scientific graph (title, labeled axes, units, etc.).

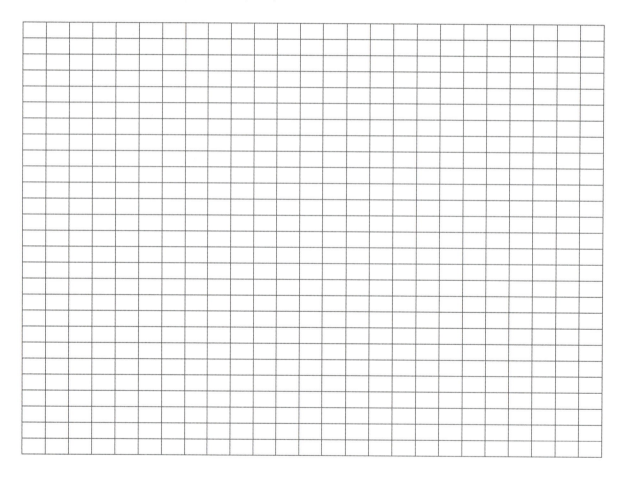

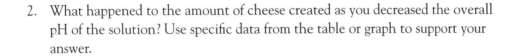

2. What happened to the amount of cheese created as you decreased the overall pH of the solution? Use specific data from the table or graph to support your answer.

3. Are there data points that do not fit the overall trend? List two potential errors that may have caused student groups to get data points that did not follow the overall class trend.

CONCLUSION AND CONNECTIONS

1. Did the amount of cheese change as the pH of the milk changed? Explain your reasoning using information from the Background section to support your answer.

2. Scientists regularly choose to share their data with other scientists around the world. In this experiment, what was the benefit that came from all the teams sharing their class data?

3. Do you think that the pH of cheese is acidic or neutral? Explain your reasoning.

4. What do you think would happen to the amount of cheese if 1% milk was used instead of whole milk? Why?

5. Lemon juice was the citric acid used in this experiment. Why do you think dentists advise people against sucking on lemons?

EXPERIMENT 6:
Acidic Milk: Teacher Pages

MEASURING PH CHANGES WHEN ACID IS INTRODUCED IN CHEESE MAKING

Acids and bases can be a challenging topic for students to grasp. Because the concepts rest on an understanding of hydrogen and hydroxide interactions among molecules, many students struggle to explain what makes an acid acidic and how it can impact other molecules. This experiment introduces acids in a way that integrates a familiar food: cheese. Using the process of making cheese, students are introduced to acids, hydrogen ions, and the pH scale of measuring acidic strength. The lab also models the cumulative nature of science by having each of the student groups complete one test and then compile the results with the rest of the class to find the relationship between the data. This combination of content, skills, and curdled milk makes for an engaging learning experience for the class.

STANDARDS ADDRESSED
National Science Education Standards: Grades 5–8

Content Standard A: Science as Inquiry
- Abilities necessary to do scientific inquiry
- Understanding about scientific inquiry

Content Standard B: Physical Science
- Properties and changes of properties in matter
- Transfer of energy

Content Standard F: Science in Personal and Social Perspectives
- Science and technology in society

Content Standard G: History and Nature of Science
- Science as a human endeavor
- Nature of science

National Science Education Standards: Grades 9–12

Content Standard A: Science as Inquiry
- Abilities necessary to do scientific inquiry
- Understanding about scientific inquiry

Content Standard B: Physical Science
- Structure of atoms
- Structure and properties of matter
- Chemical reactions

Content Standard E: Science and Technology
- Abilities of technological design
- Understanding about science and technology

Content Standard F: Science in Personal and Social Perspectives
- Science and technology in local, national, and global challenges

Content Standard G: History and Nature of Science
- Science as a human endeavor
- Nature of scientific knowledge
- Historical perspectives

VOCABULARY

Acid: Any chemical compound that will raise the amount of hydrogen ions (H^+) above the amount of hydrogen ions found in water.

Base: A solution that has an excess of OH– ions above the amount of hydroxide ions found in water. Another word for base is *alkali*.

Hydrogen ion: A hydrogen atom that has no electrons, and therefore has a positive charge. It is highly reactive.

pH: A scale that measures how acidic or basic a solution is. The scale measures from 0 to 14, with water a neutral substance with a pH of 7.

MATERIALS NEEDED, DECODED FOR THE GROCERY STORE

200 ml of emulsified colloid of liquid butterfat in H_2O (whole milk)

- Each student group will need 200 ml of whole milk. A gallon of whole milk will have enough for 18 lab groups.
- It is possible to complete the lab using 2% milk, but the amount of cheese created will be much smaller, and often too little to be shared equally within the lab group.

Citric acid (lemon juice)

- There are two ways to get lemon juice from the grocery store. You can buy lemons and juice them (each has about 30 ml of juice), or you can buy the prepackaged lemon juice in the produce section. I like the prepackaged juice because it comes in squirt bottles so it is easier for students to measure, and saves time preparing lemons. The small bottles that look like a lemon contain about 200 ml or enough for about 20 lab groups.
- Lime juice is more acidic and will change the outcome of your experiment. Make sure your acid is consistent for the entire class.

Sodium chloride, NaCl (table salt)

- Each student uses a pinch of salt for his or her cheese, so a single saltshaker will be more than enough for a class.

Plastic fork

- The plastic forks work well because they give students not only a device for scraping off the cheese but also for eating the cheese. If you are letting students use the forks as only a tool, they can be used as a class set. If you are allowing students to eat off of them as well, they can be disposed of or be washed with dish soap before being used by another student. Purchase according to the number of students in your class.

Cheesecloth or gauze cloth

- If you go to a fancy gourmet shop you may find cheesecloth. I have never found any at the grocery stores I frequent, so I buy gauze cloth in bulk. Gauze is not cheap, however, so another option is to buy heavy-duty paper towels. The paper towels will require students to double layer the funnel and squeeze out a little more liquid, but is a more cost-effective approach to the lab. Just make sure you buy strong paper towels because cheaper ones will split open and students will lose their cheese curds and have incorrect results.

Carbohydrates for tasting the cheese (crackers or bread)
- One box of crackers is all you need for the tasting. A single sleeve of crackers will cover a class of 25 students.

Dish soap
- This is necessary for cleanup. I ask students to use an amount about the size of a quarter for each glass container, and I have one bottle available for every four lab groups to share.

SAFETY HIGHLIGHTS

- The Bunsen burners and ring stands present a potential for students to burn themselves if used incorrectly. Please make sure students have had Bunsen burner safety training before allowing them to participate in this lab. As a teacher, you also need to be prepared with burn treatment options, such as running the burned area under cold water, if a student gets hurt.
- Students will be working with citric acid. Goggles are a must for protecting students' eyes, with an eyewash station and acid shower nearby for any situations that arise. Aprons and gloves are also required. If students get the acid on their skin, they should be cautious and wash the area with soap and water immediately.
- If a glass stir rod breaks, you should dispose of the entire mixture in the beaker. Even if the break is minor, you may have shards of glass in the mixture that are not visible.

Note that these safety highlights are in addition to the safety information detailed in the Safety Protocol section at the beginning of this book. Please refer to that section for additional information about safety when implementing this or any lab in this book.

PREPARATION

1. The milk should be refrigerated until it is used. The citric acid should be refrigerated as well once the bottle has been opened.

2. I recommend having a separate or labeled trash can for trash for this lab. From the gauze cloth to the milk, this can lead to a smelly lab if all trash is not thrown away in a timely manner. I make a "TRASH HERE" sign and take all the other trash cans out of the classroom so that I can dispose of the trash at the end of the school day.

3. You will want to create the template for the large class data table before the start of the lab. This can be drawn on the board, a large piece of butcher paper, or projected on a whiteboard or smartboard.

PROCEDURE

I recommend having students work in a pairs for this experiment. Each student group can handle the creation of cheese for its specific amount of acid, and the amount of cheese created is easily split between two students. There are nine different values of citric acid to be tested. If there are more student groups, I recommend having groups test the same variable, rather than increasing the number of students in a group or increasing or decreasing the amount of acid being tested

Once in groups, I often let students self-select their variable by asking for volunteers for each variable. You also can assign students a variable to test, although you may find that students are less invested in testing a variable they did not get to select themselves.

1. Begin by showing students short movie clips that involve the use of acid. I have used the 1989 *Batman* movie at the point when the Joker is created. There is also the 2008 *Batman* movie *The Dark Knight*, in which acid disfigures the face of District Attorney Harvey Dent. After identifying the acid in the scene, pause the clip before the acid interacts with the character and ask students to predict what is going to happen. They can write the prediction or share it with a partner. Have the students share their predictions aloud with the class.

2. Next, ask students to read the Background section. This will most likely be met with opposition because students want to see what is going to happen in the movie clip. Assure them that you will show the rest of the clip once they have a context for what the acid is going to do and how that relates to the experiment. After reading the background information about acids, ask students to refine their prediction about what is going to happen in the movie scene, adding an explanation of *why* they believe their explanation is correct. They can share this with their classmates, or share their predictions aloud with the entire class. Once they have clearly explained their predictions using the information in the Background section, show the rest of the movie clip.

3. Continue to have the students read about the process of making cheese. A short demonstration that allows students to understand the breakdown of the casein micelles can be conducted by having a group of 5–10 students come to the front of the classroom and huddle together. Each student represents a

casein protein and as a group they are a micelle. (You can ask the students to identify themselves, or give each student a sign to hold.) I often compare the huddled group to a school dance, showing how difficult it is for a teacher to get in between students, as there is no empty space available. Then ask the class, "So what happens if I add heat to this protein molecule? What would happen if all of you got hot and sweaty at the dance?" The students are often quick to move away from one another, demonstrating the breakdown of the micelle. This occurs with the heat and acid. As the micelle breaks down, I give each student a balloon to hold in front of him or her. The balloons are labeled *fat*. Then the students are "cooled" so they can group back together, incorporating the fat molecules. Ask the students to explain what happened to the micelle. It should have gotten bigger, now forming a curd, which is used to make cheese.

4. Finish reading the Background section and present the pH scale. If students do not have a background in pH, it will be necessary to instruct them on how to use the pH paper. Another activity is using the list of items below and placing them on a pH scale from 0 to 14. You can also share the pH scale with examples as a handout to give students a point of reference depending on the focus of your lesson:

pH Value	Item or Solution
0	Hydrofluoric acid
1	Stomach acid
2	Lemon juice
3	Orange juice
4	Tomato juice
5	Black coffee
6	Urine
7	Distilled water
8	Seawater
9	Baking soda
10	Milk of Magnesia
11	Ammonia solution
12	Soapy water
13	Bleach
14	Sodium hydroxide

5. After students finish reading the Background section, break them up into lab groups. Each lab group then needs to be assigned an experimental variable value for its individual test. The variable is the amount of citric acid with values ranging from 6 ml to 14 ml. If there are more than nine lab groups, assign multiple groups the same variable. I do not recommend testing less than 6 ml of citric acid or more than 15 ml of citric acid as it creates an end product that is not edible. These students are often upset that they do not get their final cheese, so it is better to have student groups test the same variable. You can also add values between those listed in the lab like 9.5 ml and 10.5 ml.

6. Encourage students to highlight or circle their independent variable value on the data table. This is helpful to remind them of their assigned value and so they can place their observations in the correct cell in the table.

7. Once groups are assigned their specific independent variable, you can begin the discussion of the hypothesis. Students are being asked to predict a relationship. Depending on students' prior experience with relationships, it is often helpful to use the "If x (independent variable)…then y (dependent variable response)…because (explanation)…" hypothesis model to help them write a clear hypothesis. An example of this would be, "If the amount of acid used to make the cheese increases, then the amount of cheese produced will increase because there is more acid to break down the casein micelles, forming more curds and cheese." You can model this format for students using prior experiment setups, or ask them for suggestions on how to fill in the format for this experiment.

8. Once students begin the Procedure section, make sure they are measuring the correct value of citric acid for their group. Students may ask others how much they need at the supply table and end up using the wrong amount, so I position myself near the supplies to keep an eye on their measurements.

9. Students can use Bunsen burners or hot plates to achieve the heating step with the milk. If you have younger students, I recommend hot plates on medium heat. Older students may use Bunsen burners, but depending of the size of your group, hot plates may be the safer choice.

10. Remind students to continually stir their milk. If the heat is too high, the milk can burn, which ruins the cheese and makes it nearly impossible to clean out the beaker. Many students will want to stir with the thermometer, which is not a good idea because they are designed as measuring tools, not for the utility of stirring. It takes about 10–15 minutes to heat the milk to the desired temperature depending on the flame size and ring stand setup.

11. While the milk is heating, remind students to make observations. Ask, "Do

you notice any visible changes? What is happening to the casein proteins as heat is added? Is this a physical or chemical change?"

12. When the students add the citric acid, it creates a mixture of curds and whey. The mixture looks like sour milk and tends to gross out the students. Have them identify the different components of the curdled milk from the background information, reinforcing that the curds are just the casein proteins with fat globules inside them. Students need to record their observations in the Data and Observations section of the lab.

13. The mixture is allowed to rest to allow the curds to float to the top, as well as allowing the mixture to cool. If students do not wait the full amount of time, they will not be able to handle the beaker safely. This presents the possible danger of dropping the beaker, which would break the glass, as well as present the potential for burns from the hot liquid. If students cannot handle the beaker, they need to wait longer before straining their mixture.

14. Have students use a double layer of the gauze or paper towels. In either case, allow the excess cloth to hang over the side of the funnel, which is helpful in lifting the curds out to squeeze out any remaining liquid.

15. The straining can be a little difficult for students because it is not a skill most are familiar with. I recommend demonstrating the straining with the first group with a cool beaker and have all the students watch. While demonstrating the straining method, give the following instructions to the entire class:

    (a) You do not want to spill any of the contents of your curds and whey. The data for this experiment is dependent on you creating the most cheese possible, and spilling outside the funnel will cause you to lose mass and impact the class data. Only fill the funnel to be two-thirds full and wait for it to drain to less than one-fourth before adding more to the funnel.

    (b) As the curds accumulate, it can be difficult for the liquid to strain. You can help this process by pulling the cloth (paper towel) slightly out of the funnel by 1 cm and squeezing it gently against the side of the funnel. Squeezing too hard can cause your cheese to break through and will impact your data.

    (c) If there are curds that are stuck in the beaker, use a small amount of water to rinse them out. You want every piece of curd for your mass measurement.

16. Soap is necessary to clean all the equipment thoroughly after this lab.

17. Encourage students to eat the cheese within the class period while it is fresh. The cheese should not be brought home to share.

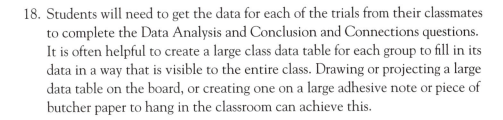
18. Students will need to get the data for each of the trials from their classmates to complete the Data Analysis and Conclusion and Connections questions. It is often helpful to create a large class data table for each group to fill in its data in a way that is visible to the entire class. Drawing or projecting a large data table on the board, or creating one on a large adhesive note or piece of butcher paper to hang in the classroom can achieve this.

DATA ANALYSIS ANSWER KEY

All the data analysis for this lab is math based. If students are struggling with the questions, I recommend using a sample data set and going through the calculations as a class on the board. Then students can use the same skills and apply them directly to their data.

1. *Draw a graph of the relationship between the amount of citric acid used (your independent variable) and the amount of cheese that was created (your dependent variable). Remember to include all elements of a scientific graph (title, labeled axis, units, etc.).*

The change in the amount of cheese created with different values of citric acid

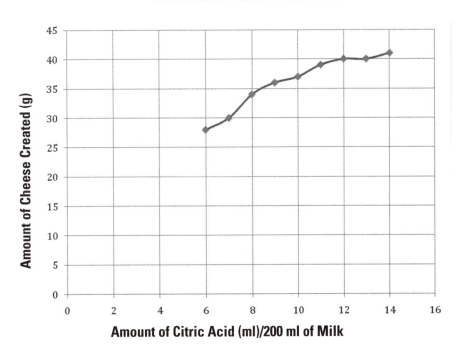

The graph will depend on the accuracy of your students, but should have a general increase in the amount of cheese created as the amount of acid was increased. These values might level off at 12 or 13 ml of acid. It is also possible that there are sudden spikes where data were inconsistent. These spikes will be addressed in a later question.

2. *What happened to the amount of cheese created as you decreased the overall pH of the solution? Use specific data from the table or graph to support your answer.*

    Students should notice that the overall amount of cheese was increasing along with the overall pH of the solution. This requires students to go back to the data table to make the connection that adding additional acid will decrease the overall pH of the solution, making it more acidic. Each student answer should cite specific data from the data table or graph for support.

3. *Are there data points that do not fit the overall trend? List two potential errors that may have caused student groups to get data points that did not follow the overall class trend.*

    Common errors cited by students include students measuring materials incorrectly, not heating the milk to the correct temperature, and losing curds in the straining process. Students should be able to identify at least two potential errors that may have affected the outcome.

CONCLUSION AND CONNECTIONS ANSWER KEY

This section of the lab offers a great opportunity to engage the entire class in discussion to clarify the main ideas of the lab and allow the students to make their own connections between science and cooking. I ask that students answer the Data Analysis questions and attempt to answer the Conclusion and Connections questions, with the understanding that we will spend time the next day discussing the Conclusions and Connections section.

1. *Did the amount of cheese change as the pH of the milk changed? Explain your reasoning using information from the Background section to support your answer.*

    The amount of cheese changed as the pH of the milk changed because the increase in hydrogen ions allowed for the creation of more curds by the casein proteins. The hydrogen ions caused more micelles to break open allowing fat globules in, creating more curds. The graph and data tables should support this explanation.

2. *Scientists regularly choose to share their data with other scientists around the world. In this experiment, what was the benefit that came from all the teams sharing their class data?*

Scientists need to share data to share the workload. If a single student team had tried to attempt this experiment on its own, it would have taken nine class periods of testing. By working as a team and communicating the data, scientists were able to arrive at the solution much more quickly.

You can compare this to other projects such as the human genome project, explaining how scientists all over the world worked collectively to tackle a problem that originally seemed impossible because of the volume of work.

3. *Do you think that the pH of cheese is acidic or neutral? Explain your reasoning.*

The pH of the cheese is going to be around 5.3–5.5. This means it is still considered acidic. This is a great test to allow the students to try in the classroom using cheese from their experiment or other cheese from the grocery store. The cheese is acidic because it still contains a higher amount of hydrogen ions from the breakdown of the casein micelles. It is closer to neutral because a lot of the hydrogen ions were left in the solution that was strained off (whey). See that students have an answer along with an explanation for their reasoning.

4. *What do you think would happen to the amount of cheese if 1% milk was used instead of whole milk? Why?*

The amount of cheese would decrease because the amount of fat in the milk is less. The fat is necessary for forming the curds, and when you decrease the amount of fat present in the milk, it means that less cheese curds can form. You can approach this question by asking what the differences are between whole milk, 1% milk, and skim milk. Why does fat make a difference? You can then refer back to the student casein micelle demonstration of the school dance at the beginning of the lab.

5. *Lemon juice was the citric acid used in this experiment. Why do you think dentists advise people against sucking on lemons?*

Lemon juice is acidic, so it has a high amount of hydrogen ions. These ions are highly reactive and cause changes in the chemicals of your mouth, especially your teeth. Your tooth enamel is sensitive to acid and can be worn away, which weakens your teeth. Dentists recommend avoiding foods with high acidity.

CROSS-CURRICULAR NOTE: TECHNOLOGY

This is an ideal opportunity to have students create their graphs using a computer spreadsheet such as Excel.

CROSS-CURRICULAR NOTE: MATH

The measurement of pH is a logarithmic scale. This is a great opportunity to connect the math skills associated with understanding logarithms to a concrete application.

CROSS-CURRICULAR NOTE: LITERACY

Acid is a strong word that evokes imagery and visual connections. These connections can be exhibited in poetry as acrostic poems. The poem allows students to use the letters in a word to inspire connections. Here is an acrostic poem for *acid*:

Angry
Caustic
Illegal
Dangerous

Students can use the names of acids found in their households and come up with acrostic poems that use words to describe the acid properties and uses.

OPTIONAL EXTENSIONS
Middle School

1. Students can use different types of milk such as powdered milk, lactose-free milk, soy milk, or goat milk to examine the difference among the cheese curds. They can measure the overall amount of cheese created by similar volumes of milk, and compare that with the percentage of casein.

2. Students can try creating cheese with different types of acids such as orange

juice, tomato juice, and lime juice. Ask, "How does changing the pH of the acid affect the amount of cheese that is created?"

3. To make this lab more inquiry based, have students create the Materials Needed and Procedure sections after being presented with the initial video and background information. Have students choose the independent variable to test as a class, allowing them to share the information. An effective way to approach this is to give students the final questions you would like them to answer for Data Analysis and Conclusion and Connections and design the experiment around those questions.

High School

1. After the initial experiment, ask students to create cheese using milk with unknown fat contents. Students can find a relationship between the amount of cheese created and the fat content of the milk used, and determine how this relates back to the structure of the casein micelle.

2. Students can explore what happens to the micelle when a basic solution such as baking soda is added back to the cheese mixture. Have students make a hypothesis and test the impact of adding solutions that are basic to the newly formed cheese.

3. Acids are found in many foods. Ask students to create a pH line that depicts the pH of their favorite cafeteria foods, and explore how acidity relates to the taste profile of food.

EXPERIMENT 7:
Berries and Bacteria: Student Pages

MEASURING HOW ACIDS AND HEAT IMPACT BACTERIA IN JAM

BACKGROUND

Have you ever had a ripe apple, a juicy strawberry, or a succulent peach? Did the juices flow into your mouth with each bite as you devoured it? On the other hand, have you ever had a piece of fruit that was less than perfect? How about a piece that was mushy, grainy, or dry, and after a bite or two you ended up throwing it in the trash? That is the problem with fruit; you have to catch it at just the right time of maturation to get the full flavor and texture. If you miss that window, your fruit comes under the attack of bacteria and enzymes and begins to decompose, leaving you with something unappealing and inedible.

The problem isn't new. In fact, ancient civilizations were the first ones to tackle the problem of keeping fruits for an extended period of time by drying the fruit to save it for later use. But it was the invention of jam that truly brought fruits to the masses. Jam is a product that preserves fruit in jars and keeps it from spoiling for an extended period of time.

How is this preservation done? The process starts with crushing up fresh fruit and taking it through a process of container sterilization, chemical reaction, and pasteurization before it arrives on the shelf of your grocery store as jam. The chemical reaction occurs when citric acids are added to change the acidity of the jam and the pectin (starch) strands of the fruit realign with sugars to create a gelatin-like structure. And there it is, the perfect addition to your peanut butter sandwich. Each step is designed to change the molecular structure of the fruit to prevent spoiling and eliminate bacteria to prolong the life of your fruit.

So how effective is the acid in removing bacteria? This experiment is designed to test how much bacteria is eliminated when acid is added to the berries in the jam-making process. You will take culture samples after crushing the berries after mixing in the acid. You will then leave the petri dishes for 48 hours and measure the differences in bacteria growth. Berries and bacteria, you say? Sounds delicious.

HYPOTHESIS

We will be taking two cultures during this experiment:

1. After crushing the berries. (This is our control setup so we can compare the results of the steps to the initial condition.)

2. After adding the acid to the berries.

What percentage of bacteria do you think the acid will be able to eliminate? Make a prediction and explain *why* you believe this will occur based on your previous knowledge and information from the Background section.

MATERIALS NEEDED PER GROUP
- Plastic knives, one for each student
- Plastic bottle
- 15 ml of citric acid (lemon juice)
- 350 ml of sucrose, $C_{12}H_{22}O_{11}$ (sugar)
- 20 ml of pectin (Pectin comes in different forms. Please check the packaging of the form you purchase to make sure you are adding it at the correct time.)
- One container *Fragaria virginiana* (strawberries)
- Metal scoop
- Glass stir rod

130

- Beaker, 600 ml
- Paper towel
- Two cotton swabs
- Plastic bag
- Two petri dishes with agar
- Graduated cylinder
- Bunsen burner and ring stand with wire mesh
- Tongs
- Indirectly vented chemical-splash goggles

PROCEDURE

1. Read through the entire procedure before beginning.

2. Put on your safety goggles and gather all your materials at your lab station. If you notice any of the materials are dirty or discolored, notify your teacher.

3. Wash each of your *Fragaria virginiana* by running them under water and running your fingers over the outside of the skin to remove any excess sediment.

4. Remove the green calyx (leafy stem) from the *Fragaria virginiana* by placing them one by one on the paper towel and cutting off the stem using the plastic knife. Keep your fingers clear of the knife as you cut.

5. Use the metal scoop to remove the inner calyx of the *Fragaria virginiana*. You can do this by pushing the metal scoop into the center of the berry and twisting the scoop in a 360° motion. This will remove the inner white part of the berry, leaving a small hole. Repeat this for all *Fragaria virginiana* in your container.

6. Cut half of the *Fragaria virginiana* into small pieces using the plastic knife on a paper towel, again being careful to keep your fingers away from the sharp end of the knife. The pieces should be smaller than 0.5 cm. Place the cut pieces in a 600 ml beaker.

7. When half of the *Fragaria virginiana* have been cut into small pieces, use a plastic bottle to crush the pieces in the beaker into a small pulp. This should be a slow motion of applying pressure to the berries until your plastic bottle stops. Then lift and repeat. You want to liquefy the pieces of *Fragaria virginiana* to have as few whole pieces as possible.

8. Finish cutting the rest of the *Fragaria virginiana*. Place the remaining pieces in the 600 ml beaker and crush them using the plastic bottle as described in step 7.

9. Next take a marker and label one petri dish "Before Acid" and the other dish "After Acid." Write your group initials on the lower corner of the petri dishes.

10. Take a cotton swab and dip an end in the 600 ml beaker with the crushed *Fragaria virginiana*. Remove the cover from your petri dish labeled "Before Acid." Gently draw a zigzag line across the plate with the cotton swab as is shown in Figure 7.1.

Figure 7.1: Petri dish with zigzag line.

11. Use two pieces of masking tape to seal the dish shut, and place the dish in a clear plastic bag.

12. Measure 15 ml of citric acid using the graduated cylinder and add to the 600 ml beaker of mashed *Fragaria virginiana*. Slowly mix the acid with the glass stir rod.

13. Take a cotton swab and dip an end in the 600 ml beaker with the crushed *Fragaria virginiana* with acid. Remove the cover from your petri dish labeled "After Acid." Gently draw a zigzag line across the plate with the cotton swab as you did to the "Before Acid" dish.

14. Use two pieces of masking tape to seal the dish shut and place it in a clear plastic bag with the other petri dish. Seal the plastic bag. You will *not* be opening the bag again to prevent the spread of bacteria but will be able to view bacteria growth over the next several days. Place the bag in the plastic container labeled "Bacteria Bin."

15. Measure 20 ml of pectin using the graduated cylinder and slowly mix the pectin into your 600 ml beaker of *Fragaria virginiana* and acid using the glass stir rod.

16. Set up a Bunsen burner and ring stand with wire mesh on the iron ring. Make sure your Bunsen burner gas intake tube is securely connected to the gas

nozzle and that the ring is set about 3 in. above the barrel of the burner (see Figure 7.2). Light the Bunsen burner to create a flame that is no more than 3 in. high. (It should not be touching the wire mesh.)

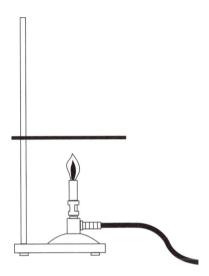

Figure 7.2: Bunsen burner and ring stand.

17. Use tongs to move your 600 ml beaker to the ring stand.

18. Heat the mixture to a full rolling boil while constantly stirring the contents with a glass stir rod. (A rolling boil is when the water doesn't stop bubbling if you stir it.)

19. Once the fruit mixture reaches a boil, remove the beaker using the tongs and mix 350 ml of sucrose into the fruit mixture so that all the sucrose dissolves. Keep in mind the beaker and the contents are hot, so use tongs to handle the beaker.

20. Once the sugar is dissolved, place it back on the ring stand to heat over the Bunsen burner. Wait for mixture to reach a full rolling boil again, and then boil for one minute, stirring constantly with the glass stir rod.

21. Remove the beaker from the ring stand and allow it to cool for two minutes.

22. Take the contents of your beaker and pour it into a paper cup labeled with your name.

23. Clean your lab table and answer the Data Analysis and Conclusions and Connections questions. You may pick up your completed product at the end of the day to take home.

DATA AND OBSERVATIONS

Procedure for Observations

1. After allowing your bacteria to incubate (grow and multiply) for 24–48 hours, observe the bacteria growth. Do *not* open the plastic bags.

2. Place your plastic bag with the bacteria cultures over a piece of graph paper. Tape the plastic bag to the graph paper and lay the paper flat on the table. You do not want to move the petri dishes around in the bag, as this will make observations difficult to track.

3. Below, draw a picture of the bacteria growth for each petri dish. Use the grid on the graph paper to match your petri dish with your observation sheet. For each square on the graph paper, if there are bacteria growing on your culture, color in the square on your observation page. Go row by row to record the presence and location of all bacteria in the petri dish.

Before Acid Petri Dish Observation

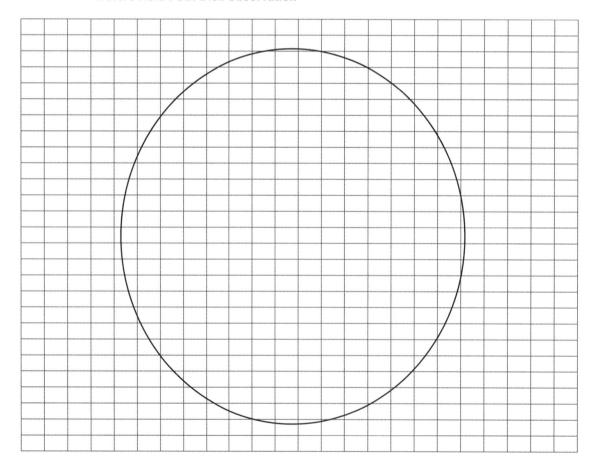

After Acid Petri Dish Observation

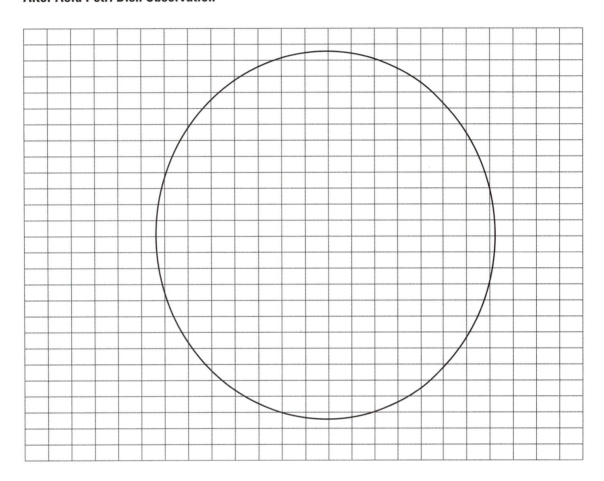

DATA ANALYSIS

For each of the following questions, be sure to explain using detail and complete sentences. If the question requires you to complete calculations, show all of your work.

1. How many squares have bacteria growing in the Before Acid petri dish?

2. How many squares have bacteria growing in the After Acid petri dish?

3. If there are approximately 125 squares in the petri dish, what is the percentage of bacteria in each dish?

Before Acid	After Acid

4. What is the change in percentage in the amount of bacteria from the Before Acid dish to the After Acid dish?

CONCLUSION AND CONNECTIONS

1. The acid changes the chemical structure of the sugars and pectin in the fruit. Do you think it is the changes in the chemical structure or the elimination of bacteria that best helps the fruit last longer? Explain using data to support your answer.

2. Explain a procedure for testing your answer to Conclusion and Connections question 1.

3. What other process during the creation of your jam could contribute to eliminating bacteria?

4. Why do some people place fruit in a freezer bag in the refrigerator?

EXPERIMENT 7:
Berries and Bacteria: Teacher Pages

MEASURING HOW ACIDS AND HEAT IMPACT BACTERIA IN JAM

This experiment uses the creation of strawberry jam to teach students about the implications of acid on bacteria as part of the sterilization and preservation of fruit. The lab initiates a discussion about how acids can be used to change the chemical composition of a substance to prevent bacteria growth. It also presents students with an opportunity to learn about culturing bacteria and making a quantitative analysis of bacteria growth using graph paper and percentages. The lab brings chemistry and biology together in a way that is informative and fulfilling.

STANDARDS ADDRESSED
National Science Education Standards: Grades 5–8

Content Standard A: Science as Inquiry
- Abilities necessary to do scientific inquiry
- Understanding about scientific inquiry

Content Standard B: Physical Science
- Transfer of energy

Content Standard C: Life Science
- Structure and function in living systems

Content Standard F: Science in Personal and Social Perspectives
- Risks and benefits
- Science and technology in society

Content Standard G: History and Nature of Science
- Science as a human endeavor
- Nature of science

National Science Education Standards: Grades 9–12

Content Standard A: Science as Inquiry
- Abilities necessary to do scientific inquiry
- Understanding about scientific inquiry

Content Standard B: Physical Science
- Chemical reactions
- Conservation of energy and increase in disorder

Content Standard C: Life Science
- The cell
- Interdependence of organisms
- Matter, energy, and organization in living systems

Content Standard E: Science and Technology
- Abilities of technological design
- Understanding about science and technology

Content Standard F: Science in Personal and Social Perspectives
- Science and technology in local, national, and global challenges

Content Standard G: History and Nature of Science
- Science as a human endeavor
- Nature of scientific knowledge
- Historical perspectives

VOCABULARY

Acid: Any chemical compound that will raise the amount of hydrogen ions (H^+) above the amount of hydrogen ions found in water.

Pectin: A long chain of pectic acid and pectinic acid molecules. Because these acids are sugars, pectin is a *polysaccharide*. In a plant, pectin is the material that joins the plant cells together. When fungus enzymes break down the pectin in fruit, the fruit gets soft and mushy.

Bacteria: Single-celled or noncellular spherical or spiral or rod-shaped organisms that reproduce by fission; important as pathogens and for biochemical properties and are found in virtually every environment on Earth (Princeton University 2006).

Sterilization: The procedure of making some object free of live bacteria or other microorganisms, usually by heat or chemical means (Princeton University 2006).

MATERIALS NEEDED, DECODED FOR THE GROCERY STORE

Plastic knife
- I recommend having enough knives for each student in the group to have one. This helps speed up the cutting of strawberries and keeps all students involved. The knives can be cleaned and used for the next class, so buy as many as you'll need for your largest single class, plus a few extras in case there is breakage. Plastic knives are sold individually in boxes of 30–50.

Plastic bottle
- I use the dropper bottles in which we place distilled water for other lab experiments. Any flat plastic surface will do; you can even use plastic forks, although the crushing will take a little longer. Each lab group will need one device for crushing the strawberries, so 10–15 will do for a class.

15 ml of citric acid (lemon juice)
- There are two ways to get lemon juice from the grocery store. You can buy lemons and juice them (each has about 30 ml of juice), or you can buy the prepackaged lemon juice in the produce section. I like the prepackaged juice because it comes in squirt bottles so it is easier for students to measure, and saves time preparing lemons. The small bottles that look like a lemon contain about 200 ml or enough for about 20 lab groups.
- Lime juice is more acidic and will change the outcome of your experiment. Make sure your acid is consistent for the entire class.

350 ml of sucrose, $C_{12}H_{22}O_{11}$ (sugar)
- Sugar is sold in as small as 5 lb. bags and increases from there. This is quite a bit of sugar for each lab group, about 3.5 cups. A 5 lb. bag will give you enough sugar for about six lab groups.

20 ml of pectin
- Pectin can be purchased at your local grocery store. It is usually sold with the glass jars in the canning section or with the gelatin. There are many different varieties of pectin depending on what type of item you are canning. For this experiment, you want to be sure to purchase fruit pectin, often advertised on the box as good for making jams and jellies. A 6-ounce box containing two packages will contain enough pectin for eight lab groups.

One container *Fragaria virginiana* (strawberries)
- Purchase one container of strawberries for each lab group. Strawberries are typically harvested between February and March in the United States, and tend to be cheapest in the late spring and early summer. I wait to do this lab until the strawberries are inexpensive, so that I can purchase a large quantity without breaking the bank.
- You can also complete this experiment with frozen strawberries; however, their bacteria content will be very low because of the freezing process.

Metal scoop
- Each student group needs a metal scoop to hull the strawberries. These are the simple metal chemistry equipment scoops that can be purchased to measure chemical powders. The ends are triangular, but rounded, making them safe for students to use.

Paper towel
- Each student group will need one paper towel to cut strawberries. A single roll of paper towels will meet the needs of more than 100 students.

Two cotton swabs
- Each student group will need two cotton swabs to take bacteria samples. These can be purchased in containers of 1,000 in the cosmetics section of the grocery store next to cotton balls. One container is enough for more than 200 lab groups.

Plastic bag
- Each student group will also need a plastic bag to seal its petri dishes. I use half-gallon bags so the two petri dishes can sit next to each other flat on the

graph paper. Once these bags are used for the bacteria incubation they will need to be discarded.

Dish soap
- This is necessary for cleanup. I ask students to use an amount about the size of a quarter for each glass container, and I have one bottle available for every four lab groups to share.

SAFETY HIGHLIGHTS
- The Bunsen burners and ring stands present a potential for students to burn themselves if used incorrectly. Please make sure students have had Bunsen burner safety training before allowing them to participate in this lab. As a teacher, you also need to be prepared with burn treatment options, such as running the burned area under cold water, if a student gets hurt.
- Students will be working with citric acid. Goggles are a must for protecting students' eyes, with an eyewash station and acid shower nearby for any situations that arise. Aprons and gloves are also required. If students get the acid on their skin, they should be cautious and wash the area with soap and water immediately.
- If a glass stir rod breaks, you should dispose of the entire mixture in the beaker. Even if the break is minor, you may have shards of glass in the mixture that are not visible.

PREPARATION
1. You will need to make petri dishes with agar for the bacteria cultures before the lab. Each group will need two petri dishes. In an effort to conserve supplies, I often ask one group to grow the bacteria for all groups at the lab table. Those groups can then share the bacteria data. The directions for preparing the petri dishes are as follows:

   (a) You'll need a clean, microwave-safe container (a quart-size bowl works well) to mix and heat the agar with water. These mixing proportions make enough nutrient agar to prepare two halves of the petri dish. Mix 1/2 tsp. agar (about 1.2 g) with 1/4 cup (60 ml) of hot water and stir. Bring this mixture to a boil for one minute to completely dissolve the agar. The mixture should be clear, with no particles floating around in the solution. Allow the mixture to cool for three to five minutes before moving to the next step.

(b) Separate the top and bottom of the petri dish and carefully fill the bottom half with warm agar nutrient solution. Use the top half to loosely cover the bottom portion (set the lid ajar to allow moisture to escape) and allow the solution to cool and harden for at least an hour.

2. Label a plastic container "Bacteria Bin." This will give students one place to put their plastic bags with petri dishes. I make one for each class period. Make sure the bins fit in a cabinet in your room, or can be easily covered in a dark cloth to allow for bacteria growth at room temperature.

3. The students will need paper cups or jars to allow the jam to cool and take it home to share. If you use jars, these need to be sterilized before placing the jam in them. This involves boiling both the jars and tops. The cost of jars can be expensive, so I just place the jam in plastic cups and allow students to take them home at the end of the day, or share with their groups the following day. It is helpful to have trays set out with class periods labeled so the jam stays organized for pickup later in the day.

4. If you are going to follow the demonstration recommendation for introducing the lab, you will need to have a piece of ripe fruit and a piece of spoiled fruit. The easiest way to do this is to buy a package of strawberries and to allow one to sit out in a warm environment for several days, while keeping the other in the refrigerator.

PROCEDURE

I recommend having students work in teams of three or four for this experiment. The final product creates about 400 ml of jam, which is plenty to share among a large group. There is also quite a significant amount of labor involved with the preparation of the strawberries, which can be shared equally by a large group. The large group size also cuts down on the total number of lab groups per class and overall cost of supplies.

1. Begin by showing students two pieces of fruit, one that is ripe, and another that has spoiled. Ask the students to share observational differences between the two pieces of fruit. Record these on the board in the following chart:

Observations of Ripe Fruit	Observations of Spoiled Fruit

2. You can use this chart to introduce the Background section of the lab. Have students read the background information about the process of making jam and make a hypothesis about how the acid will affect the overall level of bacteria that will grow in the petri dishes.

3. When creating their hypotheses, encourage students to think about where else bacteria are found, and what things are done to prevent their growth and transfer. Most students are familiar with hand sanitizer, and it can be helpful to have a bottle nearby so students can check the ingredients to see if there are any acids present. These sanitizers rely on large percentages of alcohol, which encourages a discussion about how different factors affect the environment of the bacteria and therefore, their growth potential.

4. As students begin to clean the strawberries, make sure they are putting the rinsed strawberries into a clean container. Encourage them to think about why it is necessary to rinse the strawberries. Ask, "Does that get rid of bacteria throughout the entire fruit? Why or why not?"

5. While preparing the strawberries, it is helpful for the students to have two containers. This way they can move the berries from one container to the other as they rinse them, then again as they cut off stems, and finally as they hull them. You can save one class set of strawberry containers to use in future classes, or you can use Tupperware containers. It is also important to remind students to wash out these containers after the initial step so they are not placing the berries back in a dirty container as they switch back and forth.

6. Students use plastic bottles to crush and liquefy the strawberries. Do not use another glass beaker to accomplish this task. It will lead to broken glass and ruined berries if the students are too aggressive with the task. Set out the mortar and pestle and ask students how the crushing process compares with this science tool. Ask students why a scientist would need a mortar and pestle in a lab. The answer is to increase the surface area to allow more compound or chemical to react when exposed to another chemical or energy source.

7. Next, students take bacteria cultures of the crushed berries. Make sure the petri dishes are clearly labeled with Before Acid and After Acid, sealed with masking tape, and then placed into the same plastic bag.

8. Students can use Bunsen burners or hot plates to achieve the heating step with the fruit mixture. If you have younger students, I recommend hot plates on medium high heat. The older students may use the Bunsen burners, but depending on the size of your group, hot plates may be the safer choice.

9. The fruit mixture becomes thick when the sugar and pectin are added. Encourage students to work together with one student holding the beaker steady with tongs, and the other student stirring the mixture together. They will need to then reheat the mixture to a rolling boil while stirring. If students quit stirring or do not stir all the way to the bottom of the beaker, the jam will burn, making it nearly impossible to get the charred sugar off of the beaker during cleanup.

10. When the jam is done, place the finished product in paper cups (you should be able to fill about 8–10 cups easily) or baby food jars that have been sterilized. Make sure the cups or jars are labeled with student names or initials to prevent confusion. To help with the cooling and gelling process, you can place the jam in a cool environment (such as a refrigerator) to help speed up the process. I encourage students to leave their jam and stop by at the end of the day to pick it up so they can take it home to share it.

11. Take all the petri dishes in plastic bags and place them in a warm dark area to allow the growth and reproduction of bacteria. It's best if you allow the bacteria to grow for at least 48 hours. If you create the jam on a Friday, then students can complete their data observations on Monday when they return to school. Depending on the initial condition of your strawberries, your bacteria growth may occur faster than that.

12. Do *not* allow the students to open the plastic bags with the bacteria cultures. It is possible that they are growing a pathogen, which is why the bags are to remain sealed for the bacteria observation and data analysis. This expectation must be clearly articulated along with the potential hazards (e.g., severe illness) that could occur if this is not followed. This is also why students tape the petri dishes closed, so if the plastic bags are accidentally opened, students can wash and disinfect their hands without exposure to the bacteria plates. It can also be a good idea to tape the bags sealed with a colored duct tape as a precaution.

13. While they are taking data, many students ask about how to count the squares around the edges because they are not complete because of the cir-

cular shape of the petri dish. Use the rule that 50% and over means to count the square as having bacteria present. This rule also works well when deciding whether to document a square or not. If it is over 50%, then count the square on your observations.

14. When the students are done making observations, the petri dishes need to be disposed of. Before disposing of dishes in the trash, the bacteria should be destroyed. Pour a small amount of household bleach over the colonies while holding the dish over the sink. *Caution:* Do not allow bleach to touch your skin, eyes, or clothes. This is a step for you to complete, not the students.

DATA ANALYSIS ANSWER KEY

All the data analysis for this lab is math based. If students are struggling with the questions, I recommend using a sample data set and going through the calculations as a class on the board. Then students can use the same skills and apply them directly to their data.

1. How many squares have bacteria growing in the Before Acid petri dish?

This answer is completely dependent on the particular variables of the experiment: the initial condition of the strawberries, the bacteria growth time, the environment for growth, and so on. Because we are completing a comparison between the petri dishes, this initial number does not need to be exact, but it should be higher than the number of colonies counted in the After Acid petri dish.

2. How many squares have bacteria growing in the After Acid petri dish?

Again, this answer depends on the particular circumstances within the lab. See if this number is less than the number of bacteria squares counted for the Before Acid petri dish.

3. If there are approximately 125 squares in the petri dish, what is the percentage of bacteria in each dish?

Again, the exact data will depend on your initial conditions, but the calculation process should be the same. Students need to take the number of squares with bacteria for each plate and divide that by the total number of squares. They will then take this decimal and multiply it by 100%. Sample student data may look as follows:

Before Acid	After Acid
56 squares ÷ 125 squares = 0.448 0.448 × 100% = 44.8%	30 squares ÷ 125 squares = 0.24 0.24 × 100% = 24%

4. *What is the change in percentage in the amount of bacteria from the Before Acid dish to the After Acid dish?*

The answer will depend on the initial conditions and on the data of each individual student, but the process should be the same. Students should subtract the percentage of bacteria in the After Acid plate from the Before Acid plate to get a difference. Sample student data might look like this:

44.8% – 24% = 20.8% difference in bacteria growth after adding the acid

CONCLUSION AND CONNECTIONS ANSWER KEY

This section of the lab offers a great opportunity to engage the entire class in discussion to clarify the main ideas of the lab and allow the students an opportunity to make their own connections between science and cooking. I ask that students answer the Data Analysis questions and attempt to answer the Conclusion and Connections questions, with the understanding that we will spend time the next day discussing the Conclusions and Connections section.

1. *The acid changes the chemical structure of the sugars and pectin in the fruit. Do you think it is the changes in the chemical structure or the elimination of bacteria that best helps the fruit last longer? Explain using data to support your answer.*

This question asks students to think about how the acid is actually contributing to the preservation process. Answers depend on students' results from the experiment. If one student group found that the bacteria growth was nearly the same for both petri dishes, then they will answer that acid changes the chemical structure of the fruit. If there was a large difference in bacteria growth on the two plates, students will support the idea that the acid actually eliminates the bacteria from the plate. It actually does both, so either answer can be viewed as correct. Students should cite results from their data analysis to support their answer.

2. *Explain a procedure for testing your answer to Conclusions and Connections question 1.*

This question asks students to create a procedure to test whether the acid kills the bacteria or just changes fruit structure. There are many ways to approach this experiment, but an example would be growing bacteria cultures from the strawberries and then adding the acid to see if it stopped their growth and reduced their numbers. Look for students to propose an experiment that would allow them to find a direct relationship between the amount of acid and their chosen element from question 1.

3. *What other process during the creation of your jam could contribute to eliminating bacteria?*

This is a good question for group discussion. Ask students what other process may have made life more difficult for the bacteria. Encourage them to think from the perspective of the bacteria. Ask, "Would your life be more difficult if someone gave you lots of sugar?" (*Answer:* No, and the bacteria like sugar, too; it is a food source that is easy to digest.) "Would life be more difficult if you had to live in boiling hot temperatures?" (*Answer:* Yes, and the bacteria would agree again. The hot temperatures kill many of the strains of bacteria that lead to the spoilage of fruit, which is why the heating is an important process in creating jam that stays edible for a longer period of time.)

4. *Why do some people place fruit in a freezer bag in the refrigerator?*

This question asks students to analyze how environments affect the ability of bacteria to grow and reproduce. In the jam, extreme heat was used to prevent bacteria growth. But you can do the exact opposite and store the fruit in cold temperatures to prevent bacteria growth. Bacteria have a temperature preference for their ideal environment that allows them to reproduce quickly and successfully. So placing the fruit in a freezer bag prevents bacteria from accessing the fruit, and the cold temperatures keep the bacteria from growing.

CROSS-CURRICULAR NOTE: MATH

This is an ideal opportunity to see percentages used in a science context. Have students explore why percentages are helpful for comparing this type of data with other groups as opposed to just comparing numbers of squares.

CROSS-CURRICULAR NOTE: LITERACY

This experiment raises the question of how many hands actually touch your food before it arrives at your dinner table. Students can research the transportation of fresh fruit, counting how many people come into contact with the fruit before it's eaten. This connection also brings up the topic of migrant labor, which can be an area of discussion and connection for older students.

OPTIONAL EXTENSIONS

Middle School

1. Encourage students to take samples of the jam throughout the process, including before heating and after heating, to see where the majority of bacteria is eliminated.

2. To make this lab more inquiry based, ask students to come up with ways to measure the amount of bacteria that has grown in each petri dish. The only rule they must follow is that they cannot unseal the tape from the petri dishes. This allows students to come up with a way to quantify the data for analysis.

3. Encourage students to look at how different edible acids affect the creation of jam using other acids such as orange juice, tomato juice, or vinegar. Ask, "What are the properties of the final jam? Does it stay preserved for the same amount of time? Why or why not?"

High School

1. Students can test which fruits have higher initial bacteria content in the grocery store by growing cultures from several fruits such as apples, strawberries, blueberries, and bananas. Analysis can include looking at the porous nature of each fruit, the indigenous location and transport time to the grocery store, and the percentage of sugar content to explain the differences in bacteria growth.

2. Students can test how quickly bacteria grow on fruit that is sitting out at room temperature by taking cultures on a piece of fruit once a day for five days. Then they can compare the amount of bacteria growth to see if the growth is linear or exponential by graphing the results.

EXPERIMENT 8:
American Mozzarella: Student Pages

CALCULATING RATES OF CHANGE FOR RENNET IN CHEESE MAKING

BACKGROUND

Legend has it that mozzarella was first made when cheese curds accidentally fell into a pail of hot water in a cheese factory near Naples, Italy...and presto—a new cheese was made, and pizza shops starting popping up all over. Well, maybe the pizza parlors are a stretch, but new cheeses are often formulated when mistakes happen, so there may be some truth in this tale. Aside from pizza, mozzarella is used in salads, pastas, sandwiches, and string cheese. With so many uses, who wouldn't want to know more about making mozzarella?

There are two common ways to make mozzarella: an acid method and a culture method. In both methods, raw milk is pasteurized and then coagulated to form curds. Pasteurization is the process of heating a beverage or other food to a specific temperature for a specific period of time in order to kill microorganisms that could cause disease, spoilage, or undesired fermentation. In the acid method, the milk proteins (casein) change structure based on the introduction of the hydrogen ion (H^+). The hydrogen ion is attractive, which breaks down the milk proteins so they can reform in a different molecular configuration to form curds. In the culture method, bacteria are used to accomplish this same breakdown of the casein. The breakdown leads to the same reformation of curd. What is the major difference between the two? *Time.* The culture method tends to take longer to form the curds because the bacteria need a longer amount of time to break down the proteins.

Once the curds reach a pH of 5.2, they are cut into small pieces and mixed with hot water and then "strung" or "spun" until long ropes of cheese form. When the proper smooth, elastic consistency is reached, the curds are formed by machine or hand into balls, which are then tossed into cold water so that they maintain their shape while they cool. They are then salted and packaged. This is a short process, usually less than eight hours from raw milk to finished cheese. The critical moment is determining exactly when the cheese is mature and ready to be strung; waiting too long can result in a mushy cheese, while stringing too early can result in a tough, dry cheese. In this experiment, you will be measuring the pH change over time that occurs during the cheese-making process along with measuring mass to calculate the reaction rate of the bacterial breakdown of casein. How fast are your bacteria at changing the reactants to the product? But more important, how long until we are able to have the final lab result: *pizza*?

HYPOTHESIS

How fast are your bacteria? Are they faster than you? For this lab we will be measuring the reaction rate of the rennet bacteria to change the acidity and composition of the milk proteins to create cheese.

Nutritionists have suggested that the adolescent human body takes about 20 minutes for casein molecules to be detected in the blood stream after drinking a glass of milk (6 g of casein in an 8 oz. glass). Will the bacteria be able to break down the casein faster or slower than your body? Make a hypothesis about whether you think the rennet bacteria will be faster or slower in creating than curds when compared to your body's digestion of casein protein. Think about your body's process of digestion and size compared to the bacteria, and explain why you think your answer is correct.

MATERIALS NEEDED PER GROUP

- 500 ml of emulsified colloid of reduced liquid butterfat in H_2O (2% milk)
- 1 g of citric acid (true lemon flavoring)
- One-fourth rennet tablet
- 2 g of sodium chloride, NaCl (table salt)
- Bunsen burner
- Ring stand
- Thermometer, 150°C and nonmercury
- Balance
- Beaker, 100 ml
- Beaker, 600 ml
- Beaker, 1,000 ml
- Glass stir rod
- Tongs
- Plastic knife
- Cheesecloth or gauze cloth
- Rubber band
- Plastic wrap
- pH paper
- Clock or stopwatches
- Indirectly vented chemical-splash goggles
- Aprons
- Gloves

PROCEDURE

1. Read through the entire procedure before beginning.

2. Put on your safety goggles, apron, and gloves, and gather all your materials at your lab station. If you notice any of the materials are dirty or discolored, notify your teacher.

3. Place 500 ml of emulsified colloid of reduced liquid butterfat in H_2O in a 1,000 ml beaker.

4. In a 100 ml beaker, dissolve 1 g of citric acid in 10 ml of water.

5. Add the citric acid solution to the emulsified colloid of reduced liquid butterfat in H_2O and stir with the glass stir rod.

6. Dissolve one-fourth of a rennet bacteria tablet in 60 ml of H_2O. Place this to the side; do not add at this time. You are sharing this solution with another group, so only one group needs to make the solution.

7. Set up a Bunsen burner and ring stand with wire mesh on the iron ring. Make sure your Bunsen burner gas intake tube is securely connected to the gas nozzle and that the ring is set about 3 in. above the barrel of the burner (see Figure 8.1). Light the Bunsen burner to create a flame that is no more than 3 in. high. (It should not be touching the wire mesh.)

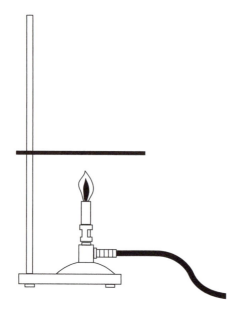

Figure 8.1: Bunsen burner and ring stand.

8. Use tongs to move your 1,000 ml beaker to the ring stand.

9. Heat the solution in the 1,000 ml beaker to 31°C on your ring stand while constantly stirring. Use your thermometer to measure the temperature of the solution, not to stir. This can cause your thermometer to break, which would ruin your final product.

10. Using tongs, remove the beaker from the heat and add 30 ml of the rennet solution, and then stir for 30 seconds. Taking too much of the rennet solution will affect the other group, so be accurate with your measurement.

11. Take a strip of pH paper to measure the pH of the solution. Do *not* disturb the solution; just place the pH paper on the surface of the liquid. Record your data in the pH measurement data table.

12. Allow the solution to remain still for 60–90 minutes while it coagulates. The only step you will be taking is measuring the pH of the solution every 10 minutes by repeating the directions in step 11.

13. After coagulation, use a knife to cut the curd into 1 cm cubes. Allow the curds to remain undisturbed for three minutes while some of the whey drains out.

14. Slowly heat the mixture to 42°C using the ring stand and Bunsen burner, and stir the mixture occasionally. Then remove the mixture from the heat using tongs and stir for 30 minutes. Trade off stirring duties with your partner, and clean your area while you are not stirring.

15. Place a double layer of cheesecloth or gauze cloth over the top of a 600 ml beaker. Push the cloth into the beaker about one-fourth of the way and then secure the cloth in place by placing a rubber band around the edges of the cloth.

16. After 30 minutes, slowly pour the mixture into the cloth to separate the curds from the whey. Allow the curds to drip-dry for 15 minutes.

17. While waiting for the curds to drip, measure 2 g of sodium chloride. Add the sodium chloride to 1,000 ml beaker containing 600 ml of water. You can use the same 1,000 ml beaker you used to make your cheese.

18. Heat the water to 70°C on the ring stand using the Bunsen burner.

19. After 15 minutes, pick up the cloth by the corners and slowly squeeze out any remaining liquid over the sink. Use the rubber band to secure the top of the cloth so the curds form a ball wrapped in gauze cloth.

20. Dispose of the liquid that dripped from the curds, and then rinse and dry the 600 ml beaker.

21. Place the curd ball in cloth back into the clean 600 ml beaker.

22. Take the warm water with sodium chloride and pour 300 ml (half) into the 600 ml beaker with the curd ball. Keep the remaining sodium chloride solution warm.

23. Allow the curd ball to soften for 60 seconds.

24. Using tongs, pour off the water and then open the cloth. Throw away the gauze. Form the curds into a ball of cheese.

25. Stretch the cheese, like taffy. Pull and twist it, and then fold it in half and pull and twist it again. Continue this for five minutes. If the cheese gets too hard to stretch, dip it into the remaining hot saltwater mixture for 30 seconds to soften it.

26. At the end of five minutes, kneed the cheese like bread until firm, and then roll it into a small ball.

27. Using a balance, measure the mass of the cheese you created. Record that measurement in the Data and Observations section.

28. Wrap the cheese in plastic wrap and label it with your group name. Place your wrapped cheese on the tray.

29. Clean your lab area and answer the Data Analysis and Conclusions and Connections questions.

PIZZA-MAKING PROCEDURE

1. Once the cheese has cooled, you can tear it apart to be eaten as string cheese or to be used on a pizza. Pizzas can be made easily using half a bagel, spaghetti sauce, and toppings of your choice like pepperoni.

2. Read through the entire procedure before beginning.

3. Put on your safety goggles, apron, and gloves, and gather all your materials at your lab station. If you notice any of the materials are dirty or discolored, notify your teacher.

4. Spread spaghetti sauce on the bagel half and lightly cover the sauce with your mozzarella and toppings.

5. Place in a toaster oven and bake at 350°F for 10–12 minutes or until the cheese is melted. Allow to cool and then enjoy.

6. Clean your lab area.

DATA AND OBSERVATIONS

pH Data Table	
Time (minutes)	pH of rennet bacteria solution
0 min	
10 min	
20 min	
30 min	
40 min	
50 min	
60 min	
70 min	
80 min	
90 min	

Mass of Cheese Created: _____ g

DATA ANALYSIS

For each of the following questions, be sure to explain using detail and complete sentences. If the question requires you to complete calculations, show all of your work.

1. If coagulation of the curd is complete at a pH of 5.2, how long did the cheese take to complete the coagulation?

2. Assuming you didn't lose any curd along the way, what was the average amount of curd made by the rennet bacteria each minute?

3. How much did the pH change during the coagulation of the casein?

4. What was the average rate of pH acidity change per minute caused by the rennet bacteria?

CONCLUSION AND CONNECTIONS

1. Was your initial hypothesis correct? Explain why or why not citing specific data.

2. What is the rate at which the human body break down casein? Is rennet faster or slower? Explain your reasoning.

3. What is the most beneficial part of working in a team to create mozzarella?

4. What do you think would happen if you used the entire tablet (rather than one-fourth) of rennet bacteria to make your cheese?

EXPERIMENT 8:
American Mozzarella: Teacher Pages

CALCULATING RATES OF CHANGE FOR RENNET IN CHEESE MAKING

This experiment will challenge you as much as your students. Whether you are a laboratory scientist or experienced chef, making mozzarella truly pushes your skills of measurement, precision, and most of all, patience. This lab is designed to be a three- to four-hour process that can be completed in a single extended class, or in a series of classes in which a section of the procedure is completed to achieve one final product. The students gain experience in measuring pH and acidity, bacteria processes, and calculating reaction rates. They also gain experience in the collaborative nature of science, and learn how working with others can lead to accomplishments that would have been difficult to achieve alone. The time and effort is well worth the learning achieved in this experience, as well as the final product: pizza.

STANDARDS ADDRESSED
National Science Education Standards: Grades 5–8

Content Standard A: Science as Inquiry
- Abilities necessary to do scientific inquiry
- Understanding about scientific inquiry

Content Standard B: Physical Science
- Properties and changes of properties in matter
- Transfer of energy

Content Standard C: Life Science
- Structure and function in living systems

Content Standard F: Science in Personal and Social Perspectives
- Science and technology in society

Content Standard G: History and Nature of Science
- Science as a human endeavor
- Nature of science
- History of science

National Science Education Standards: Grades 9–12

Content Standard A: Science as Inquiry
- Abilities necessary to do scientific inquiry
- Understanding about scientific inquiry

Content Standard B: Physical Science
- Structure of atoms
- Structure and properties of matter
- Chemical reactions
- Conservation of energy and increase in disorder

Content Standard C: Life Science
- The cell

Content Standard E: Science and Technology
- Abilities of technological design
- Understanding about science and technology

Content Standard F: Science in Personal and Social Perspectives
- Science and technology in local, national, and global challenges

Content Standard G: History and Nature of Science
- Science as a human endeavor
- Nature of scientific knowledge
- Historical perspectives

VOCABULARY

Acid: Any chemical compound that will raise the amount of hydrogen ions (H^+) above the amount of hydrogen ions found in water.

Bacteria: Single-celled or noncellular spherical or spiral or rod-shaped organisms that reproduce by fission; important as pathogens and for biochemical properties and are found in virtually every environment on Earth. (Princeton University 2006)

Reaction rate: The speed at which a reaction takes place. This also can be defined as the time it takes reactants to change to products in a chemical equation.

Reactant: A substance that is present at the start of a chemical reaction.

Product: A substance that is present at the end of the chemical reaction.

MATERIALS NEEDED, DECODED FOR THE GROCERY STORE

500 ml of emulsified colloid of reduced liquid butterfat in H_2O (2% milk)

- You definitely will need a basket for this shopping trip. Each lab group will need 500 ml of 2% milk. A gallon of milk will be enough for about seven groups. Keep in mind that if you are doing this lab as a daylong process for several class sections, you will need only enough milk for the number of lab setups you plan on running for *one class*. For example, if I have 14 lab groups in a class, but will be doing this activity as a daylong process with three classes, I only need enough milk for 14 groups because groups will be working on the same mozzarella production throughout the day and will not need new milk.

- Do *not* purchase milk that has been ultra-pasteurized. The protein is denatured at the high temperature in this type of milk and the whey proteins bind on the casein and block the rennet. This damage to the milk is irreversible and will cause you to end up with no curds. Look for another brand of milk and make sure it has not been ultra-pasteurized. Local brands are less likely to have been through this process. If no milk options are available that have not already been ultra-pasteurized, then you can make your own milk using dry milk powder and cream.

1 g of citric acid (true lemon flavoring)

- Citric acid can be purchased from a pharmacy or grocery store under the name *true lemon*. This is kept with the sugar substitutes in most grocery stores. The true lemon is a replacement for lemon flavoring and is sold in packets or bottles. A bottle will contain enough citric acid for more than 25 groups.

One-fourth rennet tablet
- This is probably the most difficult ingredient to locate. Most store employees don't know what rennet is and will suggest you go to a cheese-making store. That is not necessary. Rennet bacteria tablets are sold under the product name of Junket. Junket is sold in tablet form in boxes that are usually kept with the gelatin or pudding. The tablets go far, so you need only one-fourth of a tablet for every two groups. Each box contains eight tablets, so one box will be enough for 32 groups.

2 g of sodium chloride, NaCl (table salt)
- Each group uses salt to flavor its cheese, so a single saltshaker will be more than enough for 20 lab groups.

Plastic knife
- I recommend having one knife for each group. Plastic knives are sold individually in boxes of 30–50.

Cheesecloth or gauze cloth
- Cheesecloth can usually be found in a fancy gourmet shop. I have never found this at the grocery stores I frequent, so I buy gauze cloth from the first-aid section of the store in bulk. Gauze is not inexpensive, so another option is to buy heavy-duty paper towels. Using paper towels will require students to double layer the beaker and squeeze out a little more liquid, but this a more cost-effective approach to the lab. Make sure you buy strong paper towels, though, because the cheaper ones will split open and cause students to lose their cheese curd and have incorrect results.

Rubber band
- Each group needs one rubber band to secure its cloth to the beaker for dripping the whey from the curd.

Plastic wrap
- The plastic wrap is used to wrap the final cheese product before cooling. A single roll will be enough for more than 30 lab groups.

Clock or stopwatches
- Normally, I have students use the classroom clock to time their reactions. But because the cheese can be so time dependent, I often use timers that alert the students that they need to move on to the next step. This alleviates a lot of the problems that can arise when the lab setups are transferred from class to class. Using timers allows the new student groups to know exactly when to begin the next step instead of relying on the previous students to record the information accurately before leaving the lab. Egg timers also work well if you don't have stopwatches.

Dish soap
- This is necessary for cleanup. I ask students to use an amount about the size of a quarter for each glass container, and I have one bottle available for every four lab groups to share.

SAFETY HIGHLIGHTS

- The Bunsen burners and ring stands present a potential for students to burn themselves if used incorrectly. Please make sure students have had Bunsen burner safety training before allowing them to participate in this lab. As a teacher, you also need to be prepared with burn treatment options, such as running the burned area under cold water, if a student gets hurt.
- Students will be working with citric acid. Goggles are a must for protecting students' eyes, with an eyewash station and acid shower nearby for any situations that arise. Aprons and gloves are also required. If students get the acid on their skin, they should be cautious and wash the area with soap and water immediately.
- If a glass stir rod breaks, you should dispose of the entire mixture in the beaker. Even if the break is minor, you may have shards of glass in the mixture that are not visible.

Note that these safety highlights are in addition to the safety information detailed in the Safety Protocol section at the beginning of this book. Please refer to that section for additional information about safety when implementing this or any lab in this book.

PREPARATION

1. Refrigerate the milk until it's ready for use.

2. I recommend having a separate labeled trash can for trash for this lab. From the gauze cloth to the milk, this can lead to a smelly lab if all the trash is not thrown away in a timely manner. I make a "TRASH HERE" sign and take all the other trash cans out of the classroom so that I can dispose of the trash at the end of the school day.

PROCEDURE

I recommend having students work in teams of two for this experiment. The final product is going to be shared by all the lab groups that contribute to the final product, which could be groups from up to four classes depending on your approach to the lab.

The time breakdown for this lab is as follows:

- Initial setup of milk, acid, and rennet: 30 minutes
- Coagulation and pH measurements: 60–90 minutes
- Stirring and heating curd: 30 minutes
- Straining of curd: 15 minutes
- Twisting of curd: 10 minutes
- Total time: 150 minutes to 180 minutes (2.5 to 3 hours)

You need to look at your classes in terms of time and position within the day. I have four science sections that are 45 minutes each, and I break down the experiment in the following way:

Class 1: Setup and start of coagulation and pH measurements
Class 2: Coagulation and pH measurements
Class 3: 30-minute stir and beginning of the straining process
Class 4: Straining is finished, curd is twisted, and cheese is wrapped

If you have longer block classes, you can do the process in two 90-minute periods. It takes some creative problem solving depending on your schedule. If a lunch period occurs, you can ask for volunteers to take pH measurements during that time, or you can take them yourself and share them with the students as a class data set. I have also asked other teachers to accommodate a special schedule on the day we make mozzarella (with the promised reward of pizza) to allow this lab to take place. I have found the reward for the students completing this lab in terms of learning and enjoyment is well worth the effort.

Again, because there can be quite a bit of waiting, especially during the coagulation and straining, I often have students complete a reading on pH and acidity from their textbook to accompany this lab. Students who are there for the slower moments of the lab can complete the reading, with other classes completing the activity for homework. Other options include implementing the extension activities, such as culturing the rennet bacteria or measuring the effect the amount of acid on the flavor of the cheese. Finally, you also can have the students measure the pH and acidity of other food items to enhance their knowledge.

1. Begin by placing the students in their lab groups, and asking them to read the Background section. If students have completed Experiment 6: Acidic Milk, then they are familiar with the protein breakdown associated with casein. If they have not, then it will be helpful to use the demonstration about casein that is outlined below from the Acidic Milk lab.

    A short demonstration that helps students to understand the breakdown of the casein micelles can be conducted by having a group of 5–10 students come to the front of the classroom and huddle together. Each student represents a casein protein, and the group is a micelle. (You can ask the students to identify themselves, or give each student a sign to hold.) I often compare the huddled group to a school dance, showing how difficult it is for a teacher to get in between people, as there is no empty space available. Then ask the class, "So what happens if I add heat to this protein molecule? What would happen if all of you got hot and sweaty at the dance?" The students are often quick to move away from one another, demonstrating the breakdown of the micelle. This occurs with the heat and acid. As the micelle breaks down, I give each student a balloon to hold in front of him or her. The balloons are labeled "fat." Then the students are "cooled" so they can group back together, incorporating the fat molecules. Ask the students to explain what happened to the micelle. It should have gotten bigger, now forming a curd, which is used to make cheese.

2. This brings up the discussion of reaction rate. Ask students, "How do you measure the speed of an object? (*Answer*: By measuring the time and distance of the object.) How do you measure the speed of bacteria? Do they have a distance?" This allows you to introduce the terms *reaction rate*, *reactants*, and *product*. You can write these as definitions on the board or provide them as a handout for students to keep in their notes.

3. It is helpful to demonstrate these terms in action. Ask for two student volunteers who will accomplish the "reaction" of handing out goggles. I use the diagram below to facilitate the discussion:

Reactants	→	Products
1. The goggles 2. The students without goggles 3. The students handing out the goggles		1. The students with goggles

Ask the class, "What are the reactants in this reaction? What are the products in this process? How can I measure the rate of this reaction?" (*Answer*: By timing the students who are handing out goggles.) Go ahead and allow the students to hand out goggles while timing them. You can use this exercise as a precursor to the math in the Data Analysis section of the lab. Ask the class to consider how they would go about measuring the average number of goggles handed out by each student. Then ask students to consider how to solve for the number of goggles they could hand out in 10 seconds. You can then tie the discussion back to the creation of mozzarella. In the cheese-making process, what is the biological organism that is passing out the goggles? (*Answer*: The rennet bacteria.)

4. This will lead students to create a hypothesis. Encourage them to use background knowledge or experience to support their hypothesis and explain their reasoning.

5. As students begin the Procedure section, make sure that they are using only one-fourth of the rennet tablet for every two groups. I have only two groups at each lab area, but if you have more, it may be helpful to assign which two groups are sharing rennet before students begin the lab.

6. Students can use Bunsen burners or hot plates to achieve the heating step with the milk. If you have younger students, I recommend hot plates on medium heat. The older students may use the Bunsen burners, but depending of the size of your group, hot plates may be the safer choice.

7. Remind students to continually stir the milk during the heating process. If the heat is too high, the milk can burn, which ruins the cheese and makes it nearly impossible to clean the beaker. Many students will want to stir with the thermometer. This is not a good idea because they are designed as mea-

suring tools, not for the utility of stirring. It takes about 10–15 minutes to heat the milk to the desired temperature depending on the flame size and ring stand setup.

8. Students should *not* stir or agitate the milk solution once it reaches the coagulation stage. It needs to sit undisturbed. I ask the students to work at their desks during this time to prevent them from checking on the experiment.

9. As the students take pH measurements, monitor their results. The milk needs to achieve a pH of 5.2. Most store-bought milk begins with a pH of 6.7, with the citric acid bringing it down to around 6.2. Once the pH reaches 5.2, you can check the milk for curd formation. The curds form as a skin at the top of the beaker. If you dip in a glass rod, you should feel the skin break. This is called a "clean break," which means the curd is ready for the next step. If there is no skin, the milk will need to coagulate longer.

10. As the students reheat the mixture, the curd cubes will start to fall apart. This is expected and part of the process.

11. Have students use a double layer of the gauze or paper towels. In either case, allow the excess cloth to hang over the side of the beaker. This excess material is helpful for lifting the curds out to squeeze out any remaining liquid.

12. The straining can be a little difficult for the students because it is not a skill most are familiar with. I recommend demonstrating the straining with the first group that has a cool beaker and have all the students watch. While demonstrating the straining method, consider a few items to share with the entire class:

    (a) You do not want to spill any of the contents of your curds and whey. The data for this experiment are dependent on you creating the most cheese possible, and spilling outside the beaker will cause you to lose mass and impact the data. Only fill the cloth two-thirds full and wait for it to drain to less than one-fourth before adding more to the cloth.
    (b) As the curds accumulate, it can be difficult for the liquid to strain. You can help this process by pulling the cloth (or paper towel) slightly out of the beaker by 1 cm and squeezing it gently against the side of the beaker. If you squeeze too hard, it can cause your cheese to break through into the whey and will impact your results.
    (c) If there are curds that are stuck in the beaker, use a small amount of water to rinse them out. You want every last piece of curd for your mass measurement.

13. Have students place their cheese balls with labels on a single tray. This will allow you to refrigerate the cheese until you are ready to eat it.

14. Soap is necessary to clean all the equipment thoroughly after this lab.

15. At the end of this lab, I host a pizza party where the students can make their own pizzas using the mozzarella they created. I use toaster ovens, bagels, and marinara sauce. I encourage students to bring in any topping that they would like to include. I usually buy an extra bag or two of shredded mozzarella to allow all students to have ample cheese. Depending on the size of the lab groups and the number of classes participating, cheese will run out. This is a great way to allow students to share the product in a way that is fun, and the party celebrates the collaborative nature of this project.

DATA ANALYSIS ANSWER KEY

All the data analysis for this lab is math based. If students are struggling with the questions, I recommend using a sample data set and going through the calculations as a class on the board. Then students can use the same skills and apply them directly to their data.

1. *If coagulation of the curd is complete at a pH of 5.2, how long did the cheese take to complete the coagulation?*

   This is one of the answers that I wish was the same for every person who conducts this experiment. I have had the coagulation take anywhere from one hour to one and a half hours using the exact same procedure and materials. I mark the completion of coagulation when the milk mixture reaches a pH of 5.2, and students can use the data table to determine when that moment occurred.

2. *Assuming you didn't lose any curd along the way, what was the average amount of curd made by the rennet bacteria each minute?*

   To solve for this answer, students need to take the final mass of the cheese created and divide it by the time it took for coagulation to occur, which was answered in question 1. A sample student calculation is shown below:

Final Mass		Time for Coagulation		Rate Total mass
350 g	÷	80 minutes	=	4.375 g of curd per minute

3. *How much did the pH change during the coagulation of the casein?*

This depends on the initial conditions, but should be an average change of 1. Students can solve this by subtracting the final pH (5.2) from the initial pH of the milk.

4. *What was the average rate of pH acidity change per minute caused by the rennet bacteria?*

Again, this depends on specific student data. The calculation process involves taking the amount of pH change determined in question 3 and dividing it by the time of coagulation determined in question 1. For example:

pH Change		Time for Coagulation		Rate Total mass
1.0	÷	80 minutes	=	0.0125 pH change per minute

CONCLUSION AND CONNECTIONS ANSWER KEY

This section of the lab offers a great opportunity to engage the entire class in discussion to clarify the main ideas of the lab and allow the students to make their own connections between science and cooking. I ask that students answer the Data Analysis questions and attempt to answer the Conclusion and Connections questions, with the understanding that we will spend time the next day discussing the Conclusions and Connections section.

1. *Was your initial hypothesis correct? Explain why or why not citing specific data.*

For this question students will need to figure out the rate of casein digestion for humans. Students need to use the information given in the Hypothesis section of the lab—6.4 g of casein in 20 minutes—to solve this problem. Human digestion calculations should look like this:

Mass of Casein		Time for Digestion		Rate
6.4 g	÷	20 minutes	=	0.32 g per minute

2. *What is the rate at which the human body breaks down casein? Is rennet faster or slower? Explain your reasoning.*

The human digestion system prefers not to break down protein because human body systems are composed of proteins. Organs that keep our body going, such as the heart, are made of muscle, so the human body tends to go for carbohydrates and sugar to power itself. This is an answer that may require research by the students or can be a guided answer using a class discussion format to lead students to an answer.

3. *What is the most beneficial part of working in a team to create mozzarella?*

Scientists need to share data to share the workload. If a single student team had tried to attempt this experiment on its own, it would have taken the group three hours. By working as a team and communicating the data, scientists were able to complete the task more efficiently.

You can compare this to other projects such as the human genome project, explaining how scientists all over the world worked collectively to tackle a problem that originally seemed impossible because of the volume of work. Students will have different takes on why collaborating is helpful, and I encourage them to share these thoughts with their classmates. This emphasizes that science is usually not an individual effort.

4. *What do you think would happen if you used the entire tablet (rather than one-fourth) of rennet bacteria to make your cheese?*

There would have been more bacteria; therefore the coagulation rate would have increased. This relates back to chemical reaction rates and how increasing reactants can increase the creation rate of the products. You can take this opportunity to introduce the vocabulary word *catalyst* to describe how having more bacteria would speed up the process.

CROSS-CURRICULAR NOTE: MATH

This experiment provides an excellent opportunity to work with the math teacher on skills regarding averages and calculating rates.

CROSS-CURRICULAR NOTE: LITERACY

In connection with their final product, ask students to come up with a creative type of pizza that the United States is currently missing. Students should explain how they would make it, market it, and sell it. Give students a stack of pizza advertisements and let them compare and contrast aspects to decide what makes a good pizza advertisement. Ask students to design an advertisement for their new pizza and write a summary explaining their design choices.

OPTIONAL EXTENSIONS

Middle School

1. Have students explore the question, How much acid is too much? Students can experiment with adding different amounts of citric acid and discuss the effect on the taste of the cheese. The more acid you add, the more sour the cheese will become.

2. After cheese is created, it is often "aged." Students can explore how the aging process impacts the pH of cheese. They can test different cheese samples from the deli to see if there is a connection between cheese age and pH values.

High School

1. Students can grow cultures of rennet bacteria in petri dishes and measure the rate of their growth and the amount of bacteria in a tablet.

2. Students can use the data achieved in this lab to measure the amount of hydrogen ions that were introduced as the pH changed. This requires knowledge of pH as a logarithmic scale as well as Avogadro's number and molarity, but the exercise can be a great connection with acidity and pH for advanced students.

PART THREE: BIOCHEMISTRY

This section highlights how the organism yeast is able to impact the creation of foods such as pretzels and pancakes, as well as liquids such as mint ginger soda. Experiment 9: Ballpark Pretzels introduces yeast and how it uses sugar in a process of fermentation to create carbon dioxide. Students have the opportunity to look at the yeast under the microscope, learning how to create a wet mount slide to observe yeast and fermentation. Experiment 10: Cinnamon Rolls builds on the understanding of fermentation to look at how the process directly affects the creation of cinnamon rolls. This experiment highlights the role of a control set in experimental design. Experiment 11: Growing a Pancake builds on the understanding of fermentation and looks at how yeast growth and processes can be affected by environmental factors such as heat and access to resources in the creation of a sourdough starter. Experiment 12: Under Pressure moves students from looking at fermentation in baked goods to looking at yeast as a source of soda carbonization. Students create mint ginger soda while analyzing the mathematical relationship that occurs in the fermentation of sugar. Experiment 13: Regular or Diet Soda? asks students to use their understanding of yeast to design a procedure that tests the impact of sugar substitutes on the fermentation process. While creating diet and regular soda, students learn about writing a procedure as a part of experimental design. The experiments in this section yield delicious results while teaching about yeast, biological processes, environmental limiting factors, and reaction rates.

EXPERIMENT 9:
Ballpark Pretzels: Student Pages

USING MICROSCOPES TO OBSERVE YEAST FERMENTATION OF SUGAR

BACKGROUND

"Take me out to the ball game; take me out with the crowd." The pastime of baseball is not just known for the athletes and rivalries, but for the food as well. From peanuts and crackerjacks to cotton candy and pretzels, baseball games are just one example of an event where the food helps to create the memorable experience.

For this experiment, we are going to focus on the ballpark pretzel. Soft ballpark pretzels are made from simple bread dough, which has all sorts of chemistry and biology taking place within its moldable form. Dough is formed from flour and water, which locks together to form massive molecules known as gluten. The gluten is formed from two proteins: glutenin and gliadin. The gluten arrangement can be incredibly dense, creating hard products like pasta. That wouldn't make for a very soft pretzel, though, so recipes use two techniques that change the arrangement of the gluten in the dough.

The first process is incorporating yeast into the mixture. Yeast is a unicellular fungus (see Figure 9.1) that thrives on sugar to multiply. The yeast is used in pretzels to create air bubbles of carbon dioxide in the dough. These air bubbles allow the dough to double in size and become softer and lighter when baked. The second process is called kneading, where the dough is pushed, pulled, and pounded repeatedly to cause the gluten chains to line up and form new chains that are linear as opposed to globular.

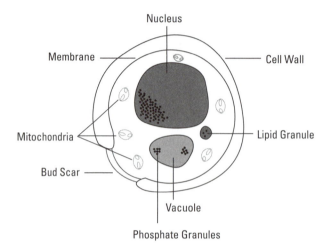

Figure 9.1: Diagram of a yeast cell and components of a yeast organism.

Finally, the pretzel is boiled in sodium bicarbonate and water. Boiling the pretzel dough before baking causes the surface starch to gelatinize into a thin, slimy coating that produces a glossy brown crust when baked. This is the final step before the pretzel is baked and paired with salt, cinnamon sugar, or mustard to be consumed by the masses.

HYPOTHESIS

We will be using yeast and sucrose when making pretzels for this experiment. Does the amount of sucrose impact the yeast's speed of fermentation? Or, is there a constant rate at which the yeast is able to synthesize sugar? We will be using a microscope to measure this process by counting the number of gas bubbles yeast makes when exposed to different levels of sugar.

Predict how you think the rate will change or stay the same as we increase the amount of sugar. Use an "If…Then…Because" statement and explain your answer using the background information provided in the previous section.

MATERIALS NEEDED PER GROUP

Materials Used Prior to Fermentation of Sugars

- One-half package of active dry *Saccharomyces cerevisiae* (baking yeast)
- 30 ml of warm dihydrogen monoxide, H_2O (water)
- 120 ml of warm dihydrogen monoxide, H_2O (water)
- 2.5 ml of sucrose, $C_{12}H_{22}O_{11}$ (sugar)
- 5 ml of sodium chloride, NaCl (table salt)
- 475–550 ml of all-purpose powdered grains (flour)
- Two pieces of filter paper
- One sheet of aluminum foil
- Lipids as needed (shortening)
- Graduated cylinder
- Balance
- Beaker, 100 ml
- Beaker, 200 ml
- Glass stir rod
- One antibacterial wipe
- Indirectly vented chemical-splash goggles
- Aprons

Materials Used After the Fermentation of Sugars

- Large beaker (over 400 ml)
- 400 ml of dihydrogen monoxide, H_2O (water for boiling)
- Bunsen burner
- Ring stand
- Tongs
- Indirectly vented chemical-splash goggles
- 10 ml of sodium hydrogen carbonate, $NaHCO_3$ (baking soda)
- Two pieces of filter paper
- Aprons

Materials for Microscope Analysis

- Active *Saccharomyces cerevisiae* solution with eyedropper (yeast solution)
- Microscope slide
- Microscope cover slip
- Microscope
- Bottles of 5% sucrose solution, 15% sucrose solution, and 30% sucrose solution
- Timer or clock

PROCEDURE FOR PRETZELS BEFORE FERMENTATION OF SUGARS

1. Read through the entire procedure before beginning.

2. Put on your safety goggles and apron, and gather all your materials at your lab station. If you notice any of the materials are dirty or discolored, notify your teacher.

3. Use an antibacterial wipe to wipe down your lab table thoroughly. You will be using this surface to create your dough, so it needs to be spotless. Cover your work area with a piece of waxed paper.

4. Once you are finished wiping down the table, thoroughly wash your hands with soap and water.

5. Begin by taking half a package of *Saccharomyces cerevisiae* and dissolving the granules in 30 ml of warm water. Mix with a glass stir rod.

6. Using a dry graduated cylinder, measure out 2.5 ml of sucrose and place on a piece of filter paper labeled "sucrose."

7. Using the same dry graduated cylinder, measure out 5 ml of sodium chloride and place on a piece of filter paper labeled "sodium chloride."

8. Measure 120 ml of warm water in a 200 ml glass beaker.

9. Add 2.5 ml of sucrose from the filter paper to the beaker with warm water. Stir to dissolve with a glass stir rod.

10. Add the *Saccharomyces cerevisiae* solution to the 200 ml beaker with the sucrose solution along with the 5 ml of sodium chloride. Stir well.

11. Using a large beaker, measure out 475 ml of all-purpose powdered grains.

12. Add the powdered grains onto the waxed paper on the lab table and create a small mountain.

13. Poke a hole in the center of your powdered grains mountain so that it looks like a volcano.

14. Pour a small amount (about 30 ml) of the sucrose *Saccharomyces cerevisiae* solution into the center of the volcano.

15. Use your hands to push the liquid and dry powdered grains together to start to mix the two together. If liquid runs out of the mountain, use the dry powdered grains to scoop it back in.

16. Repeat this process until all the liquid is incorporated into the dough. If the dough is too soft, add additional powdered grains. If the dough is too stiff, add additional water 5 ml at a time.

17. Once all the powdered grains and liquid are incorporated, use your hands (which have been washed thoroughly) to knead the dough on your lab table. Knead for 10 minutes or until your dough is stiff and elastic.

18. Grease a piece of aluminum foil with lipids. Place the dough on the foil and turn it until coated with the lipids. Cover the dough with a damp paper towel and let the dough rise on the counter until it has doubled in size. This will take about 30 minutes, during which time you are going to make microscope observations. Make sure you label the foil with your name.

19. Clean your lab area before you move to the microscope observations.

PROCEDURE FOR MICROSCOPE OBSERVATIONS

1. Read through the entire procedure before beginning.

2. Gather your lab materials at your station. Carry the microscopes with two hands, one hand at the arm and one hand on the base.

3. You will be making a wet mount slide or a microscope slide that has a liquid for viewing. Begin by taking your microscope slide. Use a flat glass slide to prepare a wet mount. The slide should be clean and free of dust or other fine particles.

4. Keeping the slide flat, place two drops of the *Saccharomyces cerevisiae* solution on the center of the slide using the plastic dropper.

5. Take a coverslip and place the edge of the coverslip on the edge of your liquid on the slide. Slowly lower the coverslip into place. If you do this too quickly, you will have large air bubbles that will make your observations difficult, so be careful.

6. Place the coverslip on top of the slide, making sure the edges of the coverslip match up with the edges of the slide. Do not press down on the coverslip.

7. Grasp the slide/coverslip combination by the outer edges. You should keep the slide as horizontal and as steady as possible. Place it on the viewing tray of your microscope.

8. Start with the lowest degree of magnification on your microscope. Use the coarse adjustment to bring the slide into view, and then the fine adjustment to fine-tune your image. Once you have achieved a clear view, increase the magnification to get a better look at the *Saccharomyces cerevisiae* cells.

9. Make an observation about the *Saccharomyces cerevisiae* and record it in your Microscope Observation Data Table. Your observation can be descriptive with words, or a diagram, or a combination of both.

10. Count the number of bubbles visible in your slide. These should be clearly defined and appear different from the *Saccharomyces cerevisiae* size. Record the number of bubbles in your data table.

11. Note the time and wait for two minutes. Do not move the slide during this time.

12. At the conclusion of two minutes, count the total number of bubbles again and record this in your data table. You can then solve for the number of bubbles created during two minutes.

13. Throw away the coverslip in the trash.

14. Wash off the *Saccharomyces cerevisiae* and dry your slide with a paper towel.

15. Repeat steps 4–14 using two drops of *Saccharomyces cerevisiae* and three drops of 5% sucrose solution from the dropper bottle.

16. Repeat steps 4–14 using two drops of *Saccharomyces cerevisiae* and three drops of 15% sucrose solution from the dropper bottle.

17. Repeat steps 4–14 using two drops of *Saccharomyces cerevisiae* and three drops of 30% sucrose solution from the dropper bottle.

18. Clean your lab area and wait for your teacher to ask you to retrieve your dough.

PROCEDURE FOR PRETZELS AFTER THE FERMENTATION OF SUGARS

1. Read through the entire procedure before beginning.

2. Put on your safety goggles and apron and gather all your materials at your lab station. If you notice any of the materials are dirty or discolored, notify your teacher.

3. Use an antibacterial wipe to wipe down your lab table thoroughly. You will be using this surface to create your dough, so it needs to be spotless.

4. Once you are finished wiping down the table, thoroughly wash your hands with soap and water.

5. Break the dough into four equal pieces.

6. Using your lab table, roll each piece into a long stick about 25 cm long and twist this into a pretzel or knot shape.

7. Set up a Bunsen burner and ring stand with wire mesh on the iron ring. Make sure your Bunsen burner gas intake tube is securely connected to the gas nozzle and that the ring is set about 3 in. above the barrel of the burner (see Figure 9.2). Light the Bunsen burner to create a flame that is no more than 3 in. high. (It should not be touching the wire mesh.)

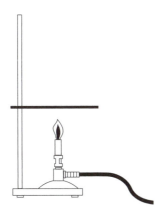

Figure 9.2: Bunsen burner and ring stand.

8. Measure 10 ml of sodium hydrogen carbonate and combine with 250 ml of water in a large 400 ml beaker.

9. Using the tongs, place the beaker on the ring stand. Bring the beaker to a boil.

10. Use the tongs to drop in one pretzel at a time and wait for them to float (about one minute). Remove the pretzel with tongs and place it on your aluminum foil with the lipids. *Safety note:* Be careful not to cause the boiling water to splash; it can cause serious skin burns.

11. Once all the pretzels have been boiled, place them in the toaster oven and bake them at 232°C (450°F) for 12 minutes or until they are golden brown.

12. Clean your lab area while you are waiting for your pretzels to be baked.

DATA AND OBSERVATIONS

Microscope Observation Data Table				
	Observations (description or graphic is acceptable)	Number of bubbles in initial slide	Number of bubbles after two minutes	Total number of bubbles created
Saccharomyces cerevisiae with no sucrose				
Saccharomyces cerevisiae with 5% sucrose solution				
Saccharomyces cerevisiae with 15% sucrose solution				
Saccharomyces cerevisiae with 30% sucrose solution				

DATA ANALYSIS

For each of the following questions, be sure to explain using detail and complete sentences. If the question requires you to complete calculations, show all of your work.

1. Create a bar graph that shows the number of bubbles created by the yeast when combined with different amounts of sucrose. Remember to include all elements of a scientific graph (title, labeled axes, units, legend, etc.).

2. What was the rate of bubbles being created for each of the *Saccharomyces cerevisiae* slides? Show your work in the table below.

	Number of bubbles created	Time for bubble creation (seconds)	Rate of bubbles created per second
Saccharomyces cerevisiae with no sucrose			
Saccharomyces cerevisiae with 5% sucrose			
Saccharomyces cerevisiae with 15% sucrose			
Saccharomyces cerevisiae with 30% sucrose			

CONCLUSION AND CONNECTIONS

1. Was your initial hypothesis correct? Restate your hypothesis and identify whether you were correct or incorrect, using data to support your answer.

2. Why is it necessary for the dough to be kneaded? What process does this accomplish? What would you expect dough to look like if it had not been kneaded?

3. Why does the dough need time to rise? What process is occurring during this period? What would you expect dough to be like if it had not been given time to rise?

4. If you wanted to speed up the rising time for the pretzels, how would you alter the procedure?

EXPERIMENT 9:
Ballpark Pretzels: Teacher Pages

USING MICROSCOPES TO OBSERVE YEAST FERMENTATION OF SUGAR

This experiment provides a hands-on lab experience for students to begin their investigation into yeast and the fermentation of sugars. The experiment allows students to view the yeast under the microscope, gaining skills in using the microscope and creating wet mounts. In connection with these observations, students also get to experience a practical application of yeast fermentation to create soft pretzels. The visual and hands-on experiences creating yeast and watching it rise provide an excellent context for understanding the process of fermentation that is viewed under the microscope, and create a memorable, edible lab.

STANDARDS ADDRESSED
National Science Education Standards: Grades 5–8

Content Standard A: Science as Inquiry
- Abilities necessary to do scientific inquiry
- Understanding about scientific inquiry

Content Standard B: Physical Science
- Properties and changes of properties in matter

Content Standard C: Life Science
- Structure and function in living systems

Content Standard F: Science in Personal and Social Perspectives
- Science and technology in society

Content Standard G: History and Nature of Science
- Science as a human endeavor
- Nature of science

National Science Education Standards: Grades 9–12

Content Standard A: Science as Inquiry
- Abilities necessary to do scientific inquiry
- Understanding about scientific inquiry

Content Standard B: Physical Science
- Structure of atoms
- Structure and properties of matter
- Chemical reactions

Content Standard C: Life Science
- The cell
- Matter, energy, and organization in living systems

Content Standard E: Science and Technology
- Abilities of technological design
- Understanding about science and technology

Content Standard F: Science in Personal and Social Perspectives
- Science and technology in local, national, and global challenges

Content Standard G: History and Nature of Science
- Science as a human endeavor
- Nature of scientific knowledge
- Historical perspectives

VOCABULARY

Yeast: Any of various unicellular fungi of the genus *Saccharomyces*, especially *S. cerevisiae*, reproducing by budding and from ascospores and capable of fermenting carbohydrates (*The American Heritage Dictionary of the English Language* 2000).

Gluten: The mixture of proteins, including gliadins and glutelins, found in wheat grains, which are not soluble in water and which give wheat dough its elastic texture (*The American Heritage Dictionary of the English Language* 2000).

Wet mount slide: A microscope slide that contains a liquid material for viewing and uses a coverslip.

MATERIALS NEEDED, DECODED FOR THE GROCERY STORE

One-half package of active dry *Saccharomyces cerevisiae* (baking yeast)
- Yeast can be purchased in the section of your grocery store with the baking powder and flour. Yeast is usually sold in packages for less than $1. One package will work for two lab groups, so base your purchase on the number of lab groups that will be conducting this experiment.
- Make sure that the yeast has not expired. If you purchase yeast and want to use it later in the year, store it in a cool, dry area.

2.5 ml of sucrose, $C_{12}H_{22}O_{11}$ (sugar)
- Sugar is sold in as small as 5 lb. bags, and increases from there. A 5 lb. bag will give you enough sugar for more than 100 lab groups for this experiment.

5 ml of sodium chloride, NaCl (table salt)
- Each group uses salt in the creation of its dough, so a single salt container will be more than enough for 20 lab groups. The salt also can be used later for adding additional flavor to the finished pretzel.

475–550 ml of all-purpose powdered grains (flour)
- You will want a shopping cart for this material. The students need quite a bit of flour for this lab, but it actually isn't as much as you might think. I purchased one 25 lb. bag of flour (around $20) and have been using it for three years. A 5 lb. bag of flour will give you enough for at least four groups. I think the larger bags are worth the cost (and the weight).

Lipids as needed (shortening)
- One can of shortening is all you need for years of this lab. Students need a small amount to grease their aluminum foil so the dough does not stick while rising or cooking. You could purchase a nonstick cooking spray as well, but the shortening option is cheaper and lasts longer.

Aluminum foil
- Each lab group will need a sheet of aluminum foil to use for its dough when it is rising, as well as for cooking. I have students use the same sheet to save money. Rolls are sold in varying lengths, but a 75-yard roll will work for 100 lab groups.

Antibacterial wipe
- Each lab group will need to wipe down its work area thoroughly before placing the flour and dough on the counter. I give each group one wipe, so a typical tube will last for about 60 lab groups, depending on the number of sheets.

10 ml of sodium hydrogen carbonate, $NaHCO_3$ (baking soda)
- The baking soda goes into the water that pretzels are boiled in to create the hard outer shell. A single box of baking soda will work for about 25 lab groups. I recommend placing the baking soda in a large beaker with a metal scoop for the students to measure the necessary volume. In the box the powder is difficult to pour and often ends up spilling, even when a funnel is used.

Dish soap
- This is necessary for cleanup. I ask students to use an amount about the size of a quarter for each glass container, and I have one bottle available for every four lab groups to share.

SAFETY HIGHLIGHTS
- The Bunsen burners and ring stands present a potential for students to burn themselves if used incorrectly. Please make sure students have had Bunsen burner safety training before allowing them to participate in this lab. As a teacher, you also need to be prepared with burn treatment options, such as running the burned area under cold water, if a student gets hurt.
- If a glass stir rod breaks, you should dispose of the entire mixture in the beaker. Even if the break is minor, you may have shards of glass in the mixture that are not visible.
- Because students will be handling the food during the dough-making process, it is important that their work area is sterilized with antibacterial wipes and then covered with a food-safe material such as waxed paper before placing food on the counter. If there is concern about the cleanliness and sanitation of the table or counter space, students need to create their dough in a sterilized bowl.

Note that these safety highlights are in addition to the safety information detailed in the Safety Protocol section at the beginning of this book. Please refer to that section for additional information about safety when implementing this or any lab in this book.

PREPARATION

1. You will need to make an active yeast solution for the students to use in the microscope observation period that occurs while the yeast is rising. Take half a package of the dry yeast and mix it with 30 ml of warm water. Add the label "Caution: Active Organism Environment" and include a small plastic eyedropper. (I typically use disposable droppers when working with yeast so I don't need to worry about cleaning and sterilizing them.)

2. You also need to prepare sucrose dropper bottles for the microscope observation. I think it is best to have these prepared for students because of the time limit factor, but you can ask your students to make these solutions if you would like them to have experience making solutions of different concentrations. Making the solutions ahead of time also eliminates the amount of materials necessary for this step.

    (a) Measure 100 ml of warm water in a glass beaker. Measure 5 ml of sugar and pour it into the warm water. Stir until all the sugar is suspended. Then pour the solution evenly among three plastic dropper bottles, labeling each dropper bottle "5% Sucrose Solution."
    (b) Repeat step a for a 15% sugar solution by mixing in 15 ml of sugar and labeling the bottles "15% Sucrose Solution."
    (c) Repeat step a for a 30% sugar solution by mixing 30 ml of sugar and labeling the bottles "30% Sucrose Solution."
    (d) This will give you nine dropper bottles. If you have more student groups than nine, you can easily double the values to make more dropper bottles of each concentration.

PROCEDURE

I recommend having students work in teams of three or four for this experiment. The final product creates four small pretzels, which is plenty to share among a large group. There is also a significant amount of labor involved with the preparation of the dough, which can be shared equally by a large group. The large group size also cuts down on the total number of lab groups per class and the overall cost of supplies.

This lab requires sticking to a tight schedule if you are going to fit the entire process into a 90-minute period. If you have 45-minute classes, you can always have one group begin the dough-making process and complete microscope observations, and have the second class finish the pretzels and complete microscope observations while waiting for the pretzels to bake.

When I have completed this lab with large student groups (40 or more students), I have taken the entire class through the lab step-by-step rather than have all students attempt the procedure on their own. Although this makes the lab more directed, it alleviates the continuous calls for teacher attention from lab groups around the room. It also allows you to direct the times when cleaning is appropriate.

1. Begin by placing the students in lab groups and asking them to read the Background section. You can introduce the activity by asking them what their favorite foods are at sporting events to provide context and connections for each of the students.

2. Once students have read the Background section and moved to writing their hypothesis, I like to show them products that contain yeast, such as canned biscuits, crescent rolls, and sliced bread. I allow students to pass these around to help them see that sugar (sucrose) is a component in all of these breads. This also can initiate a discussion about the different densities and consistencies of each of these products.

3. This lab is broken down into three parts: pretzels before fermentation, microscope observations, and pretzels after fermentation. I instruct students to handle each part as a separate lab. This controls the materials that are out, the use of space, and the safety concerns at each moment in the classroom. I have also completed the lab when all the materials were out at one time, but found it was a bit chaotic and overwhelming. I recommend placing *only* the materials needed for the pretzels before fermentation out at the outset of the lab. The other two sets of materials can be kept in large boxes or containers that are not set out but will be exchanged when the students are ready to move on.

4. The students will be creating their dough on the flat tabletop or countertop. Students can complete these steps on a piece of waxed paper or in a large mixing bowl if you have concerns about the sanitation of your tabletops. I have asked students to bring in plastic or metal mixing bowls in the past.

5. The mountains of dough are messy. Preparing students for the messiness will prevent some screams that might occur when liquid leaks out of the dough. Although there are four students in each lab group, only two need to

be involved in the hands-on incorporation of the liquid. Another student can pour liquid in the mountain, while the fourth can be cleaning out used glassware. Remind them of the importance of adding small amounts of liquid at a time so it doesn't leak off the table. *Safety note*: Immediately wipe up any liquids spilled on the floor to prevent a slip/fall hazard.

6. When the dough is finished and students are covering it with a damp paper towel, make sure the towels are not constricting the dough from rising. It is often helpful to walk around and pull the paper towels off the dough and place them back about 15 minutes into the rising process.

7. When you reach the microscope observations, it is important to show your students how to correctly carry the microscopes with two hands—one on the base and one on the arm—if they are moving them from a cabinet or central supply area to their work area.

8. Depending on their experience with microscopes, it may be helpful to demonstrate a wet mount for the entire class before sending the students off to make their own observations.

9. If you are running short on time, you can prepare the slides and microscopes to allow students to view in a rotation. Do not leave the lights of the microscope on, as this can overheat and kill the yeast.

10. For the pretzel twisting technique, take the two ends of the dough rope and twist them together. Then fold the twisted end back over and attach to the center of the loop of dough. I encourage students to create whatever shape they want, keeping in mind if all the dough is packed together in a ball, they will have raw dough in their final product.

11. When the pretzels are placed in the water with the baking soda, the water will fizz up and potentially spill over the edge of the beaker. This is important to know so you can keep an eye on students' Bunsen burner flames. If a flame goes out, students need to immediately turn off the gas valve so gas does not leak into the room.

12. The most difficult part of this lab is removing the boiled pretzels from the beaker of water. I have the students use two pairs of tongs. Some pretzels may fall apart, but students can put them back together before they bake.

13. There are two options for baking the pretzels: First, you can ask the staff in your cafeteria to help you with the baking process. Most schools have rules about students not being in the school kitchen, so check with your administrative staff. The second option is to use toaster ovens. I have had several donated so that I am up to four toaster ovens, which works well for cooking

pretzels in rotation for up to 35 students. You can get inexpensive toaster ovens for around $25. These ovens have made other labs possible as well without bothering the kitchen staff.

14. I handle the baking of pretzels, and require that all the students in a single group have all their pretzels on a single piece of aluminum foil that can fit in the toaster oven. This cuts down on baking time, allowing you to bake four pretzels at once. I also do not hand out a single pretzel until the entire lab is clean.

15. Students can add salt, cinnamon sugar, or other condiments to their pretzels after they are baked. If these condiments are placed on the pretzels before the baking, they often burn, so it is better to add them after baking is complete.

16. Once the pretzels have cooled, tear the aluminum foil sheet into four pieces and allow each student to take his or her pretzel while working on their data analysis.

DATA ANALYSIS ANSWER KEY

All the data analysis for this lab is math based. If students are struggling with the questions, I recommend using a sample data set and going through the calculations as a class on the board. Then students can use the same skills and apply them directly to their data.

1. *Create a bar graph that shows the number of bubbles created by the yeast when combined with different amounts of sucrose. Remember to include all elements of a scientific graph (title, labeled axes, units, legend, etc.).*

Bubbles Produced by Yeast in Two Minute Observation with Different Levels of Sucrose

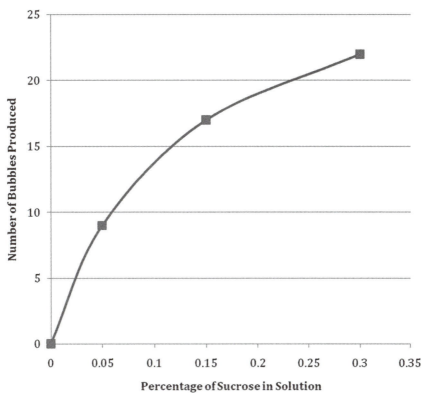

2. *What was the rate of bubbles being created for each of the* Saccharomyces cerevisiae *slides? Show your work in the table below.*

Each student will have slightly different numbers, but those numbers should show the trend that more bubbles are created as the sucrose content increases. To find the rate of bubbles created, students need to take the total number of bubbles created and divide that number by 120 seconds. (Watch that they do not use two minutes because that is not the unit format in the table.) Here is a sample showing student data and calculations:

	Number of bubbles created	Time for bubble creation (seconds)	Rate of bubbles created per second
Saccharomyces cerevisiae with no sucrose	0	120 seconds	0 bubbles/second
Saccharomyces cerevisiae with 5% sucrose	9	120 seconds	0.075 bubbles/second
Saccharomyces cerevisiae with 15% sucrose	17	120 seconds	0.142 bubbles/second
Saccharomyces cerevisiae with 30% sucrose	22	120 seconds	0.183 bubbles/second

CONCLUSION AND CONNECTIONS ANSWER KEY

This section of the lab offers a great opportunity to engage the entire class in discussion to clarify the main ideas of the lab and allow the students to make their own connections between science and cooking. I ask that students answer the Data Analysis questions and attempt to answer the Conclusion and Connections questions, with the understanding that we will spend time the next day discussing the Conclusions and Connections section.

1. *Was your initial hypothesis correct? Restate your hypothesis and identify whether you were correct or incorrect, using data to support your answer.*

   Students will have different initial answers based on their specific hypotheses, but everyone should identify that the trend in the graph shows that the rate of bubble creation increases as the sucrose content increases. This is demonstrated by the rise in the graph.

2. *Why is it necessary for the dough to be kneaded? What process does this accomplish? What would you expect dough to look like if it had not been kneaded?*

   The dough is kneaded to realign the gluten chains to make the dough smooth and more elastic. If the dough had not been kneaded, it would have turned out lumpy with an inconsistent texture because of globular gluten concentrations being different throughout the dough.

3. *Why does the dough need time to rise? What process is occurring during this period? What would you expect dough to be like if it had not been given time to rise?*

The dough needs a chance to rise to give the yeast organisms an opportunity to ferment the sugars in the dough and produce the air bubbles that make the bread light and fluffy. Dough that was not given time to rise would be dense with no air bubbles because the yeast would not have time to produce the gas.

4. *If you wanted to speed up the rising time for the pretzels, how would you alter the procedure?*

There are two common answers for this question. One approach would be to increase the amount of sugar. Based on the student data, higher sucrose content produces more bubbles, and therefore should cause the yeast to rise faster. The other answer would be to increase the amount of yeast. By increasing the amount of yeast, there are more microorganisms completing the fermentation reaction, and therefore the yeast should rise faster. A third approach would be to heat the temperature of the rise environment to promote the fermentation process. Any of these answers, or a combination of the three, is acceptable.

CROSS-CURRICULAR NOTE: MATH

This experiment provides an excellent opportunity to work with the math teacher on skills such as rates and percentages. Students can also look at the graph to see whether the trend fits linear growth or exponential growth.

CROSS-CURRICULAR NOTE: LITERACY

There is a real-world connection between this lab and sporting venues. Students can research how much money is generated from the sales of pretzels at a nearby ballpark or stadium. How do pretzel sales compare to the sales of potato chips? Ask students to write a persuasive argument for why pretzels are a better choice for a snack when compared to chips. They should use data from their research to support their argument.

OPTIONAL EXTENSIONS

Middle School

1. Students can determine the effect of temperature on glucose fermentation. They can test temperatures such as 4°C, room temperature, 26°C, 32°C, 36°C, 41°C, and 49°C.

2. Students can compare fermentation of different sugars by baker's yeast (*Saccharomyces cerevisiae*) and brewer's yeast (*Sacc. pastorianus*, or *S. bayanus*). Optional sugars include glucose, fructose, sucrose, maltose, lactose, galactose, and starch.

3. Ask students to break down the lab procedure for creating pretzels and identify where chemical changes are taking place and where physical changes are taking place to study the difference between the two processes.

High School

1. You could modify this lab to incorporate more inquiry by having students create a procedure for measuring the relationship between sugar concentration and yeast fermentation.

2. Have students look at the actual process of fermentation as anaerobic respiration. Students can compare and contrast this model to the aerobic respiration of the Krebs cycle, glycolysis, and electron transport chain.

3. Students can look at the cellular structure of yeast. Ask, "How does the yeast cell compare with the human cell? What organelles are similar, and which are different?" This line of questioning can lead into a discussion about early life on Earth and evolution.

EXPERIMENT 10:
Cinnamon Rolls: Student Pages

CREATING A CONTROL SET TO ANALYZE THE ROLE OF YEAST IN BAKED GOODS

BACKGROUND

Have you ever taken part in a food fight? There are foods flying left and right, and all you can think about is how you don't want to get mustard on your new shirt. But instead of worrying about stains, you really should be thinking about density.

Why density? Density is the measurement of an object's mass per unit of volume (see Figure 10.1, p. 198). Objects of different density can often be the same size but have a very different mass. For example, a kickball and a bowling ball are about the same size, but their masses are very different, so the items have different densities. Density is one of the many characteristics that can be used to describe matter.

So why does all of this matter in a food fight? The density of the object will determine the amount of force with which it will impact you. Back to the bowling ball and kickball example, it would be a lot less painful to be hit by a kickball (which has a small density) as opposed to a bowling ball (which has a large density). Although the two are the same size, the difference in density changes the impact.

In this experiment we will be investigating how the density of a cinnamon roll can change when yeast is removed from the procedure. Yeast is a biological agent that thrives on sugar to multiply. The yeast is used in cinnamon rolls to create air bubbles of carbon dioxide in the dough. These air bubbles allow the dough to double in size and become softer and lighter when baked. You will be investigating what happens to the density of the rolls when the yeast is removed. What does a change in density taste like? You will find out in this lab, which will not only improve your knowledge of science but also make you a more formidable opponent in your next food fight.

Mass Measured by a Balance

Density = $\dfrac{\text{Mass Measured by a Balance}}{\text{Volume Measured by Beaker or Area (Length × Width × Height)}}$

Figure 10.1: Density is a measurement of matter that can be determined by dividing mass by volume.

HYPOTHESIS

How will the density change in the final cinnamon roll if yeast is not used in the dough-making process? Will the density increase, decrease, or stay the same? Write your prediction, and explain why you believe this will be the outcome using the background information to support your answer.

SETUP

For this experiment we will be changing the amount of yeast that is present in two batches of cinnamon rolls. Then we will test the difference in density between the roll with yeast and the roll without. To be able to compare the two rolls and say with certainty that it was the yeast that caused the density outcome, we need to keep all other variables the same. These are our *controlled variables*. This allows us to keep our experiment consistent so we can determine whether yeast impacts the density.

Read the condensed procedure below for making cinnamon rolls. Circle the values that need to remain the same for both cinnamon roll tests.

> *In a large mixing bowl beat the eggs, sugar, and salt for the dough mixture. Combine the warm mile and margarine and add to the egg mixture. Slowly add 4 cups flour and beat well. Add the yeast and mix thoroughly. Add the remaining 4 cups flour and mix for 7 minutes. Place the dough in an oiled bowl and cover with plastic wrap. Let the dough rise to double its size, about 1 hour. (Food Network n.d.)*

Using this as your guide, circle the controlled variables in the Materials Needed and Procedure sections. These values will stay the same for both groups. There is only one value that will change between trials, the *independent variable*. Write *independent variable* in the Materials Needed and Procedure sections next to the value that will change in the two trials.

Your lab group will be assigned one value of the independent variable to test. Your final product will either contain yeast or not contain yeast. Write your independent variable here:

My independent variable for my assigned trial is:

_____.

Cross out steps or materials that do not apply to your trial in the Materials Needed and Procedure sections.

MATERIALS NEEDED PER GROUP

Dough Materials

- One *Gallus domesticus* ova (egg)
- 45 ml of sucrose, $C_{12}H_{22}O_{11}$ (sugar)
- 1.5 ml of sodium chloride, NaCl (table salt)
- 120 ml of warm emulsified colloid of liquid butterfat in H_2O (whole milk)
- 30 g of margaric or heptadecanoic acid (margarine)
- 475 ml of powdered grains (flour)
- One package of active dry *Saccharomyces cerevisiae* (yeast)
- 20 ml of warm dihydgrogen monoxide, H_2O (water)
- Fats and oils (as needed)
- Aluminum foil
- Beaker, 200 ml
- Beaker, 600 ml
- Graduated cylinder
- Glass stir rod
- Balance
- Ruler
- Antibacterial wipe
- Indirectly vented chemical-splash goggles
- Aprons
- Gloves
- Paper towel

Filling Materials

- 30 g of margaric or heptadecanoic acid (margarine)
- 120 ml of brown sucrose, $C_{12}H_{22}O_{11}$ (brown sugar)
- 10 ml of *Cinnamomum zeylanicum* (cinnamon)
- Plastic knife

PROCEDURE

1. Read through the entire procedure before beginning.

2. Put on your safety goggles, apron, and gloves, and gather all your materials at your lab station. If you notice any of the materials are dirty or discolored, notify your teacher.

3. Use an antibacterial wipe to wipe down your lab table thoroughly. You will be using this surface to create your dough, so it needs to be spotless. Have students place a piece of waxed paper on the surface.

4. Once you are finished wiping down the table, thoroughly wash your hands with soap and water.

5. Begin by taking a package of *Saccharomyces cerevisiae* and dissolving the granules in 20 ml of warm water in a 200 ml beaker. Mix with a glass stir rod.

6. In the same 200 ml beaker, mix one *Gallus domesticus* ova, 45 ml of sucrose, and 1.5 ml of sodium chloride and stir with the glass stir rod.

7. Measure out 120 ml of warm emulsified colloid of liquid butterfat in H_2O in a graduated cylinder and add to the 200 ml beaker.

8. Using the balance, measure out 30 g of margaric acid and add to the ova mixture in the 200 ml beaker.

9. Using a large beaker, measure out 475 ml of all-purpose powdered grains.

10. Add the powdered grains to the lab table on the foil and create a small mountain. Then poke a hole in the center of your powdered grains mountain so that it looks like a volcano. Pour a small amount (about 30 ml) of the ova mixture. Using your hands, push the liquid and dry powdered grains together to start to mix the two substances. If liquid runs out of your mountain, use dry powdered grains to scoop it back in.

11. Repeat this process until all the liquid is incorporated into the dough. If the dough is too soft, add additional powdered grains. If the dough is too stiff, add additional water, 5 ml at a time.

12. Once all the powdered grains and liquid are incorporated, use your hands (which have been washed thoroughly) to knead the dough on your lab table. This may take up to seven minutes until the dough is stiff and elastic.

13. Grease a piece of aluminum foil with fat and oil. Place the dough on the foil and turn it until coated with the fat and oil. Cover the dough with a damp paper towel and let the dough rise on the counter until it doubles in size.

This will take about 20–30 minutes, during which time you should clean your lab area. Make sure you label the foil with your name.

14. After the dough has risen, roll out the dough into a 25 cm × 25 cm square.

15. Take 30 g of margaric acid and spread it evenly across the dough square. Sprinkle on the 120 ml of brown sucrose and 10 ml of *Cinnamomum zeylanicum*.

16. Roll the dough square up into a cylinder starting with the bottom edge.

17. Once you have a cylinder, cut it into equal pieces to distribute within your group. (If you have three people in your lab group, cut the cylinder into three pieces, and so on.)

18. Place the rolls back on your oiled aluminum foil and bake for 15 minutes at 178°C (350°F).

19. Clean your lab area while you are waiting for the rolls to bake.

20. Once your rolls are done, you will take several measurements to calculate the density of your rolls. Use the balance to find the mass of all the rolls created. You can remove the mass all at once or one roll at a time and add the masses together. Record this mass in your Density Data Table.

21. Now find the volume of your rolls. Stack all of your rolls on top of each other and measure the height in centimeters with a ruler. Record this height in your Density Data Table.

22. Next measure the diameter of your roll in centimeters with a ruler. Record this measurement in your Density Data Table.

23. Take your plastic knife and cut your roll in half. Share half of your roll with the group you were paired with that ran the other trial with a different independent variable. Taste both rolls and record your observations in the Taste Test Data Table.

24. Answer Data Analysis and Conclusion and Connections questions.

DATA AND OBSERVATIONS

Density Data Table			
	Mass (g)	Total height of rolls (cm)	Diameter of rolls (cm)
Rolls without *Saccharomyces cerevisiae*			
Rolls with *Saccharomyces cerevisiae*			

Taste Test Data Table	
	Taste observations
Rolls without *Saccharomyces cerevisiae*	
Rolls with *Saccharomyces cerevisiae*	

DATA ANALYSIS

For each of the following questions, be sure to explain using detail and complete sentences. If the question requires you to complete calculations, show all of your work.

1. The area of a circle can be calculated using the following equation:

$$\text{Area} = \pi \times \text{Diameter}$$

Calculate the area of the rolls made with *Saccharomyces cerevisiae* and the area of the rolls made without *Saccharomyces cerevisiae* in the table below. Show all your work.

	Area of roll (cm^2)
Rolls without *Saccharomyces cerevisiae*	
Rolls with *Saccharomyces cerevisiae*	

2. The volume of the rolls can be calculated by using the following equation:

$$\text{Volume} = \text{Area} \times \text{Height}$$

Calculate the volume of the rolls made with *Saccharomyces cerevisiae* and the volume of the rolls made without *Saccharomyces cerevisiae* in the table below. Show all your work.

	Volume of roll (cm³)
Rolls without *Saccharomyces cerevisiae*	
Rolls with *Saccharomyces cerevisiae*	

3. The density of the rolls can be calculated by using the following equation:

$$\text{Density} = \text{Mass} \div \text{Volume}$$

Calculate the density of the rolls made with *Saccharomyces cerevisiae* and the density of the rolls made without *Saccharomyces cerevisiae* in the table below. Show all your work.

	Density of roll (g/cm³)
Rolls without *Saccharomyces cerevisiae*	
Rolls with *Saccharomyces cerevisiae*	

CONCLUSION AND CONNECTIONS

1. Was your initial hypothesis correct? Please restate your hypothesis and identify whether you were correct or incorrect using data to support your answer.

2. Why would the density for the two rolls be different because of changing the amount of yeast? Explain using your taste observations to support your answer.

3. List two examples of starch products that you think are made with yeast and two examples of starch products that you think are not made with yeast.

4. Identify the other material (besides yeast) that would have caused the exact same difference in density if it were removed from the procedure.

5. In the following diagram, the objects have settled into a specific position based on density. Which item has the highest density? Which liquid has the lowest density? Explain how you arrived at your answer.

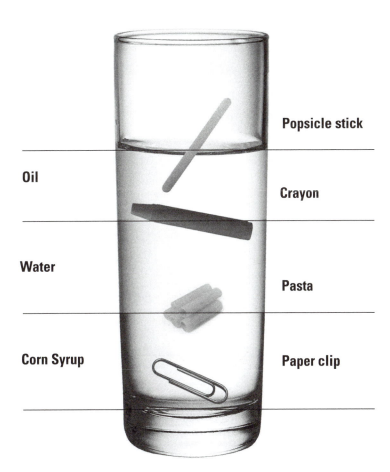

Popsicle stick

Oil

Crayon

Water

Pasta

Corn Syrup

Paper clip

EXPERIMENT 10:
Cinnamon Rolls: Teacher Pages

CREATING A CONTROL SET TO ANALYZE THE ROLE OF YEAST IN BAKED GOODS

This experiment presents a unique approach to biological agents by using the lens of density to look at the impact of yeast organisms in sugar fermentation. The hands-on activity allows students to investigate how the presence or lack of yeast can affect the overall density of a cinnamon roll. Students calculate density using a dimensional analysis that incorporates basic geometry skills, which makes the lab an excellent opportunity for a cross-curricular lesson with math. In addition to the biology and math content, the lab also looks at experimental design, asking students to identify the controlled variables within the experiment. Students are given one procedure, which they modify based on their assigned independent variable. This approach builds their understanding of the scientific method, knowledge of yeast reactions, and math application skills.

STANDARDS ADDRESSED
National Science Education Standards: Grades 5–8

Content Standard A: Science as Inquiry
- Abilities necessary to do scientific inquiry
- Understanding about scientific inquiry

Content Standard B: Physical Science
- Properties and changes of properties in matter

Content Standard C: Life Science
- Structure and function in living systems

Content Standard E: Science and Technology
- Understanding about science and technology

Content Standard F: Science in Personal and Social Perspectives
- Science and technology in society

Content Standard G: History and Nature of Science
- Science as a human endeavor
- Nature of science

National Science Education Standards: Grades 9–12

Content Standard A: Science as Inquiry
- Abilities necessary to do scientific inquiry
- Understanding about scientific inquiry

Content Standard B: Physical Science
- Structure of atoms
- Structure and properties of matter
- Chemical reactions

Content Standard C: Life Science
- The cell
- Matter, energy, and organization in living systems

Content Standard E: Science and Technology
- Abilities of technological design
- Understanding about science and technology

Content Standard F: Science in Personal and Social Perspectives
- Science and technology in local, national, and global challenges

Content Standard G: History and Nature of Science
- Science as a human endeavor
- Nature of scientific knowledge
- Historical perspectives

VOCABULARY

Density: The measurement of an object's mass per unit of volume.

Controlled variables: Factors that are not being tested and therefore are held constant throughout the experiment.

Controlled experiment: An experiment in which only one factor is being changed (the independent variable), and the other variables are being held constant to create a control group to create a standard to measure the change.

MATERIALS NEEDED, DECODED FOR THE GROCERY STORE

One *Gallus domesticus* ova (egg)
- Each student group will need one egg for this experiment. Eggs are sold by the dozen, so one box provides for 12 student groups.

45 ml of sucrose, $C_{12}H_{22}O_{11}$ (sugar)
- Sugar is sold in 5 lb. bags, and increases from there. A 5 lb. bag will give you enough sugar for more than 50 lab groups for this experiment.

1.5 ml of sodium chloride, NaCl (table salt)
- Each group uses salt in the creation of its dough, so a single salt container will be more than enough for 40 lab groups.

120 ml of warm emulsified colloid of liquid butterfat in H_2O (whole milk)
- Each student group will need 120 ml of whole milk. A gallon of whole milk will be enough for 30 lab groups.

30 g of margaric or heptadecanoic acid (margarine) for dough plus 30 g of margaric or heptadecanoic acid for filling (margarine)
- Each student group will need 60 g of margarine for their entire lab (half for making the dough, half for making the filling). This is half a stick of margarine. Most margarine is sold in packages with four sticks, so each box will be enough for eight lab groups.

475 ml of powdered grains (flour)
- You will want a shopping cart for this material. The students need quite a bit of flour for this lab, but it actually isn't as much as you might think. I purchased one 25 lb. bag of flour (around $20) and have been using it for

three years. A 5 lb. bag of flour will give you enough for at least four groups. I think the larger bags are worth the cost (and the weight).

One package of active dry *Saccharomyces cerevisiae* (yeast)
- Yeast can be purchased in the baking section of your grocery store with the baking powder and flour. Yeast is normally sold in packages for less than $1. One package will work for one lab group, but only half of the lab groups are using yeast. You only need to buy packets for half of your total number of lab groups. You want to make sure that the yeast is not expired. If you purchase yeast and want to use it later in the year, make sure you store it in a cool, dry area.

Fats and oils (as needed)
- One can of shortening is all you need for years of this lab. Students need a small amount to grease their aluminum foil so the dough does not stick while rising. You also could purchase a nonstick cooking spray, but the shortening option lasts longer and is less expensive.

Aluminum foil
- Each lab group will need a sheet of aluminum foil to use for its dough when it is rising, as well as for cooking. I have students use the same sheet to save money. Rolls are sold in varying quantities, but a 75 yd. roll will work for 100 lab groups.

Plastic knife
- I recommend having one knife for each group. The knives can be cleaned and used for the next class, so buy as many as your largest single class, plus a couple of extras in case there is breakage. Plastic knives are sold individually in boxes of 30–50.

Antibacterial wipe
- Each lab group will need to wipe down its work area thoroughly before placing the flour and dough on the counter. I give each group one wipe, so a typical tube will last for about 60 lab groups, depending on the number of sheets.

120 ml of brown sucrose, $C_{12}H_{22}O_{11}$ (brown sugar)
- Brown sugar can be purchased in the area of the store with white sugar, flour, and other baking items. Brown sugar is often sold in 2 lb. bags, so it will cover almost eight lab groups. *Note*: Brown sugar is not a product that has a long shelf life once the bag is opened. Even if you squeeze out the air and seal it,

it usually gets hard after a few months. I only buy the exact amount I need, rather than buying extra and keeping it for next year.

10 ml of *Cinnamomum zeylanicum* (cinnamon)
- Spice bottles come in a variety of sizes, so it is difficult to predict exactly how many bottles will get you through a set number of lab groups. Most spice bottles have around 4 oz., which is enough for 11 or 12 lab groups.
- When you put out the cinnamon, I recommend placing it in a beaker with a metal scoop. If you leave it in the shaker bottle, students tend to measure out too much, or it gets stuck in the funnel, and a large amount can be wasted.

Cream cheese icing
- You will notice that this item is not included on the student materials list. This is an optional item if you want your final product to look like cinnamon rolls that are sold in stores and food courts. I have found that this cost was not quite worth the difference in taste and that the students enjoyed the rolls without the icing, so the choice is yours.
- If you do offer icing, make sure you do this *after* students have made their mass and dimensional measurements. It will obviously add mass and make measuring more challenging.

Dish soap
- This is necessary for cleanup. I ask students to use an amount about the size of a quarter for each glass container, and I have one bottle available for every four lab groups to share.

SAFETY HIGHLIGHTS
- If a glass stir rod breaks, you should dispose of the entire mixture in the beaker. Even if the break is minor, you may have shards of glass in the mixture that are not visible.
- Because students will be handling the food during the dough-making process, it is important that their work area is sterilized with antibacterial wipes and then covered with a food-safe material such as waxed paper before placing food on the counter. If there is concern about the cleanliness and sanitation of the table or counter space, students need to create their dough in a sterilized bowl.

    Note that these safety highlights are in addition to the safety information detailed in the Safety Protocol section at the beginning of this book. Please refer to that section for additional information about safety when implementing this or any lab in this book.

PREPARATION

1. The milk should be warm for this lab so that the margarine can dissolve. You can set out the milk 45 minutes before the lab or place it in a warm water bath at the start of class. Once the milk has been warmed, it should *not* go back in the refrigerator for later use because of the risk of bacteria.

2. I would also set out the margarine 20 minutes before class so that it can soften and be mixed into the liquid solution.

PROCEDURE

I recommend having students work in teams of three or four for this experiment. The final product creates three or four cinnamon rolls, which is plenty to share among a larger group. There is also a significant amount of labor involved with the preparation of the dough, which can be shared equally by a larger group. The larger group size also cuts down on the total number of lab groups per class and on the overall cost of supplies.

1. You can begin the lab by showing a video clip of a food fight. There are many options, but my favorite is the imagined food fight that takes place in Steven Spielberg's movie *Hook* between Peter and the Lost Boys. There is also the classic food fight scene from the film *Animal House* if you have older students. Any food fight scene will work if it shows different types of foods being thrown. After showing the scene, I ask students to watch the clip a second time and identify the food that they would be *least* happy about being hit with. With those foods in their minds, I create a list on the board named "Qualities of Foods I Would Not Want to Be Hit With." I ask students to share different qualities of the foods they chose from the movie. The list typically consists of a variety of adjectives like *sticky, gooey, staining, heavy*, and *hard*. I focus on words such as *hard* and *heavy*.

2. Show students a marshmallow and a tangerine. These items are about the same size, so ask, "By a show of hands, who would rather be hit by the marshmallow than the tangerine?" Most students choose the marshmallow, and the question then becomes *why?* If it isn't size, then what is it about the marshmallow that makes it more appealing?

3. This brings students to the background information. Ask them to read the Background section as a lab group. While they are doing this, wrap the

marshmallow and tangerine in aluminum foil. Make sure to do this is plain sight so all the students can see. I ask all students to get their goggles and aprons on once they are finished reading.

4. When students finish reading, ask them again *why* the marshmallow is less intimidating in the food fight. This gives students the opportunity to explain the concept of density using their own words, which helps their classmates who struggle with the reading understand the term. You can use the foil-covered objects to show that size doesn't necessary mean mass and density are the same. You can wrap up the discussion by throwing the two foil items out at a student. The student will not duck for the marshmallow, but will usually flinch when you throw what he or she thinks is the tangerine. Instead of throwing the tangerine, throw a foil-covered Ping-Pong ball that you switched out while you were finishing the discussion on density. It is an entertaining moment that helps the students "wake up" and be alert for the lab. It's important that the students have on their aprons and safety goggles as a precautionary measure before items are thrown.

5. Once students have read the Background section, move on to the Hypothesis section, which asks students to predict the relationship between the presence of yeast and the density of the cinnamon roll.

6. Move on to the Setup section and introduce the term *controlled variables* on the board. Depending on your students' background knowledge, they can create their own definition or you can provide them with one to frame the activity. Students will read a short paragraph that outlines the creation of the cinnamon rolls, circling or highlighting the controls present in the procedure. Students should circle all ingredients except for yeast, which is the independent variable. This is a good opportunity to point out that variables can also be actions, such as mixing and dough rise time, and it is important that these are kept the same as well.

7. Students are then instructed to find and label the *independent variable* in the Materials Needed and Procedure sections, which in this case is yeast. It is listed as "One package of active dry *Saccharomyces cerevisiae*" in the Materials Needed and is used in step 5 of the Procedure.

8. Assign student groups their independent variable. Half the class should be making cinnamon rolls with yeast and the other half should be making cinnamon rolls without yeast. Each lab group should be partnered with another lab group that is testing the opposite independent variable so they can share data and cinnamon rolls during the taste testing at the end of the lab. Students who are assigned to not use yeast should cross out yeast in the Materials

Needed section and in step 5 of the Procedure section at that point to remind themselves not to add that ingredient.

9. Students will be creating dough on the tabletop or countertop. You can complete this step on a piece of foil or in a large mixing bowl if you have concerns about the sanitation of your tabletops. I have asked students to bring in plastic or metal mixing bowls in the past.

10. The mountains of dough are messy. Explaining the possible messiness to students helps to prevent some screams that occur when liquid leaks out of the dough. Although there are four students in each lab group, only two need to be involved in the hands-on incorporation of the liquid. Another student can pour liquid in the mountain, while the fourth can be cleaning out used glassware. Remind students of the importance of adding small amounts of liquid at a time so the liquid doesn't leak off the table. *Safety note*: Immediately wipe up any spilled liquids on the floor to prevent a slip/fall hazard.

11. When the dough is finished and students are covering it with a damp paper towel, make sure the towels are not constricting the dough. It is often helpful to walk around and pull the paper towels off the dough and place them back on about 15 minutes into the rising process.

12. There are two options for baking the rolls: First, you can ask the staff in your cafeteria to help you with the baking process. Most schools have rules about students not being in the kitchen, so check with your administrative staff. The second option is to use toaster ovens. I have had several donated so that I am up to four toaster ovens, which work well for cooking rolls in rotation for up to 35 students. You can get inexpensive toaster ovens for around $25. These ovens have made other labs possible as well without bothering the kitchen staff.

13. I handle all the baking of rolls and require that all the students in a single group have all their rolls on a single piece of aluminum foil that can fit in the toaster oven. This cuts down on baking time, allowing you to bake six to eight rolls at once. I also do not hand out a single roll until the entire lab is clean.

14. Once the rolls have cooled, tear the aluminum foil sheet into four pieces and allow each student to take their rolls to measure and then eat while working on their data analysis.

DATA ANALYSIS ANSWER KEY

All the data analysis for this lab is math based. If students are struggling with the questions, I recommend using a sample data set and going through the calculations as a class on the board. Then students can use the same skills and apply them directly to their data.

1. *The area of a circle can be calculated using the following equation:*

$$Area = \pi \times Diameter$$

Calculate the area of the rolls made with Saccharomyces cerevisiae and the area of the rolls made without Saccharomyces cerevisiae in the table below. Show all your work.

Student answers will depend on their rolls, but the calculation process should be the same and use the equation in the question. A sample student calculation might look like this:

	Area of roll (cm²)
Rolls without *Saccharomyces cerevisiae*	Area = π × Diameter = π × 10 cm = 31.4 cm²
Rolls with *Saccharomyces cerevisiae*	Area = π × Diameter = π × 11 cm = 34.54 cm²

2. *The volume of the rolls can be calculated by using the following equation:*

$$Volume = Area \times Height$$

Calculate the volume of the rolls made with Saccharomyces cerevisiae and the volume of the rolls made without Saccharomyces cerevisiae in the table below. Show all your work.

Student answers depend on their rolls, but the calculation process should be the same and use the equation in the question. A sample student calculation might look like this:

	Volume of roll (cm³)
Rolls without *Saccharomyces cerevisiae*	Volume = Area × Height = 31.4 cm² × 8 cm = 251.2 cm³
Rolls with *Saccharomyces cerevisiae*	Volume = Area × Height = 34.54 cm² × 9 cm = 310.86 cm³

3. *The density of the rolls can be calculated by using the following equation:*

$$Density = Mass \div Volume$$

Calculate the density of the rolls made with Saccharomyces cerevisiae *and the density of the rolls made without* Saccharomyces cerevisiae *in the table below. Show all your work.*

Student answers will depend on their rolls, but the calculation process should be the same and use the equation in the question. A sample student calculation might look like this:

	Density of roll (g/cm³)
Rolls without *Saccharomyces cerevisiae*	Density = Mass ÷ Volume = 1,150 g ÷ 251.2 cm³ = 4.578 g/cm³
Rolls with *Saccharomyces cerevisiae*	Density = Mass ÷ Volume = 1150 g ÷ 310.86 cm³ = 3.699 g/cm³

CONCLUSION AND CONNECTIONS ANSWER KEY

This section of the lab offers a great opportunity to engage the entire class in discussion to clarify the main ideas of the lab and allow the students to make their own connections between science and cooking. I ask that students answer the Data Analysis questions and attempt to answer the Conclusion and Connections questions, with the understanding that we will spend time the next day discussing the Conclusion and Connections section.

1. *Was your initial hypothesis correct? Please restate your hypothesis and identify whether you were correct or incorrect using data to support your answer.*

   Students will have different initial answers based on their specific hypothesis but should identify that the trend shows that the density of the roll decreases when yeast is used. The data table in question 3 of the Data Analysis section, which shows that the density of the rolls was lower when yeast was used, supports this answer.

2. *Why would the density for the two rolls be different because of changing the amount of yeast? Explain using your taste observations to support your answer.*

   The density is different because the presence of yeast creates air bubbles within the dough, causing it to rise and gain volume. The mass used in the creation of both rolls should be close to the same, so the change in volume will cause the rolls with yeast to have a lower density. The taste observations should support this when students say it was "light" and "soft" and "chewy," supporting the presence of air pockets and higher volume.

3. *List two examples of starch products that you think are made with yeast and two examples of starch products that you think are not made with yeast.*

   - With yeast: bread, wine, beer, pretzels, coffee cake, pizza dough
   - Without yeast: biscuits, flat bread, pita bread, bran cereal

   In this answer, see that the students have found lighter, less dense products to suggest they were made with yeast.

4. *Identify the other material (besides yeast) that would have caused the exact same difference in density if it were removed from the procedure.*

   The answer is sugar. If sugar were removed, the yeast would not have the food source to go through the process of fermentation. This links back to the background information and shows that the reaction process involves more than one reactant to achieve the final product of gas bubbles in the cinnamon rolls.

5. *In the following diagram, the objects have settled into a specific position based on density. Which item has the highest density? Which liquid has the lowest density? Explain how you arrived at your answer.*

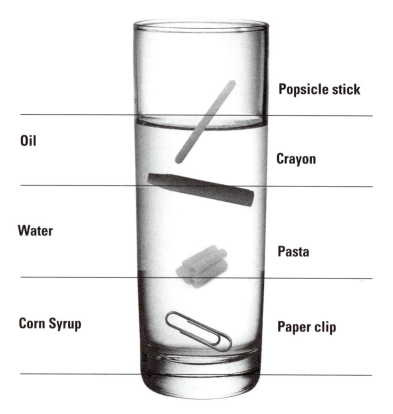

Oil

Water

Corn Syrup

Popsicle stick

Crayon

Pasta

Paper clip

The cup shows the stratification of objects based on their density. The item with the highest density is going to be the paper clip, because it settled at the bottom of the glass. The liquid with the lowest density is the oil because it settles on top of the other liquids. Student errors occur on this question because students do not correctly read that the question about highest density is asking for an object, while the second question about lowest density is asking about a liquid. This is a good opportunity to remind students about the importance of reading through an entire question and underlining important information. This question can lead to a follow-up discussion about the density of ice being less than water, which is why it floats.

CROSS-CURRICULAR NOTE: MATH

This is a great opportunity to incorporate math and geometry in a real-life application. Using the equations for area (two-dimensional) and volume (three-dimensional) creates a strong connection between math and science.

CROSS-CURRICULAR NOTE: LITERACY

There are several companies that are known for their baked goods such as Cinnabon, Pillsbury, Krispy Kreme, and Dunkin Donuts. Ask students to create a timeline that shows the progression of a company from time of origination to present. Students can compare and contrast the growth of the company to the rising of the dough in this experiment.

OPTIONAL EXTENSIONS

Middle School

1. Students can measure the volume and mass of different candies such as licorice, taffy, and chocolate to find the densities of the different candies. This can be compared with the overall health of the product determined by calories or fat content.

2. Students can measure the density of other starch products and predict the presence of yeast and the amount of time it was allowed to rise.

3. Students can make cinnamon rolls using different amounts of rise time to see how reaction time impacts the density of the roll.

High School

1. Students can identify the roll of each ingredient by creating a control set. For example, one group can create rolls without the egg, another can create rolls without the milk, and so on. Ask students how the control set informs them about the role of each ingredient in the process.

2. Students can use the density of the objects to predict the amount of carbon dioxide that was formed in the time the yeast was allowed to rise. Ask students how this rate relates back to the chemical equation for fermentation.

EXPERIMENT 11:
Growing a Pancake: Student Pages

HOW ENVIRONMENTAL FACTORS IMPACT FUNGI GROWTH IN A SOURDOUGH STARTER

BACKGROUND

Many people spend time cultivating and tending gardens that grow items such as tomatoes, herbs, strawberries, and other produce. But how many people do you know who can grow pancakes? This experiment is all about growing pancakes, or at least an ingredient—yeast— that is found in pancakes. Yeast is a fungus that can be purchased at the grocery store in granular form. To "wake up" the yeast, you can add warm water and sugar to the package to get the process of fermentation started; in this process, yeast creates CO_2 gas based on sugars.

But sometimes purchasing an item at the store isn't as satisfying as creating it yourself. Yeast is a common unicellular organism that is found in our environment and can be cultured and grown without using a store brand. This is called making a "starter" in the world of cooking.

So how do you grow yeast on your own? You have to make an inviting environment for the fungi. Once the fungi have made their home in your environment, you tend to them with nutrients and care for them in the same way people care for plants in their gardens. After a few days you have your very own yeast factory. If cared for properly, yeast starters can last for several months or even years.

In this experiment we will be making a yeast starter over the process of several days using flour and pineapple juice. If you are successful in caring for your starter, you will have the last ingredient necessary to make your own pancakes.

HYPOTHESIS

How will you know that you have grown yeast? Predict at least three characteristics of the starter you might observe that will let you know that you have grown yeast. For each observation, explain how that observation will let you know yeast is growing.

MATERIALS NEEDED PER GROUP

General Materials
- Indirectly vented chemical-splash goggles
- Aprons

Materials for Growing a Starter
- 160 ml of powdered grain (flour)
- 90 ml of *Ananas comosus* liquid with no additional sucrose (pineapple juice)
- 45 ml of warm dihydrogen monoxide, H_2O (warm water)
- Small plastic jar with lid, or plastic cup with plastic wrap
- Graduated cylinder
- Glass stir rod

Materials for Making Sourdough Pancakes
- 60 ml of fungi starter
- 120 ml of pancake mix
- 85 ml of dihydrogen monoxide, H_2O (water)
- Beaker, 400 ml
- Glass stir rod
- Griddle
- Spatula
- Powdered sucrose to taste, $C_{12}H_{22}O_{11}$ (powdered sugar)

PROCEDURE FOR GROWING A STARTER

Day 1

1. Read through the entire procedure before beginning.

2. Put on your safety goggles and apron and gather all your materials at your lab station. If you notice any of the materials are dirty or discolored, notify your teacher.

3. Using masking tape, label your plastic container with your name and your partner's name.

4. Using a graduated cylinder, measure out 50 ml of powdered grain and place it in the plastic container.

5. Add 60 ml of *Ananas comosus* liquid with no additional sucrose to the plastic container and stir with a glass stir rod.

6. Make an initial observation and record it in your Starter Observation Data Table. You will need to make an observation of your starter each day during class. Your observations can include things you notice by sight, smell, texture, or sound. Do *not* taste the starter.

7. Cover the plastic container and let it sit for 48 hours at room temperature. Your mixture can be stirred vigorously two or three times a day.

8. Wash your hands thoroughly.

Day 3

1. Put on your safety goggles and apron and gather all your materials at your lab station. If you notice any of the materials are dirty or discolored, notify your teacher.

2. Check your plastic container and make an observation to record in your Starter Observation Data Table for Day 3.

3. Using a graduated cylinder, measure out 30 ml of powdered grain and place it in the plastic container.

4. Add 30 ml of *Ananas comosus* liquid with no additional sucrose to the plastic container and stir with a glass stir rod.

5. Cover the plastic container and let it sit for 48 hours at room temperature. Your mixture can be stirred vigorously two or three times a day.

6. Wash your hands thoroughly.

Day 5

1. Put on your safety goggles and apron and gather all your materials at your lab station. If you notice any of the materials are dirty or discolored, notify your teacher.

2. Check your plastic container and make an observation to record in your Starter Observation Data Table for Day 5.

3. Using a graduated cylinder, measure out 80 ml of powdered grain and place it in the plastic container.

4. Add 45 ml of warm H_2O to the plastic container and stir with a glass stir rod.

5. Cover the plastic container and let it sit for 24 hours at room temperature.

6. Wash your hands thoroughly.

PROCEDURE FOR SOURDOUGH PANCAKES

1. Put on your safety goggles and gather all your materials at your lab station. If you notice any of the materials are dirty or discolored, notify your teacher.

2. Measure 120 ml of pancake mix into a 400 ml beaker.

3. Add 60 ml of your fungi starter and 85 ml of H_2O to the pancake mix in the 400 ml beaker. Mix thoroughly.

4. Take your batter to the hot grill to have your teacher bake your fungi. Sprinkle with powdered sucrose as desired.

5. Clean up your lab station and answer the Data Analysis and Conclusions and Connections questions.

DATA AND OBSERVATIONS

Starter Observation	
	Observations: Sight, Texture, Smell, or Sound (no Taste)
Day 1	
Day 3	
Day 5	

DATA ANALYSIS

For each of the following questions, be sure to explain using detail and complete sentences. If the question requires you to complete calculations, show all of your work.

1. What were some observations that showed you fungi were growing in your starter? Explain, citing the specific day you made that observation.

2. What do you think caused the smell of the starter? Explain using the information in the Background section to support your answer.

CONCLUSION AND CONNECTIONS

1. What were two of the conditions that made the yeast "comfortable" in the environment you created? Explain why these conditions were helpful for cultivating yeast.

2. You had to remove some of your starter to make your pancake. How could you go about replacing that starter without repeating the entire procedure?

3. The liquid used in the starter contained citric acid. Why was the presence of acid helpful in creating a starter that was safe and edible as opposed to dangerous?

4. Now that you have your starter, what kind of an environment will you keep it in to maintain its active culture?

EXPERIMENT 11:
Growing a Pancake: Teacher Pages

HOW ENVIRONMENTAL FACTORS IMPACT FUNGI GROWTH IN A SOURDOUGH STARTER

This experiment allows students to grow their own fungi. Students are asked to grow a yeast fungi culture that is called a "starter" in the world of cooking. By creating an ideal environment, students are able to cultivate wild yeast over a period of five days. The wild yeast can then be used to create a basic sourdough pancake. This lab is designed to provide a hands-on experience that highlights how fungi grow and reproduce in ideal environments, while making a connection with the culinary world in a way that is inexpensive and edible.

STANDARDS ADDRESSED
National Science Education Standards: Grades 5–8

Content Standard A: Science as Inquiry
- Abilities necessary to do scientific inquiry
- Understanding about scientific inquiry

Content Standard B: Physical Science
- Properties and changes of properties in matter

Content Standard C: Life Science
- Structure and function in living systems
- Reproduction and heredity
- Regulation and behavior
- Population and ecosystems

Content Standard E: Science and Technology
- Abilities of technological design
- Understanding about science and technology

Content Standard F: Science in Personal and Social Perspectives
- Science and technology in society

Content Standard G: History and Nature of Science
- Science as a human endeavor
- Nature of science

National Science Education Standards: Grades 9–12

Content Standard A: Science as Inquiry
- Abilities necessary to do scientific inquiry
- Understanding about scientific inquiry

Content Standard B: Physical Science
- Structure of atoms
- Structure and properties of matter
- Chemical reactions

Content Standard C: Life Science
- The cell
- Interdependence of organisms
- Matter, energy, and organization in living systems

Content Standard E: Science and Technology
- Abilities of technological design
- Understanding about science and technology

Content Standard F: Science in Personal and Social Perspectives
- Science and technology in local, national, and global challenges

Content Standard G: History and Nature of Science
- Science as a human endeavor
- Nature of scientific knowledge
- Historical perspectives

VOCABULARY

Yeast: Any of various unicellular fungi of the genus *Saccharomyces*, especially *S. cerevisiae*, reproducing by budding and from ascospores and capable of fermenting carbohydrates (*The American Heritage Dictionary of the English Language* 2000).

Limiting factor: Any environmental factor that limits the growth, reproduction, and population expansion of an individual organism. Examples include availability of food supplies, shelter, and disease.

Asexual reproduction: Reproduction by one sex that results in an identical genetic offspring.

MATERIALS NEEDED, DECODED FOR THE GROCERY STORE

160 ml of powdered grain (flour)
- Flour is sold in the area of the grocery store with sugar and other baking products. A 5 lb. bag will be enough for 14 or 15 lab groups to create a starter.
- You can purchase whatever kind of flour you would like, such as white, whole wheat, or rye. See Optional Extensions for additional ideas on using different types of flour.

90 ml of *Ananas comosus* liquid with no additional sucrose (pineapple juice)
- You can obtain pineapple juice from a can of pineapple slices, or buy pineapple juice from the juice aisle.
- It is easier to find unsweetened pineapple juice at health food grocery stores that sell organic and local products.
- The pineapple juice is used because it contains a higher level of citric acid, which helps prevent the growth of another type of bacteria that is harmful in the starter.

Small plastic jar with lid, or plastic cup with plastic wrap
- Each student group will need a plastic container to keep its starter. You can purchase small plastic containers in the grocery store in the aisle with sandwich bags and foil. You can also use plastic cups (larger than bathroom drinking cups) along with plastic wrap and a rubber band as an alternative.

120 ml of pancake mix
- I recommend buttermilk pancake mix for this recipe. Pancake mix is sold in containers of different sizes. A 40 oz. box will be enough for 10 lab groups.

Griddle
- I bring in a large electric griddle to make the pancakes. This is a time saver, and I have never had much success grilling the pancakes over a Bunsen burner. You could use a pan over a hot plate, but I think the griddle is easier, especially if you have a large number of students.

Powdered sucrose to taste, $C_{12}H_{22}O_{11}$ (powdered sugar)
- I use powdered sugar for the pancakes. It is less expensive than syrup and tends to go further. My only warning is that students will use whatever amount you put out, so I tend to ration the powdered sugar, putting out a set amount for each class.

Dish soap
- This is necessary for cleanup. I ask students to use an amount about the size of a quarter for each glass container, and I have one bottle available for every four lab groups to share.

SAFETY HIGHLIGHTS
- Students should wash their hands after working with the starter mix each day. This is to prevent the spread of any unwanted bacteria. I ask that all students wash their hands thoroughly with soap and water in our daily "hand washing parties" during this lab. You can also use hand sanitizer if there are not enough sinks for students to use.
- If any of the starter organisms appear to grow mold or show other irregularities in color, smell, or texture, disinfect the cup with bleach and throw away the starter immediately to prevent the growth and spread of unwanted pathogens.

Note that these safety highlights are in addition to the safety information detailed in the Safety Protocol section at the beginning of this book. Please refer to that section for additional information about safety when implementing this or any lab in this book.

PREPARATION

1. This lab takes five days, so make sure you begin on the Monday of a five-day school week, unless you want to send the starters home with the students and ask them to bring them back.

2. This lab can get smelly. The sourdough starter definitely has a pungent smell, and by Days 4 and 5 the smell is particularly strong. I keep the starter cups near a window but not in direct sunlight, and use plug-in air fresheners for the last day to dissipate the smell. *Safety note*: Some students may be allergic to air fresheners, in which case you should avoid using them. Whatever you do, do *not* leave any starters sitting out over the weekend. If they are unclaimed, they go in the dumpster.

PROCEDURE

I recommend that students work individually or in pairs of two for this experiment. The work and data collection is simple enough that two students are ideal for the experiment.

1. Begin with a question to the students: "What could I do to make my classroom more comfortable for you?" Have students brainstorm ideas that would make them more comfortable. Suggestions may include more comfortable furniture, different lighting, snacks and beverages, and access to video games. Then ask students, "What do you think would happen to the classroom if I did all those things?" Ideally, students would want to spend more time in the classroom, and perhaps hang out there during their free time. As more students would come to the science classroom, the student population there would grow. This analogy works well for what the students are to be doing in the lab.

2. Have students read the Background section in their lab groups. Depending on the student's background with yeast, it may be helpful to show a short Internet video of yeast under the microscope. You can also set up a few microscopes and wet mount slides using yeast from the grocery store.

3. In their hypothesis, students are asked to come up with three characteristics that would show that yeast was growing in their starter. *Note*: Students can make observations with all of their senses except for taste. There will be no tasting of the starter, so encourage them to use observations with their other four senses.

4. For this experiment, students will begin a starter, which takes about 10–15 minutes to set up. The starters will need to be covered and kept in a room-temperature environment. I recommend having trays for each of the class periods to keep the starters organized.

5. Students need to stir the starter vigorously two or three times per day. I recommend that one of these times be during their science class. The other time can be in the morning before school, at the end of the school day, lunch, or whenever they have free time. Ideally, these two times occur at least an hour or two apart. You can compare students' dedication to their yeast to having a pet because it needs to be cared for. The more thoughtful they are about caring for the yeast, the better the yeast will grow, giving them a better pancake.

6. I encourage the students to name their yeast starters to build a connection. Secondary students benefit from being able to give the fungi a name to help them recognize the starter as a living organism. The recognition that the starter is alive helps students to be invested in the detail required for growing it and learn the day-to-day procedures that support the growth of the fungi. The connection improves the experiment and makes for an enhanced discussion about how limiting factors can exist for other living organisms as well.

7. To see if the yeast is growing, students should start to see bubbles in their starter by Day 4. If there are no bubbles by that day, the starter has not worked and students should throw it away (in a trash bag that can be taken out to the dumpster) and start again. I recommend that all students make a starter, so that there are plenty of starters to be shared in the creation of pancakes if several do not grow.

8. On the final day, students can use their starter to create the sourdough pancakes. The recipe in the lab is the most basic pancake recipe that I have found to be successful. There are more complex pancake recipes, and students can be encouraged to research those recipes and bring in additional materials to upgrade their pancake products if they are interested.

9. The pancakes for this final product are cooked on a griddle. The teacher should be in charge of the griddle, although you can allow students to flip their own pancakes if they are older and you are supervising the cooking. You can try having students grill their pancakes in oiled aluminum foil using a hot plate or Bunsen burner, but I have not had much success with that approach.

DATA ANALYSIS ANSWER KEY

1. *What were some observations that showed you fungi were growing in your starter? Explain, citing the specific day you made that observation.*

   Students may have a host of observations that lead them to believe that fungi are growing. The most common observation is the formation of gas bubbles. The gas bubbles are a product of fermentation and show the presence of CO_2. Students also might note smell, a thickening of the paste, and/or a change in volume. The important part of this answer is that students relate the answer back to their data.

2. *What do you think caused the smell of the starter? Explain using the information in the Background section to support your answer.*

   The smell of the starter comes from the fermentation of sugars and the production of CO_2 by the yeast. It is also the smell of yeast that can be detected as the fungi multiply.

CONCLUSION AND CONNECTIONS ANSWER KEY

This section of the lab offers a great opportunity to engage the entire class in discussion to clarify the main ideas of the lab and allow the students to make their own connections between science and cooking. I ask that students answer the Data Analysis questions and attempt to answer the Conclusion and Connections questions, with the understanding that we will spend time the next day discussing the Conclusion and Connections section.

1. *What were two of the conditions that made the yeast "comfortable" in the environment you created? Explain why these conditions were helpful for cultivating yeast.*

   One environmental condition is the room temperature. Yeast fungi will thrive at room temperature, which is why bread is allowed to rise at room temperature. If the temperature were too hot it would kill the yeast; too cold, and the yeast would slow down and "hibernate." Another condition is the presence of flour and pineapple juice. This is a starch and sugar combination that is the ideal food for yeast, allowing them to grow and thrive. Another condition is the liquid environment. Yeast appreciates moisture for growth and movement in their environment. Students need to come up with two environmental qualities that allow for the wild yeast to grow.

2. *You had to remove some of your starter to make your pancake. How could you go about replacing that starter without repeating the entire procedure?*

This is the idea of a self-replacing starter. By adding more flour, sugar, and liquid, the yeast will continue to replicate and replace the yeast that was removed. Many people have starters that have been passed to them by friends. Once you have a yeast growth going, you can keep it alive and in production by keeping the environment free of limiting factors. A good rule to share with students during this discussion is that you want to replace the amount of starter you removed. For example, if you remove a cup of starter, you want to replace it with a cup of flour and half a cup of water.

3. *The liquid used in the starter contained citric acid. Why was the presence of acid helpful in creating a starter that was safe and edible as opposed to dangerous?*

Citric acid allows yeast fungi to live but prevents other dangerous bacteria from growing because it is an acid. The hydrogen ion concentration is a destructive limiting factor for many bacteria. You can allow students to research the specific bacteria types that are prevented in yeast starters by including citric acid.

4. *Now that you have your starter, what kind of an environment will you keep it in to maintain its active culture?*

Again, fungi want an ideal environment that is free of limiting factors. This environment includes a nice room temperature (although the starter also can be kept in the refrigerator as well), plenty of flour and moisture, and movement in the mixture. Students are encouraged to take their starter home to share in their personal kitchens. If they are going to keep it for an extended period of time, I encourage them to transfer the starter into a glass jar with a stronger seal.

CROSS-CURRICULAR NOTE: MATH

Ask students, "How do you take a recipe and alter it to fit the needs of your group?" Then have students make conversions for the recipe in order to create enough pancakes to feed the entire class, then the entire grade, then the entire school.

CROSS-CURRICULAR NOTE: LITERACY

This experiment focuses on the needs of the yeast to grow and develop. Read the picture book *If You Give a Pig a Pancake* by Laura Numeroff. This book talks about the needs of a pig if you give him a pancake. Ask students to write a short story with a similar structure; the story should outline the needs of the yeast to become incorporated into a pancake.

OPTIONAL EXTENSIONS

Middle School

1. Students can grow starters with different types of flour such as whole grain and rye. Have them look at the yeast under the microscope and determine how the organisms are different. Then students can bake with these different starters, and examine what changes occur when they use different types of flour.

2. Students can examine samples of the starter over an extended period of time and measure the amount of organisms in a sample under the microscope. Using this observation, they can estimate the total number of yeast organisms in a starter, and see how adding resources like sugar and flour impacts the population.

High School

1. Students can take a sample from the starter to view under the microscope to look for evidence of asexual reproduction occurring among the yeast.

2. Make the lab more inquiry based by asking students to create a recipe for growing a starter based on the background information. Encourage students to design an experiment to find the ideal growing environment for yeast.

3. Ask students to analyze the cellular structure of yeast. Based on this structure, ask students to construct what they believe the best environmental conditions would be for the organism, relating each condition back to the organism's physical structure. This is an ideal opportunity to discuss adaptation with students and even begin to discuss early life on Earth and evolution.

EXPERIMENT 12:
Under Pressure: Student Pages

DETERMINING THE MATHEMATICAL RELATIONSHIP FOR YEAST FERMENTATION IN THE CREATION OF MINT GINGER SODA

BACKGROUND

As a student, you are always under pressure: under pressure to get a project finished, to win a game, to ask another student to the school dance, and to do an amazing job on your science lab writeup. All of these pressures aren't necessarily equal, which brings us to this lab in which you will be measuring the volume created by the pressure of homemade mint ginger soda.

Mint ginger soda is an example of a carbonated beverage. Carbonated beverages also go by the name *soda pop* because of the popping noise the beverages make when the can or bottle is opened. So how do you get a beverage to be carbonated? There are actually several techniques to infuse a liquid with gas, but for this lab you will be using a biological agent: yeast.

Yeast is a bacterium that feeds on sugar in a process called *fermentation* to form two products, one of which is carbon dioxide. The chemical equation for fermentation is as follows:

$$\text{Yeast} + \underset{\text{(sugar)}}{C_6H_{12}O_6} \rightarrow \underset{\text{(ethanol)}}{2C_2H_5OH} + \underset{\text{(carbon dioxide)}}{2CO_2}$$
$$\underset{\text{(fungi)}}{}$$

If you place yeast in a container and seal it, you can measure the amount of fermentation that is taking place based on the amount of gas that is produced. This information can be useful in telling you about the fermentation rate.

So relax; this lab is all about creating pressure, not crumbling under it. Take a deep breath and get excited about making your own mint ginger soda.

HYPOTHESIS

Is the relationship between the amount of gas produced over time by yeast linear or exponential? (Linear means the yeast rate of producing gas is constant. Exponential means the yeast rate of producing gas is faster over time.) Make a hypothesis and explain your prediction using background information.

MATERIALS NEEDED PER GROUP

- 20 g of *Zingiber officinale* root (ginger root)
- 1060 ml of dihydrogen monoxide, H_2O (water)
- 10 *Mentha sachalinensis* leaves (mint leaves)
- 120 ml of sucrose, $C_{12}H_{22}O_{11}$ (sugar)
- One-half package of yeast
- Plastic knife, one per student
- Paper towel
- Cheesecloth or gauze cloth
- Rubber band
- Beaker, 600 ml
- Beaker, 1000 ml
- Graduated cylinders
- Balance
- Bunsen burner and ring stand
- Tongs
- Glass stir rod
- Empty plastic bottles with lids
- Erlenmeyer flask, 250 ml
- Balloon (nonlatex)
- Metric measuring tape
- Indirectly vented chemical-splash goggles
- Aprons

PROCEDURE

1. Read through the entire procedure before beginning.

2. Put on your safety goggles and apron, and gather all your materials at your lab station. If you notice any of the materials are dirty or discolored, notify your teacher.

3. Set up a Bunsen burner and ring stand with wire mesh on the iron ring. Make sure your Bunsen burner gas intake tube is securely connected to the gas nozzle and that the ring is set about 3 inches above the barrel of the burner (see Figure 12.1). Light the Bunsen burner to create a flame that is no more than 3 in. high. (It should not be touching the wire mesh.)

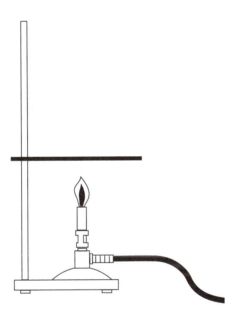

Figure 12.1: Bunsen burner and ring stand.

4. Measure 500 ml of H_2O into a 1,000 ml beaker. Use the tongs to place the beaker on the ring stand, and then bring the water to a boil.

5. While waiting for the water to boil, use the balance to measure a piece of *Zingiber officinale* root that is between 20 and 30 g.

6. Use the plastic knife to peel the bark off the *Zingiber officinale* root. The bark is fairly soft, so it shouldn't take a lot of pressure. Make sure you are using the knife to peel away from yourself and your fingers. Discard the bark in the trash.

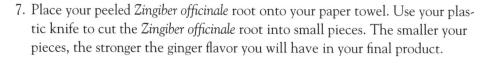

7. Place your peeled *Zingiber officinale* root onto your paper towel. Use your plastic knife to cut the *Zingiber officinale* root into small pieces. The smaller your pieces, the stronger the ginger flavor you will have in your final product.

8. Take the pieces of *Zingiber officinale* and add to the 1,000 ml beaker of boiling water.

9. Tear 10 *Mentha sachalinensis* leaves into small pieces. Add the *Mentha sachalinensis* leaves to the 1,000 ml beaker of boiling water. *Safety note:* Cautiously add the pieces to the boiling water because the water can splash and cause serious burns.

10. Once the mint ginger water boils, reduce the size of the flame to allow the solution to simmer for eight minutes.

11. Use the tongs to remove the beaker from the ring stand. Allow the solution to cool for 10 minutes.

12. While you are waiting for the solution to cool, place a double layer of cheesecloth or gauze over the top of a 600 ml beaker. Push the cloth into the beaker about one-fourth of the way and then secure the cloth in place by placing a rubber band around the edges of the cloth.

13. Dissolve half a package of yeast in 60 ml of warm water. Place this to the side.

14. Strain the mint ginger solution through the cloth and into the 600 ml beaker.

15. Remove the cloth and remaining matter and dispose into the trash.

16. Using a graduated cylinder, measure 120 ml of sucrose. Use a glass stir rod to mix this into the mint ginger solution until thoroughly dissolved.

17. Add the 60 ml of yeast solution to the 600 ml beaker and stir with a glass stir rod.

18. Measure 150 ml of the mint ginger yeast solution into a 250 ml Erlenmeyer flask. Fill the entire remainder of the flask with water, all the way to the lip. Label the flask with your name.

19. Place a balloon over the top of the flask. Secure the balloon in place with a rubber band so no air is leaking.

20. Use the metric measuring tape to find the circumference of the deflated balloon. Record the measurement in your Gas Volume Data Table. You will be taking a measurement every day in class for the rest of the week. Place your flask in the designated area for your class.

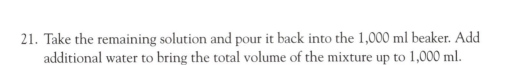

21. Take the remaining solution and pour it back into the 1,000 ml beaker. Add additional water to bring the total volume of the mixture up to 1,000 ml.

22. Fill your bottle, leaving 5 cm of air space at the top. Place the cap on the bottle. Squeeze out as much air as possible so the liquid rises all the way to the top, and then seal the bottle.

23. Label your bottle clearly with your name.

24. The bottles will be a bit difficult to stand up because of the lack of pressure. This will improve over time, but for the rest of class, lay the bottles on their sides.

25. Clean your lab area and answer the Data Analysis and Conclusions and Connections questions.

26. On Day 4, move the bottles to a cool environment to refrigerate before drinking on Day 5.

DATA AND OBSERVATIONS

Gas Volume Data Table	
	Circumference of balloon (cm)
Day 1	
Day 2	
Day 3	
Day 4	
Day 5	

DATA ANALYSIS

For each of the following questions, be sure to explain using detail and complete sentences. If the question requires you to complete calculations, show all of your work.

1. The equation for circumference of a circle is:

    $$C = 2\pi \times radius$$

    Using this equation and the data obtained in your experiment, solve for the radius of each day's balloon in the table below. Be sure to show your work.

	Radius of balloon
Day 1	
Day 2	
Day 3	
Day 4	
Day 5	

2. The equation for volume of a sphere is:

    $$Volume = 4/3 \times \pi \times (radius)^3$$

    Using this equation and the data obtained in Data Analysis question 1, solve for the volume of each day's balloon in the table below. Be sure to show your work.

	Volume of balloon
Day 1	
Day 2	
Day 3	
Day 4	
Day 5	

3. Create a line graph that shows change in gas volume created when compared to time. Remember to include all elements of a scientific graph (title, labeled axes, units, etc.).

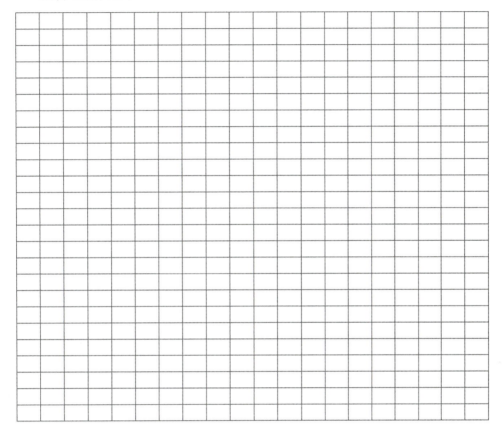

CONCLUSION AND CONNECTIONS

1. Was your initial hypothesis correct? Restate your hypothesis and identify whether you were correct or incorrect, using data to support your answer.

2. How large do you think the balloon would be if you measured the volume tomorrow? Explain how you arrived at your answer.

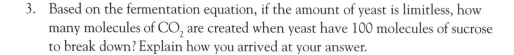

3. Based on the fermentation equation, if the amount of yeast is limitless, how many molecules of CO_2 are created when yeast have 100 molecules of sucrose to break down? Explain how you arrived at your answer.

4. What would happen to your soda bottles if you allowed the yeast to continue to ferment for another two weeks?

5. Why do you think that soda pop manufacturers do not use yeast in the creation of their product?

EXPERIMENT 12:
Under Pressure: Teacher Pages

DETERMINING THE MATHEMATICAL RELATIONSHIP FOR YEAST FERMENTATION IN THE CREATION OF MINT GINGER SODA

This experiment presents a different approach to using the biological agent of yeast in a liquid format. Rather than using the yeast in a baking procedure, the fermentation process is highlighted as part of the creation of a carbonated beverage. In this case, mint ginger soda is created to show students how yeast forms carbon dioxide when digesting sugar molecules. The experiment takes one day, with observations and fermentation taking place over the course of a week. Students then use geometry equations about circumference and volume of a sphere to calculate the volume of gas created by the yeast. This is an ideal lab for doing cross-curricular work with math because it also looks at describing the data trend as linear or exponential. From the calculations to the carbonation, this lab incorporates skills and content in a hands-on learning experience that is exciting for all involved.

STANDARDS ADDRESSED
National Science Education Standards: Grades 5–8

Content Standard A: Science as Inquiry
- Abilities necessary to do scientific inquiry
- Understanding about scientific inquiry

Content Standard B: Physical Science
- Properties and changes of properties in matter

Content Standard C: Life Science
- Structure and function in living systems
- Regulation and behavior

Content Standard E: Science and Technology
- Abilities of technological design
- Understanding about science and technology

Content Standard F: Science in Personal and Social Perspectives
- Science and technology in society

Content Standard G: History and Nature of Science
- Science as a human endeavor
- Nature of science

National Science Education Standards: Grades 9–12

Content Standard A: Science as Inquiry
- Abilities necessary to do scientific inquiry
- Understanding about scientific inquiry

Content Standard B: Physical Science
- Structure of atoms
- Structure and properties of matter
- Chemical reactions

Content Standard C: Life Science
- The cell
- Interdependence of organisms
- Matter, energy, and organization in living systems

Content Standard E: Science and Technology
- Abilities of technological design
- Understanding about science and technology

Content Standard F: Science in Personal and Social Perspectives
- Population growth
- Science and technology in local, national, and global challenges

Content Standard G: History and Nature of Science
- Science as a human endeavor
- Nature of scientific knowledge
- Historical perspectives

VOCABULARY

Yeast: Any of various unicellular fungi of the genus *Saccharomyces*, especially *S. cerevisiae*, reproducing by budding and from ascospores and capable of fermenting carbohydrates (*The American Heritage Dictionary of the English Language* 2000).

Fermentation: The conversion of carbohydrates into alcohols and carbon dioxide in a biochemical reaction facilitated by microorganisms. The equation for fermentation is as follows:

$$\underset{\text{(fungi)}}{\text{Yeast}} \quad + \quad \underset{\text{(sugar)}}{C_6H_{12}O_6} \quad \rightarrow \quad \underset{\text{(ethanol)}}{2C_2H_5OH} \quad + \quad \underset{\text{(carbon dioxide)}}{2CO_2}$$

Pressure: The force applied to a unit area of surface, measured in pascals (SI unit) or in dynes (cgs unit); the compressed gas exerts an increased pressure (Princeton University 2006).

Linear relationship: A relationship in which a fixed change in x, y increases or decreases by a fixed amount.

Exponential relationship: A relationship in which a fixed change in x, y gets multiplied by a fixed amount.

MATERIALS NEEDED, DECODED FOR THE GROCERY STORE

20 g of *Zingiber officinale* root (ginger root)
- Fresh ginger root is available in the produce section of the grocery store, often in a basket near other root products like turnips. I have also seen it sold with fresh herbs. The root is sold by the pound and is a relatively inexpensive purchase. One pound is about 450 g, which will cover 20 lab groups.

10 *Mentha sachalinensis* leaves (mint leaves)
- These are also sold in the produce section with other fresh herbs. If leaves aren't available, you can use mint flavoring (which is available in the spice section of the store). Each group needs about 10 mint leaves, so a bunch will cover anywhere from 10 to 15 lab groups.

120 ml of sucrose, $C_{12}H_{22}O_{11}$ (sugar)
- Sugar is sold in the area of the grocery store with flour and other baking products. A 5 lb. bag will be enough for about 15 lab groups.

One-half package of yeast
- Yeast can be purchased in the baking section of the store with the baking powder and flour. Yeast is sold in packages for less than $1. One package will work for two lab groups, so base your quantity on the number of lab groups that will be completing this lab.
- Make sure that the yeast is not expired. If you purchase yeast and want to use it later in the year, make sure you store it in a cool, dry area.

Plastic knife
- I recommend having one knife for each student. This is helpful in allowing the students to chop up the ginger root faster by splitting it up. The knives can be cleaned and used for the next class, so buy as many as you'll need for your largest class, plus a few extras in case there is breakage. Plastic knives are sold individually in boxes of 30–50.

Cheesecloth or gauze
- You can usually find cheesecloth in a gourmet shop. I have never found any at the grocery stores I frequent, so I buy gauze cloth in bulk. This can be found in the first-aid section of the store or in a school nurse's office. Each student group needs two pieces to fit over the mouth of a 600 ml beaker.

Rubber band
- Each group needs a rubber band to secure its cloth to the beaker for straining the liquid from the ginger and mint pieces.

Empty plastic bottles with lids
- There are two ways I have approached this in the past. The first is to purchase a large case of water (18–24 plastic bottles). The students dump out the water in class, or into a gallon container to be used later as distilled water. Then each student can have a water bottle to fill with mint ginger soda. The cost of a case of water varies from $5 to $8. The second option is to ask students to bring in their own soda bottles. If your school sells soda or juice in plastic bottles at lunch, the students can reuse those containers. The only problem I had with this approach was that students had containers of all different sizes, making the division of soda unequal among the groups. If you go this route, give them a maximum size the bottle can be. It's also a good idea to buy an extra case of water for students who do not bring a bottle.

Balloon
- Each student group will need one balloon to gather gas. Purchase only nonlatex balloons. You want regular party balloons, not water balloons or

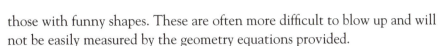

those with funny shapes. These are often more difficult to blow up and will not be easily measured by the geometry equations provided.

- Balloons can be fairly expensive at grocery stores, where they cost up to $4 for a package of eight. Party stores, however, sell balloons in packages of 100 for about the same price.

Metric measuring tape
- This tape is necessary to measure around the circumference of the balloon. If you do not have measuring tapes, you can use a piece of string or yarn and compare it to a ruler or meterstick.

Paper towel
- Each student group will need one paper towel to cut its ginger root. A single roll of paper towels will meet the needs of more than 100 students.

Dish soap
- This is necessary for cleanup. I ask students to use an amount about the size of a quarter for each glass container, and I have one bottle available for every four lab groups to share.

SAFETY HIGHLIGHTS

- The Bunsen burners and ring stands present a potential for students to burn themselves if used incorrectly. Please make sure students have had Bunsen burner safety training before allowing them to participate in this lab. As a teacher, you also need to be prepared with burn treatment options, such as running the burned area under cold water, if a student gets hurt.
- If a glass stir rod breaks during mixing, you should dispose of the entire mixture. Even if the break is minor, you may have shards of glass in the mixture that are not visible.
- It is important to note that students are creating pressure inside a sealed bottle. If this pressure continues to build without being released, the bottle will explode. This could be either a large mess, or worse, a student getting hit in the eye with an accelerating bottle lid. I have students mature the liquid and consume the beverage at school. This prevents any issues with overfermentation or bottles with too much pressure occurring outside the lab environment. *Safety note*: Bottles must be depressurized upon completing the experiment to prevent danger of explosion.

Note that these safety highlights are in addition to the safety information detailed in the Safety Protocol section at the beginning of this book. Please refer to that section for additional information about safety when implementing this or any lab in this book.

PREPARATION

1. This lab takes five days, so make sure you begin on a Monday of a five-day school week. If you continue the lab over a weekend, it will be more difficult for students to use the data to determine the type of mathematical relationship that is being exhibited by the yeast.

2. Set aside plastic bins for the balloon-covered flasks. Label each bin with the class period. I have found that bins protect the glassware better than trays, and because they are out for a week, this is a beneficial step to take.

3. It is also helpful to have a separate space set aside for the mint ginger soda bottles to ferment. This should be separate from the glass flasks (again, to prevent breakage), and should be labeled clearly before the start of the lab.

PROCEDURE

I recommend that students work in groups of two for this experiment. The recipe makes plenty of mint ginger soda (enough for about two and a half bottles), and when groups are larger, students get a bit upset about the amount they receive. The work and data collection is also simple enough that two students are ideal for the experiment.

1. An effective introduction to this activity can be asking students to close their eyes and make a sound observation. Once they all have their eyes closed, open a can of soda, cracking the seal loudly. It is best to do this in the middle of the student's desks rather than the front of the room so everyone can hear clearly. Put the soda can under a cardboard box and ask students to open their eyes and identify what they heard. Have them share their observations with a partner, and then share with the entire class. Record observations on the board. Inevitably, a student will tell you the noise was made by a soda can. This is a great opportunity to distinguish between an observation (which was required to be made by sound) and an inference.

2. Once students have shared their ideas, pull out the soda can. As students give you the "I told you so," ask them, "Why does the can make that sound when

250

being opened? What is going on inside the can?" While students share their ideas, you can also ask them, "Would it make a difference if I shook the can before opening it? Why?" (If you decide to demonstrate this, have a bucket ready for the overflowing liquid.)

3. As the discussion continues, ask students to read the Background section with their partners, highlighting any information that is new for them. If they have done the previous labs with yeast, they are usually familiar with the microorganism, but the formula for fermentation is new. Write all new information on the board because the fermentation equation is helpful to have as a reference during this experiment.

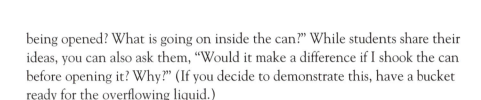

Fermentation

$$\text{Yeast} \ + \ C_6H_{12}O_6 \ \rightarrow \ 2C_2H_5OH \ + \ 2CO_2$$
$$\text{(fungi)} \quad\quad \text{(sugar)} \quad\quad\quad \text{(ethanol)} \quad\quad \text{(carbon dioxide)}$$

4. Student groups can then move on to creating a hypothesis. Introduce the vocabulary for linear relationships and exponential relationships on the board under the "new information" section. I also include sketches about what the graphs look like for each type of relationship, as shown below.

Linear relationship   Exponential relationship

Ask students to share examples of linear relationships (speed with constant acceleration, the cost of lunch if you are only buying one item, etc.) as well as examples of exponential relationships (world population, interest, etc) with their partners. Then have two lab groups share ideas with each other.

5. Once students have completed their hypothesis, they can begin the lab. The lab starts with getting the water boiling. It takes 500 ml of water a while to boil, so it is best that students get this part started before they start working on the ginger root.

6. Students should measure the ginger root so that it falls in a range of 20–30 g. The exact value is not important; anything over 20 g will have a strong ginger flavor. The limit of 30 g is to prevent the students from wasting supplies.

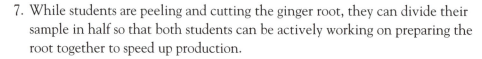

7. While students are peeling and cutting the ginger root, they can divide their sample in half so that both students can be actively working on preparing the root together to speed up production.

8. While they are cutting, ask the students, "What is the reason for cutting up the ginger into such small pieces? How does that increase your flavor?" (*Answer*: Cutting the pieces increases surface area, allowing more of the ginger flavor to be infused in the water.)

9. Measuring the deflated balloons can be a little difficult, but have students do their best with the measuring tape to get a circumference. They also can lay the balloon flat to measure on the table.

10. Students will need to measure the change in circumference of their balloon every day for the week. At this time many of them want to check on their soda's progress as well. I know a soda is "done" when the bottle has regained its initial shape and held it for about 12–24 hours. This is an easy way to tell the soda is ready for consumption.

11. On Thursday, place the mint ginger soda bottles in a cool place, like a refrigerator so students can enjoy them cold the next day.

12. On Friday, after making their final observation, students can drink their mint ginger soda during class. I do not allow them to take the soda home because of the potential safety problems that could occur if the bottle becomes too pressurized.

13. Sometimes the soda bottles have sediment from the yeast that forms along the bottom. Students should not drink the sediment; it does not taste very good, although it is not harmful.

DATA ANALYSIS ANSWER KEY

All the data analysis for this lab is math based. If students are struggling with the questions, I recommend using a sample data set and going through the calculations as a class on the board. Then students can use the same skills and apply them directly to their data.

1. The equation for circumference of a circle is:

$$C = 2\pi \times radius$$

Using this equation and the data obtained in your experiment, solve for the radius of each day's balloon in the table below. Be sure to show your work.

Student answers will depend on their solution, but the calculation process should be the same, and should use the equation provided in the question. A sample student calculation might look like this:

	Radius of balloon
Day 1	10 cm / 2π = 1.59 cm
Day 2	11 cm / 2π = 1.75 cm
Day 3	13 cm / 2π = 2.07 cm
Day 4	17 cm / 2π = 2.70 cm
Day 5	25 cm / 2π = 3.97 cm

2. *The equation for volume of a sphere is:*

$$Volume = 4/3 \times \pi \times (radius)^3$$

Using this equation and the data obtained in Data Analysis question 1, solve for the volume of each day's balloon in the table below. Be sure to show your work.

Student answers will depend on their solution, but the calculation process should be the same, and should use the equation provided in the question. A sample student calculation might look like this:

	Volume of balloon
Day 1	$4/3 \times \pi \times (1.59 \text{ cm})^3 = 16.837 \text{ cm}^3$
Day 2	$4/3 \times \pi \times (1.75 \text{ cm})^3 = 22.45 \text{ cm}^3$
Day 3	$4/3 \times \pi \times (2.07 \text{ cm})^3 = 37.153 \text{ cm}^3$
Day 4	$4/3 \times \pi \times (2.70 \text{ cm})^3 = 82.44 \text{ cm}^3$
Day 5	$4/3 \times \pi \times (3.97 \text{ cm})^3 = 262.01 \text{ cm}^3$

3. *Create a line graph that shows change in gas volume created when compared to time. Remember to include all elements of a scientific graph (title, labeled axes, units, etc.).*

Student answers will depend on their solution, but the graphs should show a similar trend. A sample student graph is provided here.

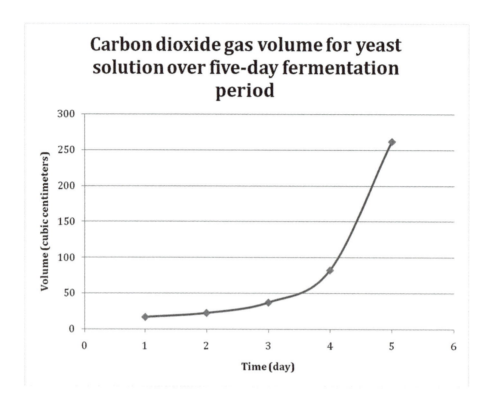

Carbon dioxide gas volume for yeast solution over five-day fermentation period

CONCLUSION AND CONNECTIONS ANSWER KEY

This section of the lab offers a great opportunity to engage the entire class in discussion to clarify the main ideas of the lab and allow the students to make their own connections between science and cooking. I ask that students answer the Data Analysis questions and attempt to answer the Conclusion and Connections questions, with the understanding that we will spend time the next day discussing the Conclusions and Connections section.

1. *Was your initial hypothesis correct? Restate your hypothesis and identify whether you were correct or incorrect, using data to support your answer.*

   Students will have different initial answers based on their specific hypothesis, but should identify that the correct trend is exponential. The graph in question 3 of the Data Analysis section, which shows that the volume of the balloon was increasing with a curved line of best fit, demonstrates this relationship.

2. *How large do you think the balloon would be if you measured the volume tomorrow? Explain how you arrived at your answer.*

    If the volume was measured tomorrow, it should increase exponentially, meaning the value based on the student data would be more than twice the value listed on Day 5. Students can arrive at the answer in one of two ways. One way is to extrapolate using the graph they created and predict the position of the line following an exponential curve on Day 6. The other option is to figure out what the actual exponential increase would be for the radius and then calculate it through to volume. Either procedure is acceptable.

3. *Based on the fermentation equation, if the amount of yeast is limitless, how many molecules of CO_2 are created when yeast have 100 molecules of sucrose to break down? Explain how you arrived at your answer.*

    The correct answer is that there would be 200 molecules of CO_2. Using the chemical equation provided in the Background section, for every one sugar molecule the yeast creates two molecules of carbon dioxide. Students can observe this relationship by looking at the numbers that come before the compound is listed in the chemical equation. Occasionally, I have students try to follow an exponential growth pattern to get this answer, or they can approach it by using the number of carbon atoms in sucrose in the subscript of the chemical formula. It is important to point out that it is the numbers listed prior to the chemical formula that deal with amounts of molecules present in a reaction.

4. *What would happen to your soda bottles if you allowed the yeast to continue to ferment for another two weeks?*

    The soda bottles would explode. Based on the exponential growth pattern, the amount of gas trapped in the bottle would get so high that the bottle would no longer be able to hold the contents and would explode because of the pressure.

5. *Why do you think that soda pop manufacturers do not use yeast in the creation of their product?*

    There are a number of ways to answer this question. Students might refer to taste, to consumer's apprehension about organisms in food, or to the exponential growth factor that would cause the bottles to explode. Any of these answers are acceptable; the goal is for students to apply their lab experiences to a real-world context.

CROSS-CURRICULAR NOTE: MATH

This is an ideal opportunity to incorporate math and geometry in a real-life application. This lab presents an opportunity to team-teach with a math teacher so students can make observations and use their math skills for data analysis.

CROSS-CURRICULAR NOTE: LITERACY

Share the lyrics for the song "Under Pressure" by Queen. Ask, "How are the themes of this song related to the experiment?" Ask students to create another set of lyrics to be added to the song based on their experiences in the lab.

OPTIONAL EXTENSIONS

Middle School

1. Another way to introduce carbonation quickly to a liquid is to use dry ice. The liquid can be prepared without the yeast, and then students can add dry ice to create a carbonized beverage. *Safety note:* Dry ice is hazardous and needs to be handled with a protective cloth or leather gloves. Handling without protection can freeze skin cells and cause injuries similar to a burn.

2. Encourage students to create labels and a marketing campaign for the mint ginger soda within the school. If there is an entrepreneur or business course, students can team with that class to sell the soda, comparing cost of supplies and money earned through sales. Students can then donate the proceeds (if there are any) to a charity of their choice.

3. Encourage students to design alternative methods for measuring the amount of gas produced by fermentation aside from the balloon. Ask students how they can measure an exact amount of gas produced using an alternative method of measurement.

High School

1. Have students use Newton's ideal gas law to calculate the exact amount of pressure within the soda bottles using Standard Temperature and Pressure, which corresponds to 273 K (0°C) and 1 atm of pressure. This requires knowledge of Avogadro's number and moles, but provides another math analysis about gas and pressure.

2. Ask students to design an experiment that compares the pressure in a soda can to the pressure created by the fermentation process. Based on the chemical equation, how long would the liquid need to ferment to have the same pressure as an average soda can?

256

EXPERIMENT 13:
Regular or Diet Soda? Student Pages

DEVELOPING A PROCEDURE TO TEST HOW SUGAR COMPARES TO SUGAR SUBSTITUTES IN YEAST FERMENTATION

BACKGROUND

Scientists work in many different fields, helping industries incorporate the latest research and technology to improve their products and services. The food industry is no different. Scientists are hired by major brands such as Kraft, Gerber, and Nestle to make their products taste better, stay fresh longer, and be healthier. With rising rates in obesity, many companies are looking at how they can offer products with the same flavor, but with less fat, sugar, oils, and/or carbohydrates.

One of the approaches that many product manufacturers have taken is the use of sugar substitutes to improve nutritional values. Figure 13.1 shows the molecular structures for both sugar and a sugar substitute. Notice the similarities in both molecules, which explain how sugar substitutes can be similar in taste and why they are used in place of sugar in recipes. By using sugar substitutes such as Splenda, Truvia, or NutraSweet, companies are able to not only lower the calories of their products but also save money in the production because many sugar substitutes are cheaper than real sugar.

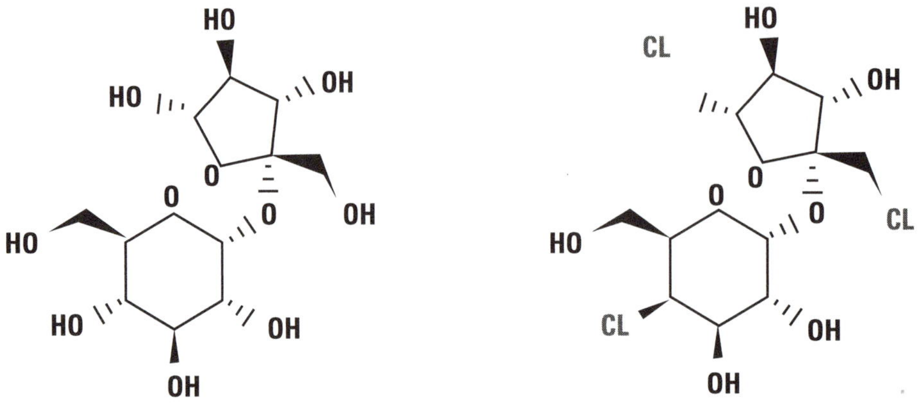

Sucrose

Sucralose
(Splenda)

Figure 13.1: Molecular diagrams for sucrose and sucralose (a sugar substitute).

In this experiment you will have the opportunity to design a procedure that creates two different kinds of blueberry soda: one with regular sugar and the other with a sugar substitute. Not only will you be able to see if there is a taste difference, but you also will be measuring how changing the sugar affects our carbonation efforts with yeast. Yeast is a biological organism that uses sugar as a food source, producing carbon dioxide gas. Does yeast prefer the original product more that the sugar substitute? We shall see who wins this taste test.

HYPOTHESIS

How will the sugar substitute impact the creation of carbon dioxide by the yeast? Predict whether you think the amount of carbon dioxide will increase, decrease, or remain the same when a sugar substitute is used compared with when regular sugar is used. Explain your reasoning using the background information to support your prediction.

MATERIALS NEEDED PER GROUP

- 100 ml of frozen *Vaccinium corymbosum* (frozen blueberries)
- 400 ml of dihydrogen monoxide, H_2O (water)
- 80 ml of sucrose or sucrose substitute (sugar or sugar substitute)
- Half a package of yeast
- Plastic fork, one per student
- Cheesecloth or gauze cloth
- Rubber band
- Beaker, 400 ml
- Beaker, 600 ml
- Beaker, 1,000 ml
- Graduated cylinders
- Balance
- Bunsen burner and ring stand
- Tongs
- Glass stir rod
- Empty plastic bottles with lids
- Erlenmeyer flask, 250 ml
- One-holed stopper for the Erlenmeyer flask
- 8 cm tube to fit the hole in the stopper
- 60+ cm of flexible tubing that fits the copper tube
- Clock or timer
- Indirectly vented chemical-splash goggles
- Aprons

PROCEDURE

Teacher Initials: _____

SETUP

No, your lab is not missing a page. The Procedure section is intentionally blank because you are going to be creating the procedure for this experiment. Scared? Don't be, because we will be going through this process together.

Procedures in science are very similar to recipes in cookbooks. It is important that you are very specific about what you are going to do so that someone could take your procedure, follow it, and achieve similar results. When writing a scientific procedure you need to follow these rules:

- Describe your method step by step (each step should be numbered and should include all related ideas).
- Write sequentially, in the order you perform each step.
- Give directions in the imperative mood (use the command form of the verb).
- Write clearly and concisely. Be very specific. Never assume anything!
- Use the correct names of all equipment, materials, places, and objects.

To help you along in this process, I will give you three tools. First, I have already created the device for measuring the release of gas by your soda. This device is going to be referred to as the gas collection setup (see Figure 13.2). This setup is already provided at your lab stations. You do not need to describe how to build this device, only how to use it.

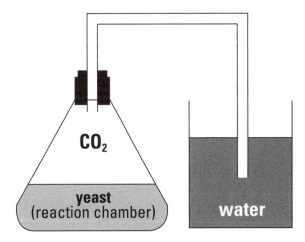

Figure 13.2: Gas collection setup.

Second, I have provided a general overview of the steps associated with this lab. This is not a procedure, as it does not follow the guidelines given above. Use this general information and the Materials Needed section to write a scientific procedure for this experiment.

For this experiment, you will be making two different blueberry sodas: one with sugar and the other with a sugar substitute. To make blueberry soda, you want to smash your blueberries and boil them with half of your water. Once the soda reaches a boil, turn down the heat and let it simmer for eight more minutes. Allow the solution to cool and then strain out the blueberries, leaving just the flavored soda. Mix in your sugar or sugar substitute and half a package of yeast. Pour your soda into a flask and hook up to the stopper in the gas collection setup. Make sure the flexible tube is under water and wait for bubbles to begin forming, which may take up to five minutes. Once the bubbles form, count the number of bubbles that are released from the tube for three minutes and record this. Then mix your soda solution with the rest of your water, and fill your plastic bottles, leaving them one-fourth empty. Squeeze out the air and seal the bottles. Allow fermenting for three to five days before drinking.

Last, but certainly not least, let's take a moment to identify your independent variable, dependent variable, and controlled variables. Each group will be testing only the sugar or sugar substitute. You will get the data from the other test from another lab group. You will be measuring the amount of bubbles that form over three minutes. With that knowledge, fill out the following table and have your teacher initial it before beginning to write your procedure.

	Blueberry soda experiment
Independent variable	
Dependent variable	
Controlled variables	

Teacher initials: _____

Once you have your procedure written, bring it to be checked and initialed by your teacher. This will most likely take you two or three drafts before you have it right. Do not get discouraged; it is just like writing drafts in your English class. You are not expected to get it perfect the first time. Good luck!

DATA AND OBSERVATIONS

Blueberry Soda Carbon Dioxide Data Table		
	Our trial: Number of carbon dioxide bubbles counted in three minutes	_____'s trial: Number of carbon dioxide bubbles counted in three minutes
Blueberry soda with sugar		
Blueberry soda with sugar substitute		

DATA ANALYSIS

For each of the following questions, be sure to explain using detail and complete sentences. If the question requires you to complete calculations, show all of your work.

1. Calculate the average number of carbon dioxide bubbles created in three minutes for the blueberry soda with sugar using the values from your data table.

2. Calculate the average number of carbon dioxide bubbles created in three minutes for the blueberry soda with sugar substitute using the values from your data table.

CONCLUSION AND CONNECTIONS

1. Restate your hypothesis and identify whether you were correct or incorrect, using data to support your answer.

2. Why do you think the yeast reacted this way to the sugar substitute? Explain using your knowledge of yeast obtained from the Background section.

3. Fill out the table below to list three sets of products that you have tried that use sugar and a sugar substitute. You can use the internet if you need to look up products.

Sugar product	Sugar substitute product
1.	1.
2.	2.
3.	3.

4. Do you think any or all of the sets of products listed in your answer to Conclusions and Connections question 3 taste different? Choose one pair of products and compare and contrast them using the Venn diagram below. Be sure to label your circles.

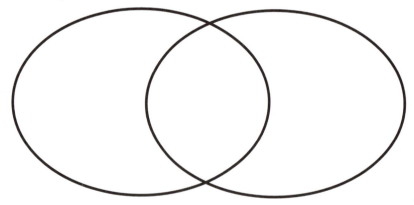

EXPERIMENT 13:
Regular or Diet Soda? Teacher Pages

DEVELOPING A PROCEDURE TO TEST HOW SUGAR COMPARES TO SUGAR SUBSTITUTES IN YEAST FERMENTATION

If your students are ready to take on more responsibility in the lab, then this is the experiment for you. This experiment guides students through the process of creating their own procedure to test a given independent variable. Students are instructed about the proper format for a procedure, and are given tools to support their efforts, such as the lab setup, identification of variables, and a general overview to convert into scientific procedure format. The experiment allows students to get comfortable with the process of creating a procedure so that they can start directing their own experiments in the near future. This opportunity for skill improvement is embedded in a lab experience that tests the impact of using a sugar substitute with yeast in the creation of blueberry soda. The final product provides the perfect motivation for students to work hard to write a detailed procedure, while gaining knowledge about microorganisms in food products.

STANDARDS ADDRESSED
National Science Education Standards: Grades 5–8

Content Standard A: Science as Inquiry
- Abilities necessary to do scientific inquiry
- Understanding about scientific inquiry

Content Standard B: Physical Science
- Properties and changes of properties in matter

Content Standard C: Life Science
- Structure and function in living systems
- Regulation and behavior
- Population and ecosystems

Content Standard E: Science and Technology
- Abilities of technological design
- Understanding about science and technology

Content Standard F: Science in Personal and Social Perspectives
- Personal health
- Risk and benefits
- Science and technology in society

Content Standard G: History and Nature of Science
- Science as a human endeavor
- Nature of science

National Science Education Standards: Grades 9–12

Content Standard A: Science as Inquiry
- Abilities necessary to do scientific inquiry
- Understandings about scientific inquiry

Content Standard B: Physical Science
- Structure of atoms
- Structure and properties of matter
- Chemical reactions

Content Standard E: Science and Technology
- Abilities of technological design
- Understanding about science and technology

Content Standard F: Science in Personal and Social Perspectives
- Personal and community health
- Science and technology in local, national, and global challenges

Content Standard G: History and Nature of Science
- Science as a human endeavor
- Nature of scientific knowledge
- Historical perspectives

VOCABULARY

Variable: A factor that can change or influence an outcome.

Independent variable: The factor or variable that is being tested, or the variable that scientists choose to change in the experiment. This also can be called the *experimental variable* or *manipulated variable*.

Dependent variable: The variable that describes what happens as a result of changing the independent variable. This variable is measured to find changes that occur when the independent variable is changed. This can also be called the *responding variable*.

Controlled variables: These are factors that are not being tested and therefore are held constant throughout the experiment.

Controlled experiment: An experiment in which only one factor is being changed (the independent variable), and the other variables are being held constant to create a control group to create a standard to measure the change.

Yeast: Any of various unicellular fungi of the genus *Saccharomyces*, especially *S. cerevisiae*, reproducing by budding and from ascospores and capable of fermenting carbohydrates (*The American Heritage Dictionary of the English Language* 2000).

Fermentation: The conversion of carbohydrates into alcohols and carbon dioxide in biochemical reactions facilitated by microorganisms. The equation for fermentation is as follows:

$$\underset{\text{(fungi)}}{\text{Yeast}} \;+\; \underset{\text{(sugar)}}{C_6H_{12}O_6} \;\rightarrow\; \underset{\text{(ethanol)}}{2C_2H_5OH} \;+\; \underset{\text{(carbon dioxide)}}{2CO_2}$$

MATERIALS NEEDED, DECODED FOR THE GROCERY STORE

100 ml of frozen *Vaccinium corymbosum* (frozen blueberries)
- Frozen blueberries can be purchased in the freezer section of your grocery store. The frozen variety is cheaper than the fresh, and is available year-round, which is why I suggest that type for this lab. A 1 lb. bag will cover about four lab groups.

80 ml of sucrose or sucrose substitute (sugar or sugar substitute)
- Sugar is sold in the area of the grocery store with flour and other baking products. A 5 lb. bag will be enough for around 22 lab groups.
- For the sugar substitute you can use any sugar substitute you find that is

cheap and available. I recommend using Splenda, but you can use whatever substitute you prefer. The lab specifically does not require a certain brand to allow you to choose what is best for your class and budget.

- Keep in mind that lab groups will need only one of these two ingredients, and they will be running only one trial.

Half a package of yeast

- Yeast can be purchased in the area of your grocery store with the baking powder and flour. You want fast-acting yeast for this lab. Yeast is sold in packages for less than $1. One package will work for two lab groups, so base your purchase on the number of lab groups that will be conducting this lab.
- Make sure that the yeast has not expired. If you purchase yeast and want to use it later in the year, make sure you store it in a cool, dry area.

Plastic fork

- I recommend having one fork for each student. This is helpful in allowing the students to smash the blueberries. The forks can be cleaned and used for the next class, so buy as many as you will need for your largest class, plus a few extras in case there is breakage. Plastic forks are sold individually in boxes of 30–50.

Cheesecloth or gauze cloth

- You usually can find cheesecloth in a gourmet shop. I have never found any at the grocery stores I frequent, so I buy gauze cloth in bulk. This can be found in the first-aid section of the grocery store, or in a school nurse's office. Each student group needs two pieces to fit over the mouth of a 600 ml beaker.

Rubber band

- Each group needs a rubber band to secure its cloth to the beaker for straining the liquid from the blueberry pieces.

Empty plastic bottles with lids

- There are two ways I have approached this in the past. The first is to purchase a large case of water (18–24 plastic bottles). The students dump out the water in class or into a gallon container to be used later as distilled water. Then they can each have one water bottle to fill with blueberry soda. The cost of a case of water varies from $5 to $8. The other option is to ask students to bring in their own soda bottles. If your school sells soda or juice in plastic bottles at lunch, the students can reuse those containers. The only problem I had with this approach was that students had containers of all different sizes, making the division of blueberry soda unequal across the

groups. If you go this route, give students a maximum size the bottle can be. I also recommend buying an extra case of water for students who do not bring a bottle.

Dish soap
- This is necessary for cleanup. I ask students to use an amount about the size of a quarter for each glass container, and I have one bottle available for every four lab groups to share.

SAFETY HIGHLIGHTS

- The Bunsen burners and ring stands present a potential for students to burn themselves if used incorrectly. Please make sure students have had Bunsen burner safety training before allowing them to participate in this lab. As a teacher, you also need to be prepared with burn treatment options, such as running the burned area under cold water, if a student gets hurt.
- If a glass stir rod breaks during mixing, you should dispose of the entire mixture. Even if the break is minor, you may have shards of glass in the mixture that are not visible.
- It is important to note that students are creating pressure inside a sealed bottle. If this pressure continues to build without being released, the bottle will explode. This could result in either a large mess, or worse, a student getting hit in the eye with an accelerating bottle lid. I have students mature the liquid and consume the beverage at school. This prevents any issues with overfermentation or bottles with too much pressure occurring outside the lab environment. *Safety note:* Bottles must be depressurized upon completing the experiment to prevent danger of explosion.

Note that these safety highlights are in addition to the safety information detailed in the Safety Protocol section at the beginning of this book. Please refer to that section for additional information about safety when implementing this or any lab in this book.

PREPARATION

1. This lab requires only a single day of actual testing; however, it does require several class periods for students to create their procedures, and then several days before they can drink their blueberry soda. It is helpful to have a separate space set aside for the blueberry soda bottles to ferment. This should be clearly labeled before the start of the lab.

2. Blueberries need to be thawed before the lab begins. You can place them in a refrigerator a day or two before the lab, and then set them out to bring them to room temperature the morning of your lab. I keep the blueberries in a plastic container when setting them out so they do not leak.

3. The gas collection setup needs to be assembled for each of the student groups (see Figure 13.1). The setup is fairly simple:

    (a) The materials for this setup include a one-holed stopper for the 250 ml flask, an 8 cm tube to fit the hole in the stopper, 60 cm of flexible tubing that fits the tube in the stopper, and a 400 ml beaker half-filled with water.

    (b) Place the tube into the hole in the stopper. Connect the flexible tubing to the end of the tube that will be outside the flask. (Use the slope of the stopper to help you; you want the flexible tube to be attached to the tube coming out of the side of the stopper with the larger diameter.) The flexible tube will be placed in the 400 ml beaker half-filled with water.

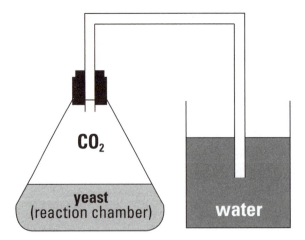

Figure 13.1: Gas collection setup.

    (c) There are a few helpful hints for this setup. You want as little tubing as possible, and all tubing should have a small radius. Otherwise, you do not get to see as many bubbles forming. If you are not getting any bubbles, you can siphon the air out of the tube to create a minivacuum. I would not recommend that the students complete this step; it needs to be handled by a teacher.

PROCEDURE

I recommend that students work in groups of two for this experiment. The recipe makes plenty of blueberry soda (enough for about two and a half bottles), and when groups are larger, students may get a bit upset about the amount they receive. The work and data collection is also simple enough that two students are ideal for the experiment.

1. This lab can be introduced with a simple compare and contrast of two products, one that contains sugar and a similar product that contains a sugar substitute. My personal choice for this experiment is Coke and Diet Coke, but you can use any two products that students are familiar with.

2. Draw a large Venn diagram on the board. Have students give individual characteristics of Coke and Diet Coke, as well as characteristics the two products share. Place the characteristics in their appropriate place on the diagram. Characteristics can include parent company, logo design, taste, ingredients, and nutritional values. It is helpful to have a few soda cans to circulate among the lab groups to help this process.

3. One of my favorite contrasting characteristics to demonstrate is the difference in density between the two products. Fill a large clear container with water. Place the Coke and Diet Coke cans in the water. Notice that the Diet Coke can floats, while the Coke can sinks. This shows a difference in density, which can be attributed to the different types of sugar that each product uses. This is a great transition into the Background section of this lab.

4. Have students read the Background section about differences in products containing sugar and sugar substitutes. Give them an opportunity to make a prediction about how a sugar substitute will perform when compared with the fermentation of sugar by the yeast.

5. Ask students to move on to the Procedure section, and they will quickly realize that it is missing. Guide them through an introduction to writing a scientific procedure using the information in the Setup section to frame your discussion.

6. As part of introducing the steps for writing a clear procedure, I write the following procedure on the board:

How to Make a PB&J
1. Get your materials
2. Place the peanut butter on the bread, and add the jelly.
3. Eat

Ask students, "Could you make a peanut butter and jelly sandwich using these directions? The directions are unclear. Maybe I should put the jar of peanut butter on top of the loaf of bread. Does that get me a peanut butter sandwich? Maybe I should dump the jelly into the jar of peanut butter. Does that make a sandwich?" This demonstration illustrates the importance of descriptive language and how being unclear in a procedure can cause you to come up with an incorrect outcome.

7. Before students start writing their procedures, go over the variables with all the student groups. This is a good time to assign each group whether they are testing the sugar or sugar substitute in their trial. Ask students to circle or highlight their assigned variable so they do not forget.

8. Compare the process of writing a procedure to writing a first draft in students' humanities classes. Ask, "What is the purpose of the first draft? Is it supposed to be perfect immediately?" This will eliminate some of the frustration that students will experience when you critique their first attempt at writing a procedure.

9. Once students have a completed procedure, encourage them to go and help other groups. I do not allow for testing until all groups have an approved procedure. This allows for students to become the teachers and create a learning community.

10. During the experiment, when students are mashing blueberries, ask, "What is the reason for smashing the blueberries into such small pieces? How does that increase the flavor?" (*Answer*: Smashing the berries into small pieces increases the surface area, allowing more of the blueberry flavor to be infused in the water.)

11. Remind students to label their soda bottles with their name and class so they get the correct liquid back.

12. Students will want to check on their soda's progress. A soda is "done" when the bottle has regained its initial shape and held it for about 12–24 hours. This is an easy way to tell the soda is ready for consumption.

13. The day before giving the sodas to the students, place the soda bottles in a cool place, like a refrigerator, so students can enjoy the soda cold the next day.

14. When the soda is cool, students can drink it during class. I do not allow them to take the soda home because of the potential safety problems that could occur if the bottle becomes too pressurized.

15. Sometimes the soda bottles have sediment from the yeast that forms along the bottom. Students should not drink the sediment; it does not taste very good, although it is not harmful.

DATA ANALYSIS ANSWER KEY

All the data analysis for this lab is math based and involves students using their individual data. If students are struggling with the questions, I recommend using a sample data set and going through the calculations as a class on the board. Then students can use the same skills and apply them directly to their data.

1. *Calculate the average number of carbon dioxide bubbles created in three minutes for the blueberry soda with sugar using the values from your data table.*

   Student answers will depend on their solution, but the calculation process should be the same. A sample student calculation might look like this:

   48 bubbles + 56 bubbles = 104 bubbles ÷ 2 = Average of 52 bubbles in three minutes

2. *Calculate the average number of carbon dioxide bubbles created in three minutes for the blueberry soda with sugar substitute using the values from your data table.*

   Student answers will depend on their solution, but the calculation process should be the same as the process outlined in Data Analysis question 1.

CONCLUSION AND CONNECTIONS ANSWER KEY

This section of the lab offers a great opportunity to engage the entire class in discussion to clarify the main ideas of the lab and allow the students to make their own connections between science and cooking. I ask that students answer the Data Analysis questions and attempt to answer the Conclusion and Connections questions, with the understanding that we will spend time the next day discussing the Conclusion and Connections section.

1. *Restate your hypothesis and identify whether you were correct or incorrect, using data to support your answer.*

   Students will have different answers based on their specific hypothesis, but they should identify that the correct trend is that the amount of bubbles decreases when a sugar substitute is used. The data table and the averages obtained in Data Analysis questions 1 and 2 support this relationship.

2. *Why do you think the yeast reacted this way to the sugar substitute? Explain using your knowledge of yeast obtained from the Background section.*

   Sugar substitutes are exactly that: a substitute. They do not have the exact molecular structure that yeast is looking for in a food sources. The yeast will utilize the sugar that is naturally present in the blueberries, so you get some reaction, but the reaction is not as great as it would be if sugar were present.

3. *Fill out the table below to list three sets of products that you have tried that use sugar and a sugar substitute. You can use the internet if you need to look up products.*

Sugar product	Sugar substitute product
1.	1.
2.	2.
3.	3.

Aside from Coke and Diet Coke, there are many products that use sugar substitutes. Some examples include sugar-free gum, fat-free yogurt, gelatin desserts, juice beverages, and frozen desserts. Encourage students to pick out products they eat, because this helps create a stronger context for this lab experience.

4. *Do you think any or all of the sets of products listed in your answer to Conclusions and Connections question 3 taste different? Choose one pair of products and compare and contrast them using the Venn diagram below. Be sure to label your circles.*

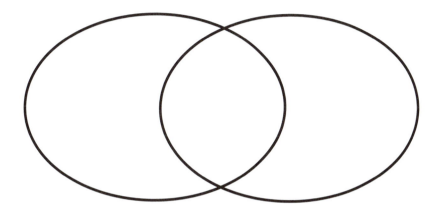

Students can choose any two products they are familiar with. Characteristics for the compare-and-contrast sections can include, but are not limited to, parent company, logo design, taste, ingredients, and nutritional values. Students should be familiar with this format based on the introduction demonstration recommended for this experiment.

CROSS-CURRICULAR NOTE: MATH

Students can look at the nutritional labels on different brands of sodas. Many of the values are often measured in different units. Encourage students to convert all the values to the same unit to see how it changes their understanding of exactly how much nutrition is in the soda. This is a great connection with math conversions and reiterates the importance of units in measurement and data collection.

CROSS-CURRICULAR NOTE: LITERACY

With the concern over the health of U.S. citizens increasing, many people have looked at banning the sale of sodas from educational institutions to improve healthy eating habits among students. Ask students, "What other changes could the United States make to improve health, and do you agree with these changes?" Students also can write an argument to debate whether Halloween should be discontinued and replaced by a healthy holiday.

OPTIONAL EXTENSIONS

Middle School

1. You can increase the level of difficulty based on your students' previous experiences by removing any of the elements provided to support their creation of the procedure. This could include asking students to analyze the gas collection setup and write a procedure for setting this up, asking them to identify the variables from the hypothesis, or not giving them the general overview of the procedure.

2. Ask students to look at regular and healthy versions of the same product. Ask, "What are the chemical similarities and differences?" Encourage students to design a test to see which substance gives the body more energy to perform an exercise task.

High School

1. Students can test multiple sugar substitutes using the same method as this experiment and compare the amount of carbon dioxide created to the chemical structure of the sugar substitute.

2. Students can measure the rate of gas produced over time. They can calculate the number of moles of carbon dioxide created and based on this information calculate the amount of ethanol produced by balancing the fermentation chemical equation.

3. Students can analyze how sugar is digested compared to sucralose or other sugar substitutes. Ask, "How are the two molecules similar, and how do those similarities translate into similar properties like taste? How are the two molecules different, and how do those differences affect digestion?"

PART FOUR:
MOLECULAR STRUCTURE

This final section highlights how the molecular structure of chemicals and compounds can affect the physical characteristics of food. These relationships are highlighted in the creation of sugar-based candies. In Experiment 14: Crystal Carbohydrates, students are introduced to the structure of sugar molecules and how these molecules can be arranged into chains to create crystallized sugar. Students create crystallized sugar and compare its physical qualities to qualities of sugar where crystallization is impeded by the type of sugar and acid. Students design a data table to highlight the importance of qualitative data organization. Experiment 15: Strong Sugar Science asks students to use the experimental design skills introduced in the 14 previous experiments to create an experiment that finds a relationship between temperature and sugar structure. This experiment is the culmination of the book and allows students to direct the inquiry into the molecular structure of sugar.

EXPERIMENT 14:
Crystal Carbohydrates: Student Pages

CREATING A DATA TABLE TO ANALYZE HOW SUGAR STRUCTURE IMPACTS THE FORMATION OF BUTTERSCOTCH CANDY

BACKGROUND

From the title of this experiment alone, I know that I have your attention. That's right; in this lab we are working with sugar. The average U.S. student consumes about 40 lbs. of sugar each year! And this desire for sugar is nothing new. Cravings for sweets date back to the 16th century when a teaspoon of sugar sold for almost $5. Can you imagine what a piece of candy would have cost?

But why is sugar so good? Sugar, which goes by the scientific name *sucrose*, is an ideal energy source for the human body. Figure 14.1 shows the molecular structure of sucrose, which is made up of carbon, oxygen, and hydrogen atoms.

The sucrose molecule packs a lot of calories (human energy units) into a small amount of substance. It is also easy for the human body to digest, providing instant energy.

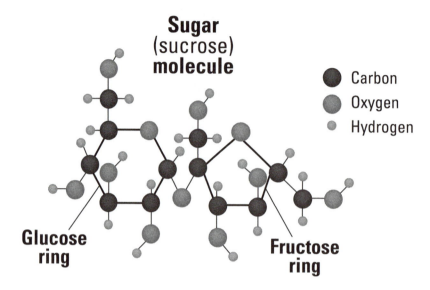

Figure 14.1: Sugar (sucrose) molecule.

With all these good qualities, why do people warn you to stay away from eating too many sweets? Although sucrose provides energy, the body quickly synthesizes that energy. This causes you to experience a sugar "high" before you "crash" and your body is left feeling tired. Second, sucrose is often considered to be an empty calorie source because it doesn't come along with the vitamins and minerals that our body requires. Finally, once the body has absorbed enough sugar, the remaining sucrose is converted into fat stores, which can lead to health problems. So what is the lesson here? Sugar can be consumed in moderation. It isn't healthy to eat all 40 lbs. in one day; however, you certainly do not have to completely remove it from your diet.

In what form do you consume sugar? It is found in almost all foods from fruits to cereals, but in its most highly concentrated form, sugar is obtained through candy. Candy aligns the chains of sugar in a way that is pleasing to the mouth and body. These molecules will interact like Legos that lock together to form crystals, similar to what is seen in rock candy. However, not all sweets want crystallization of sugar. You can prevent crystallization from occurring using a couple of methods, such as adding acid. Acid breaks down the chain into its two subparts—glucose and fructose—making it difficult for the sugar molecules to stay together. You can also add other sugars into the mix, like glucose, to prevent the

280

crystals from forming. Finally, you can use fats like butter to prevent the sucrose molecules from locking into place.

In this experiment, several lab groups will create the sucrose candy of butterscotch using the acid method of preventing crystallization. Several other lab groups will prepare their candy with a mix of different kinds of sugars. One other group will volunteer to make its candy without the acid to see the difference in how sugar reacts when it starts to make chains. We will then compare sugar structures of all three methods to observe the differences in structure.

HYPOTHESIS

What are the major differences that occur when sucrose is crystallized versus when it is incorporated with other sugars? Predict at least three characteristics of sugar structures that are chained and crystallized that are different from sucrose molecules that are not in crystal format. For each observation, explain how this relates back to the information presented in the Background section.

SETUP

Before you begin to look at the Materials Needed and Procedures sections, you will need to create a data table for recording your observations about crystallized versus noncrystallized sugar structures. When creating data tables, you want to follow the following rules:

1. Make sure your data table has a title. This title should explain what information is presented in the table to make it easier to identify.

2. Your independent variable should be stated on a different axis from your dependent variable.

3. Identify units of measurement when necessary.

4. Use a straight edge when creating your table, or use graph paper.

With these rules in mind, use your hypothesis to identify your independent and dependent variables. Read through the Materials Needed and Procedures sections. Then create a data table for recording your data and observations for this experiment. Have your teacher initial your completed data table before moving on with the experiment.

MATERIALS NEEDED PER GROUP

- 60 ml of brown sucrose, $C_{12}H_{22}O_{11}$ (brown sugar) or 60 ml of glucose solution (Karo syrup)
- 30 ml of solid fatty acid (butter)
- 60 ml of white sucrose, $C_{12}H_{22}O_{11}$ (white sugar)
- 60 ml of dihydrogen monoxide, H_2O (water)
- 5 ml of acetic acid solution (vinegar)
- 1 g of sodium chloride, NaCl (table salt)
- 1.5 ml of *Vanilla planifola* liquid (vanilla flavoring)
- Beaker, 400 ml
- Thermometer, 150°C and nonmercury
- 10 ml graduated cylinder
- 100 ml graduated cylinder
- Balance
- Aluminum foil
- Waxed paper
- Beaker tongs
- Bunsen burners and iron rings with wire gauze
- Glass stir rod
- Indirectly vented chemical-splash goggles
- Aprons
- Gloves

PROCEDURE FOR GROUPS USING ACID

1. Read through the entire procedure before beginning.

2. Put on your safety goggles, apron, and gloves, and gather all your materials at your lab station. If you notice any of the materials are dirty or discolored, notify your teacher.

3. Measure 60 ml of brown sucrose using the graduated cylinder and place in the 400 ml beaker.

4. Measure 60 ml of white sucrose using the graduated cylinder, place in the 400 ml beaker, and mix with a glass stir rod.

5. Add 60 ml of H_2O and 5 ml of the acetic acid solution to the mixture of sucrose in the 400 ml beaker. Stir thoroughly with the glass stir rod.

6. Use the balance to measure 1 g of sodium chloride and add to the mixture in the 400 ml beaker.

7. Finally, add the 30 ml of solid fatty acid to the mixture in the beaker. Stir the contents together with the glass stir rod.

8. Set up a Bunsen burner and ring stand with wire mesh on the iron ring. Make sure your Bunsen burner gas intake tube is securely connected to the gas nozzle and that the ring is set about 3 in. above the barrel of the burner (see Figure 14.2). Light the Bunsen burner to create a flame that is no more than 3 in. high. (It should not be touching the wire mesh.)

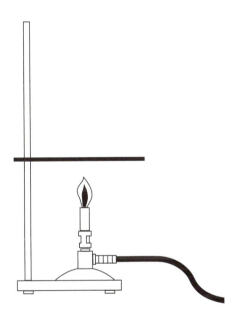

Figure 14.2: Bunsen burner and ring stand.

9. Using the tongs, place the beaker on the ring stand. Slowly heat the mixture while stirring constantly. If you heat the mixture too quickly or do not stir it, you will burn your sucrose and ruin your candy.

10. Slowly increase the size of the flame. Stir the mixture until all the sugar is dissolved and the beaker contains a clear mixture. Bring the mixture to a boil. Once the mixture is boiling, you do not need to stir.

11. While waiting for the sucrose to boil, have one partner fold a piece of aluminum foil into a 13 cm × 19 cm mold. Double layer the aluminum foil to prevent leaks.

12. Grease the mold with a solid fatty acid. Be generous because if you miss a spot, the sucrose will stick.

13. Continue to heat the sucrose mixture until it reaches 130°C. Use the thermometer to measure the temperature, not to stir. Stirring could cause the tool to break, leaving you with a ruined batch of sucrose.

14. Remove the beaker from heat using the tongs. Add 1.5 ml of *Vanilla planifola* liquid, but do not stir.

15. Using the tongs, pour the solution into the well-greased mold. Let the mixture cool before cutting it into squares. *Safety note*: Use caution in this step because the hot solution will seriously burn your skin if spilled.

16. Squares of sucrose can be individually wrapped using waxed paper.

17. Place your beaker, thermometer, and glass stir rod underneath a stream of hot water for one minute. Allow the items to sit in hot water while completing other observations in the lab.

18. Compare a piece of your candy with groups that had a different procedure. Make visual, touch, and taste observations to compare and contrast the sugar structures. Record these observations in your sugar structure table.

19. Clean your area while you are waiting for the butterscotch to cool.

PROCEDURE FOR GROUPS USING DIFFERENT TYPES OF SUGAR

1. Read through the entire procedure before beginning.

2. Put on your safety goggles, apron, and gloves, and gather all your materials at your lab station. If you notice any of the materials are dirty or discolored, notify your teacher.

3. Measure 60 ml of glucose solution using the graduated cylinder and place it in the 400 ml beaker.

4. Measure 60 ml of white sucrose using the graduated cylinder and place it in the 400 ml beaker and mix with a glass stir rod.

5. Add 60 ml of H_2O to the mixture of sucrose in the 400 ml beaker. Stir thoroughly with the glass stir rod.

6. Use the balance to measure 1 g of sodium chloride and add to the mixture in the 400 ml beaker.

7. Finally, add the 30 ml of solid fatty acid to the mixture in the beaker. Stir the contents together with the glass stir rod.

8. Set up a Bunsen burner and ring stand with wire mesh on the iron ring. Make sure your Bunsen burner gas intake tube is securely connected to the gas nozzle, and that the ring is set about 3 in. above the barrel of the burner (see Figure 14.3). Light the Bunsen burner to create a flame that is no more than 3 in. high. (It should not be touching the wire mesh.)

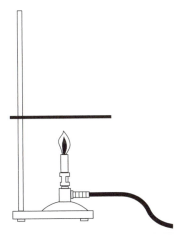

Figure 14.3: Bunsen burner and ring stand.

9. Using the tongs, place the beaker on the ring stand. Slowly heat the mixture while stirring constantly. If you heat the mixture too quickly or do not stir it, you will burn your sucrose and ruin your candy.

10. Slowly increase the size of the flame. Stir the mixture until all the sugar is dissolved and the beaker contains a clear mixture. Bring the mixture to a boil. Once the mixture is boiling, you do not need to stir.

11. While waiting for the sucrose to boil, have one partner fold a piece of aluminum foil into a 13 cm × 19 cm mold. Double layer the aluminum foil to prevent leaks.

12. Grease the mold with a solid fatty acid. Be generous because if you miss a spot, the sucrose will stick.

13. Continue to heat the sucrose mixture until it reaches 130°C. Use the thermometer to measure the temperature, not to stir. Stirring could cause the tool to break, leaving you with a ruined batch of sucrose.

14. Remove the beaker from heat using tongs. Add 1.5 ml of *Vanilla planifola* liquid, but do not stir.

15. Using the tongs, pour the solution into the well-greased mold. Let the mixture cool before cutting it into squares. *Safety note*: Use caution in this step because the hot solution will seriously burn your skin if spilled.

16. Squares of sucrose can be individually wrapped using waxed paper.

17. Place your beaker, thermometer, and glass stir rod underneath a stream of hot water for one minute. Allow items to sit in hot water while completing other observations in the lab.

18. Compare a piece of your candy with groups that had a different procedure. Make visual, touch, and taste observations to compare and contrast the sugar structures. Record these observations in your sugar structure table.

19. Clean your lab area while you are waiting for your butterscotch to cool.

PROCEDURE FOR GROUP CREATING CRYSTALLIZED SUGAR

1. Read through the entire procedure before beginning.

2. Put on your safety goggles, apron, and gloves, and gather all your materials at your lab station. If you notice any of the materials are dirty or discolored, notify your teacher.

3. Measure 60 ml of brown sucrose using the graduated cylinder and place it in the 400 ml beaker.

4. Measure 60 ml of white sucrose using the graduated cylinder and place in the 400 ml beaker and mix with a glass stir rod.

5. Add 60 ml of H_2O to the mixture of sucrose in the 400 ml beaker. Stir thoroughly with the glass stir rod.

6. Use the balance to measure 1 g of sodium chloride and add to the mixture in the 400 ml beaker.

7. Stir the contents together with the glass stir rod.

8. Set up a Bunsen burner and ring stand with wire mesh on the iron ring. Make sure your Bunsen burner gas intake tube is securely connected to the gas nozzle, and that the ring is set about 3 in. above the barrel of the burner (see Figure 14.4). Light the Bunsen burner to create a flame that is no more than 3 in. high. (It should not be touching the wire mesh.)

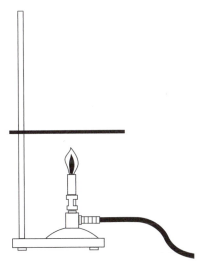

Figure 14.4: Bunsen burner and ring stand.

9. Using the tongs, place the beaker on the ring stand. Slowly heat the mixture while stirring constantly. If you heat the mixture too quickly or do not stir it, you will burn your sucrose and ruin your candy.

10. Slowly increase the size of the flame. Stir the mixture until all the sugar is dissolved and the beaker contains a clear mixture. Bring the mixture to a boil. Once the mixture is boiling, you do not need to stir.

11. While waiting for the sucrose to boil, have one partner fold a piece of aluminum foil into a 13 cm × 19 cm mold. Double layer the aluminum foil to prevent leaks.

12. Grease the mold with a solid fatty acid. Be generous because if you miss a spot, the sucrose will stick.

13. Continue to heat the sucrose mixture until it reaches 130°C. Use the thermometer to measure the temperature, not to stir. Stirring could cause the tool to break, leaving you with a ruined batch of sucrose.

14. Remove the beaker from heat using tongs. Add 1.5 ml of *Vanilla planifola* liquid, but do not stir.

15. Using the tongs, pour the solution into the well-greased mold. Let the mixture cool before cutting it into squares.

16. Squares of sucrose can be individually wrapped using waxed paper.

17. Place your beaker, thermometer, and glass stir rod underneath a stream of hot water for one minute. Allow items to sit in hot water while completing other observations in the lab.

18. Compare a piece of your candy with groups that had a different procedure. Make visual, touch, and taste observations to compare and contrast the sugar structures. Record these observations in your sugar structure table.

19. Clean your lab area while you are waiting for your butterscotch to cool.

DATA AND OBSERVATIONS

Teacher Initials: _____

DATA ANALYSIS

For each of the following questions, be sure to explain using detail and complete sentences. If the question requires you to complete calculations, show all of your work.

1. What were two observations that you could use to identify whether acid was used in the production of a candy? Explain, citing the specific senses that allowed you to make that observation.

2. What were two observations that you could use to identify whether different sugars were used in the production of a candy? Explain, citing the specific senses that allowed you to make that observation.

CONCLUSION AND CONNECTIONS

1. Draw a picture of what you think the sucrose molecules look like in candies formed through each of the listed procedures. Label your diagrams.

Candy formed with acid	Candy formed with different sugars	Candy formed with only sucrose

2. List two situations in which sugar would be the ideal food source. For each example, use the information presented in the Background section to support your answer.

3. List one situation in which sugar would not be an ideal food source. Explain why using the information presented in the Background section to support your answer.

4. What other items go through crystallization? Give two additional examples of materials that crystallize when placed together.

5. What do you think would have happened if you had stretched and pulled the sugar while it was cooling? What properties would you expect to see in sugar that had undergone these physical manipulations?

EXPERIMENT 14:
Crystal Carbohydrates: Teacher Pages

CREATING A DATA TABLE TO ANALYZE HOW SUGAR STRUCTURE IMPACTS THE FORMATION OF BUTTERSCOTCH CANDY

This experiment takes a molecular view of sugar formation, introducing the sucrose molecule and how it can be arranged in different formations to create materials with very different qualities. The lab introduces students to the concept that the characteristics of their favorite foods come from how those foods are arranged at a molecular level. Students use basic observations such as taste and sight to contrast different butterscotch candy recipes. Students use these observations to address the molecular structure of the sugar. While looking at the composition of the sugars, students also are introduced to the skill of creating a data table. The data table creation is helpful because it not only organizes information but also highlights that qualitative observations are recognized as data in the same way that we use mathematics and numbers. This written element paired with the taste of old-fashioned butterscotch makes for an exciting approach to molecular chemistry.

STANDARDS ADDRESSED
National Science Education Standards: Grades 5–8

Content Standard A: Science as Inquiry
- Abilities necessary to do scientific inquiry
- Understanding about scientific inquiry

Content Standard B: Physical Science
- Properties and changes of properties in matter
- Transfer of energy

Content Standard E: Science and Technology
- Abilities of technological design
- Understanding about science and technology

Content Standard F: Science in Personal and Social Perspectives
- Personal health
- Risk and benefits
- Science and technology in society

Content Standard G: History and Nature of Science
- Science as a human endeavor
- Nature of science

National Science Education Content Standards: Grades 9–12

Content Standard A: Science as Inquiry
- Abilities necessary to do scientific inquiry
- Understanding about scientific inquiry

Content Standard B: Physical Science
- Structure of atoms
- Structure and properties of matter
- Chemical reactions

Content Standard E: Science and Technology
- Abilities of technological design
- Understanding about science and technology

Content Standard F: Science in Personal and Social Perspectives
- Personal and community health
- Science and technology in local, national, and global challenges

Content Standard G: History and Nature of Science
- Science as a human endeavor
- Nature of scientific knowledge
- Historical perspectives

VOCABULARY

Sucrose: A crystalline disaccharide of fructose and glucose, $C_{12}H_{22}O_{11}$, found in many plants but extracted as ordinary sugar mainly from sugar cane and sugar beets, widely used as a sweetener or preservative and in the manufacture of plastics and soaps. Also called *saccharose* (*The American Heritage Dictionary of the English Language* 2000).

Glucose: A monosaccharide sugar, $C_6H_{12}O_6$, occurring widely in most plant and animal tissue. It is the principal circulating sugar in the blood and the major energy source of the body (*The American Heritage Dictionary of the English Language* 2000).

Fructose: A very sweet sugar, $C_6H_{12}O_6$, occurring in many fruits and honey and used as a preservative for foodstuffs and as an intravenous nutrient. Also called *fruit sugar*, *levulose* (*The American Heritage Dictionary of the English Language* 2000).

Crystallize: To cause to form crystals or assume a crystalline structure (*The American Heritage Dictionary of the English Language* 2000).

Calorie: A unit of energy-producing potential equal to this amount of heat that is contained in food and released upon oxidation by the body. Also called *nutritionist's calorie* (*The American Heritage Dictionary of the English Language* 2000).

MATERIALS NEEDED, DECODED FOR THE GROCERY STORE

60 ml of brown sucrose, $C_{12}H_{22}O_{11}$ (brown sugar)
- Brown sugar can be purchased in the area of the store with white sugar and flour. Brown sugar is often sold in 2 lb. bags, so it will cover almost 16 lab groups. *Note:* Brown sugar is not a product that has a long shelf life once the bag is opened. Even if you squeeze out the air and seal it, the sugar usually gets hard after a few months. I buy only the exact amount I need, rather than buying extra and keeping it for next year.

60 ml of glucose solution (Karo syrup)
- Karo syrup is usually sold in the store area with maple syrup. Keep in mind that this supply is for only half of the lab groups (those who are assigned the creation of candy with different types of sugar). The bottles come is a variety of sizes, so look at the ml measurements on the side of the bottle and divide by 60 to find the number of lab groups each bottle contains. In my experience an average-size bottle covers about 10 lab groups.

- I recommend light corn syrup, rather than dark syrup, but this is purely an aesthetic choice.

30 ml of a solid fatty acid (butter)
- This is one-fourth cup of butter. All of your lab groups aside from the group that is creating candy with just sugar will need this item. Each stick constitutes a cup of butter, and packages of butter tend to come in four, therefore a box will work for 16 lab groups. *Note:* Students will need additional butter to grease their trays. I tend to purchase one extra stick of butter per class period for this effort.

60 ml of white sucrose, $C_{12}H_{22}O_{11}$ (white sugar)
- Sugar is sold in the area of the grocery store with flour and other baking products. A 5 lb. bag will be enough for around 30 lab groups.

5 ml of acetic acid solution (vinegar)
- Vinegar is often sold in the baking aisle along with baking soda and other dry goods. This is a small amount of vinegar and is only necessary for the lab groups assigned to create candy with acid. One bottle will work for more than 50 lab groups.

1 g of sodium chloride, NaCl (table salt)
- Each group uses a small amount of salt in its candy procedure, so a single salt container will be more than enough for 40 lab groups.

1.5 ml of *Vanilla planifola* liquid (vanilla flavoring)
- Vanilla extract can be purchased in the spice section of the store. I recommend using vanilla extract instead of vanilla flavoring, but that is just a personal preference. A 2 oz. bottle contains almost 60 ml or enough for 24 lab groups.

Aluminum foil
- Each lab group will need a sheet of aluminum foil to create its mold for cooling the candy. Rolls are sold in varying quantities, but a 75 yd. roll will work for 50 lab groups.

Dish soap
- This is necessary for cleanup. I ask students to use an amount about the size of a quarter for each glass container, and I have one bottle available for every four lab groups to share.

SAFETY HIGHLIGHTS

- The Bunsen burners and ring stands present a potential for students to burn themselves if used incorrectly. Please make sure students have had Bunsen burner safety training before allowing them to participate in this lab. As a teacher, you also need to be prepared with burn treatment options, such as running the burned area under cold water, if a student gets hurt.

- The liquid sugar in this lab reaches extremely high temperatures and can cause second- and third-degree burns if it touches the skin. It is very important to be with the students for the pouring process. If you have concerns about your students pouring hot liquids, I recommend doing this lab with additional adults in the room and having only adults pour the sugar. Students need to be made aware of this risk at the outset of the lab.

- Students will be working with vinegar, which is an acid. Goggles, aprons, and gloves are a must for protecting students' eyes, with an eyewash station and acid shower nearby for any situations that arise. If students get the acid on their skin, they should be cautious and wash the area with soap and water immediately.

- If a glass stir rod breaks during mixing, you should dispose of the entire mixture. Even if the break is minor, you may have shards of glass in the mixture that are not visible.

Note that these safety highlights are in addition to the safety information detailed in the Safety Protocol section at the beginning of this book. Please refer to that section for additional information about safety when implementing this or any lab in this book.

PROCEDURE

I recommend having students work in teams of two or three for this experiment. The final product creates between 10 and 15 pieces of candy depending on how large students cut the pieces, which is plenty to share among a larger group. There is also a significant amount of labor involved with the preparation of heating the sugar, which can be shared equally by a larger group. The larger group size also cuts down on the total number of lab groups per class and overall cost of supplies.

1. The topic of sugar is an instant attraction for students. Begin by having students read the Background section about sugar and its positive and negative effects on the human body. Reading this section as a class allows students an opportunity to share their experiences with the classmates, such as their favorite candies, memories of having too much sugar, and so on. These connec-

tions help all students create a context for this experiment and the discussion of sugars.

2. When explaining how sugars form chains, the Lego block analogy is a great way to demonstrate the creation of sugar chains and crystals. Using Lego blocks, you can demonstrate how the sugars hook together in a linear fashion to create a crystal. I create a small wall using Lego blocks of the same size and color to represent the sucrose molecules.

3. When explaining the process of preventing crystallization, use a Lego block that is a different size and color. Show how this negatively affects the pattern and structural integrity of the wall. This demonstration also can be done using basic building blocks or textbooks.

4. Assign students to their groups, stating which procedure they are going to test. Have the students circle their procedure title within the lab and cross out the others so that they follow the correct directions.

5. An optional addition is to assign each procedure a color such as red, blue, and green. Tell students, "If you are creating butterscotch with acid, use green food coloring in your candy" or "If you are creating butterscotch with other sugars, use blue food coloring in your candy," and so on. This creates a visual key for students to know what process was used to create each type of butterscotch.

6. Students can then write a hypothesis about what types of characteristics they would expect to find in candies with a crystal sugar structure. For those groups that are struggling, relate this back to the Lego demonstration. Ask, "What would you expect a food to look like that had that kind of clear organization? What would it feel like in your mouth if you took a bite of it?"

7. Students are then asked to create their own data table. Many students struggle with the idea of creating a data table when there are no numbers involved in data. It is important to express that data tables are useful for organizing information, not just numerical values. Students can work within their groups to create their data table before getting teacher approval. A sample data table is included below, although there is more than one way to set up the table.

	Taste	Texture	Smell
Butterscotch formed with acid			
Butterscotch formed with different sugars			
Butterscotch formed with only sucrose			

8. Students can use Bunsen burners or hot plates to achieve the heating step with the mixture. If you have younger students, I recommend hot plates on medium high heat. The older students may use the Bunsen burners, but depending on the size of your group, hot plates may be the safer choice.

9. Students need to be constantly stirring the sugar while it is heating until the sugar substance goes clear (showing all sugar is dissolved). The sugar will start off thick, and get thinner and turn clear as it heats. If the sugar starts to turn a dark shade of brown, that means it is burning and needs to be removed from the heat immediately. At one point as the sugar heats, it starts to bubble up and increase in volume. You can stir only the top layer to get the solution to calm back down.

10. Make sure the students are stirring with the glass stir rods and not the thermometers. Using thermometers to stir can cause them to break and ruin the final product.

11. When students put the vanilla into the hot sugar, it will often pop back at them because of the temperature differential. It can help to have students wait 60 seconds before adding the vanilla.

12. Upon pouring out the sugar, students need to immediately place their beakers, thermometers, and glass stir rods in hot water. Cold water will cause the glass to crack because of the temperature differential. Run these items under hot water immediately for one to two minutes and then allow the items to soak in hot water to prevent sugar from cooling on the beaker.

13. Students need to wait about five to seven minutes for the sugar to cool before they cut it. If they let it cool to a point that it hardens, they can break the sugar pieces apart to be "butterscotch bark." The shape of the final candy is not important.

14. Have students trade pieces of candy for their observations. This way all students get a chance to test each kind of candy. The one or two groups that made the crystallized sugar will need to give up all of their candy. I give them store-bought butterscotch in exchange for volunteering to make the crystallized sugar product.

15. Once students are done trading candy, they can finish cleaning the lab area and work on their Data Analysis and Conclusion and Connections questions.

EXPERIMENT 14 Crystal Carbohydrates: Teacher Pages

DATA ANALYSIS ANSWER KEY

1. *What were two observations that you could use to identify whether acid was used in the production of a candy? Explain, citing the specific senses that allowed you to make that observation.*

   Students will have different answers based on the observations in their particular data table. Observations include that the candy was smooth in touch, taste, and appearance. When put in your mouth it is slippery, which leads you to believe that there is no crystallization, meaning the candy may have been produced with an acid that prevents sugars forming in crystals.

2. *What were two observations that you could use to identify whether different sugars were used in the production of a candy? Explain, citing the specific senses that allowed you to make that observation.*

   Students will have different answers based on the observations in their particular data table. Observations include that the candy was smooth in touch, taste, and appearance. These are the same observations that were listed in question 1. This is correct, and highlights that you cannot distinguish how crystallization was prevented.

CONCLUSION AND CONNECTIONS ANSWER KEY

This section of the lab offers a great opportunity to engage the entire class in discussion to clarify the main ideas of the lab and allow the students to make their own connections between science and cooking. I ask that students answer the Data Analysis questions and attempt to answer the Conclusion and Connections questions, with the understanding that we will spend time the next day discussing the Conclusion and Connections section.

1. *Draw a picture of what you think the sucrose molecules look like in candies formed through each of the listed procedures. Label your diagrams.*

Candy formed with acid	Candy formed with different sugars	Candy formed with only sucrose

300

NATIONAL SCIENCE TEACHERS ASSOCIATION

For this question, I look that students have attempted some sort of diagram of molecules and labeled them correctly as sucrose. Ideally, their drawings reflect the organization of molecules so that the last box shows crystals, and the other two show the molecules in a bit of disarray.

2. *List two situations in which sugar would be the ideal food source. For each example, use the information presented in the Background section to support your answer.*

   Students can list any situation in which a person is lacking energy and needs a quick pick-me-up. For example, when you are taking a test, eating a mint may give you a sudden burst of energy to keep your muscles and mind going. Sugar is quickly metabolized by the body and delivers the energy to where it is needed.

3. *List one situation in which sugar would not be an ideal food source. Explain why using the information presented in the Background section to support your answer.*

   Any situations that require strength and energy for an extended period of time are not ideal for using sugar as your source of energy. This could be playing in a sporting event, participating in a school play, or running a marathon. The sugar metabolizes quickly, leaving the body tired and lacking in energy.

4. *What other items go through crystallization? Give two additional examples of materials that crystallize when placed together.*

   Salts and minerals go through crystallization, as does ice. Students can research these items on the internet if they need additional resources.

5. *What do you think would have happened if you had stretched and pulled the sugar while it was cooling? What properties would you expect to see in sugar that had undergone these physical manipulations?*

   The physical movement will actually alter the chains of sucrose while they are still hot. This is what happens when taffy is made; properties of taffy include striations in the appearance; a softer, more malleable texture; and fewer crystals. Students are often surprised that a physical action can change the actual structure of the substance on a molecular level. If students have completed either of the experiments with cheese, you can relate this answer back to their experiences with casein molecules. You also can relate it to the process of kneading dough.

CROSS-CURRICULAR NOTE: MATH

There are multiple types of sugars used in this experiment, and these sugars have different molecular structures. Students can analyze the different chemical make-ups and geometric structures to compare and contrast the different types of sugars and how they affected the formation of the candy.

CROSS-CURRICULAR NOTE: LITERACY

Although there are many types of sugars, they do not always have the same qualities. Compare these similarities and differences to synonyms in English. How does changing a word to a similar word affect the sentence? For example: *That boy was big.* If you change the word to *huge, massive,* or *voluminous,* how does that change the meaning of the sentence? Students can draw pictures of how each word changes their perception of the image, or generate their own sentences with synonym changes.

OPTIONAL EXTENSIONS

Middle School

1. Students can research different recipes for making butterscotch and other candies. Based on the recipes, ask students to identify whether or not the sugar will be crystallized.

2. Help students grow sugar crystals to look at how temperature can impact the shape and structure of the crystal. Students can grow crystals using different types of sugars to see how they affect the characteristics of the crystal.

3. In order to make this lab more inquiry based, ask students to design an experiment that shows a relationship between sugar characteristics and thermal temperature. Students can do background research to learn about what temperatures to start and stop with.

High School

1. Encourage students to look at how the molecular structure of sugar changes with crystallization. Ask, "What characteristics of the sucrose molecule allow crystallization to occur?"

2. Students can explore whether crystallization occurs in sugar substitutes. Encourage students to create a new "candy temperature chart" for sugar substitutes explaining how temperature affects the final product.

3. Many items can crystallize, such as salts. Have students explore how the structure of salts relates to the structure of sugar. This can be observed through molecular models, microscopes, and hand lenses.

EXPERIMENT 15:
Strong Sugar Science: Student Pages

DEVELOPING AN EXPERIMENT TO FIND THE RELATIONSHIP AMONG HEAT, SUGAR STRUCTURE, AND TENSILE STRENGTH FOR CANDY

BACKGROUND

Sugar (sucrose) is a dynamic compound. The molecules can arrange themselves into different structures to create different types of candy, all of which have very different properties. Table 15.1 shows how temperature can be used to create these different structures.

Candy temperature chart.			
Name of structure	Temperature (based on sea level)	Description	Common uses
Thread	108°C–118°C	The syrup drips from a spoon, forms thin threads in water.	Syrup
Soft ball	118°C–120°C	The syrup easily forms a ball while in cold water, but flattens once removed.	Fudge
Firm ball	123°C–125°C	The syrup will form a stable ball, but loses its round shape once pressed.	Caramel candies
Hard ball	125°C–133°C	The syrup holds a ball shape, but remains sticky.	Marshmallows
Soft crack	135°C–155°C	The syrup will form firm but pliable threads.	Taffy
Hard crack	160°C–168°C	The syrup will crack if you try to mold it.	Lollipops
Caramel	169°C and above	The syrup will turn golden at this stage.	Pralines

For this experiment, we will be testing the strength of three of these kinds of candies. We will test the firm ball, soft crack, and hard crack phases of sucrose.

You might be wondering how we will be doing this. Well, you are going to decide that. This experiment is going to be designed and implemented by you. You will be determining the hypothesis, materials, procedure, variables, controls, and so on. This will give you a chance to direct what you do in the lab and how you measure the final outcome. There will be guidance and checkpoints throughout the lab to make sure you are on the right track. Channel your inner scientist, grab your goggles, and let's get started.

SETUP

In order to get started, it is important to have a question that you are trying to answer. For this particular lab, you are looking to answer, "What is the relationship between the type of sugar structure and how much weight the structure can hold?"

HYPOTHESIS

Make a prediction about the relationship between type of sugar structure and strength. Provide an explanation for your prediction.

VARIABLES

It is helpful to identify variables for this experiment, before moving into designing a procedure. Take a moment to identify the following variables. Have your teacher initial the page before moving on with the experiment.

Independent Variable: _____
Dependent Variable: _____
Control Variables (list at least three):
_____
_____
_____

Teacher Initials: _____

PROCEDURE

1. Using these variables, you will need to figure out how you are going to test the relationship between sugar structure and strength. Remember the steps for writing a good scientific procedure:
    *   Describe your method step by step. Each step should be numbered and should include all related ideas.
    *   Write sequentially in the order you perform each step.
    *   Give directions in the imperative mood. Use the command form of the verb.
    *   Write clearly and concisely. Be very specific. Never assume anything!
    *   Use the correct names of all equipment, materials, and objects.

2. To help you design your procedure, I will provide you with a basic sugar recipe that you can use to create the sugar solution for your experiment. I will also provide you with a list of materials needed to create the sugar solution. You can refer to these steps in your procedure simply by writing "Use the provided scientific procedure to create a sugar solution." Keep in mind that this is just the sugar solution, not the final sugar structure. Make sure you add additional materials to the Materials Needed list as you use them in your procedure.

3. Once you have your procedure, bring it to be checked and initialed by the teacher. This will most likely take you two or three drafts before you have it right. Do not get discouraged; this is just like writing drafts in your English class. You are not expected to get it perfect the first time. Good luck!

MATERIALS NEEDED PER GROUP

Sugar Solution Materials

*   30 ml of glucose solution (Karo syrup)
*   60 ml of white sucrose, $C_{12}H_{22}O_{11}$ (sugar)
*   15 ml of dihydrogen monoxide, H_2O (water)
*   1 g of citric acid (true lemon flavoring)
*   1 g of sodium chloride, $NaCl$ (table salt)
*   Beaker, 200 ml
*   Thermometer, 150°C and nonmercury
*   Graduated cylinder, 10 ml
*   Graduated cylinder, 100 ml
*   Balance
*   Beaker tongs
*   Bunsen burners and iron rings with wire gauze

- Glass stir rod
- Indirectly vented chemical-splash goggles
- Aprons
- Gloves
- Optional flavoring and food coloring

Additional Materials

PROCEDURE FOR CREATING SUGAR SOLUTION

1. Read through the entire procedure before beginning.

2. Put on your safety goggles, gloves, and apron, and gather all your materials at your lab station. If you notice any of the materials are dirty or discolored, notify your teacher.

3. Measure 30 ml of glucose solution using the graduated cylinder and place it in the 250 ml beaker.

4. Measure 60 ml of white sucrose using the graduated cylinder and place it in the 250 ml beaker and mix with a glass stir rod.

5. Add 15 ml of H_2O to the mixture of sucrose in the 250 ml beaker. Stir thoroughly with the glass stir rod.

6. Use the balance to measure 1 g of sodium chloride and add to the mixture in the 250 ml beaker.

7. Finally, add 1 g of citric acid to the mixture in the beaker. Stir the contents together with the glass stir rod.

8. Set up a Bunsen burner and ring stand with wire mesh on the iron ring. Make sure your Bunsen burner gas intake tube is securely connected to the gas nozzle and that the ring is set about 3 in. above the barrel of the burner (see Figure 15.1). Light the Bunsen burner to create a flame that is no more than 3 in. high. (It should not be touching the wire mesh.)

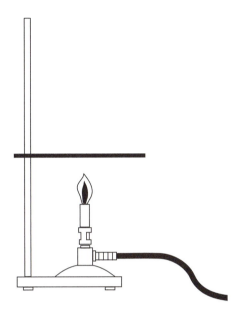

Figure 15.1: Bunsen burner and ring stand.

9. Using the tongs, place the beaker on the ring stand. Slowly heat the mixture while stirring constantly. If you heat the mixture too quickly or do not stir it, you will burn your sucrose and ruin your candy.

10. Upon completion of heating, wait 90 seconds and then you can add 1.25 ml of your choice of flavoring and three drops of food coloring.

PROCEDURE

Teacher Initials: _____

DATA AND OBSERVATIONS

Note the following rules when creating data tables:

1. Make sure your data table has a title. This title should explain what information is presented in the table to make it easier to identify.

2. State your independent variable on a different axis from your dependent variable in the data table.

3. Identify units of measurement when necessary.

4. Use a straight edge or graph paper when creating your table.

With these rules in mind, use the variables identified in the Setup section to create a data table for recording your data.

DATA ANALYSIS

1. Create a graph that shows the relationship between the structure of the sugar and the strength. Remember to include all elements of a scientific graph (title, labeled axis, units, etc.).

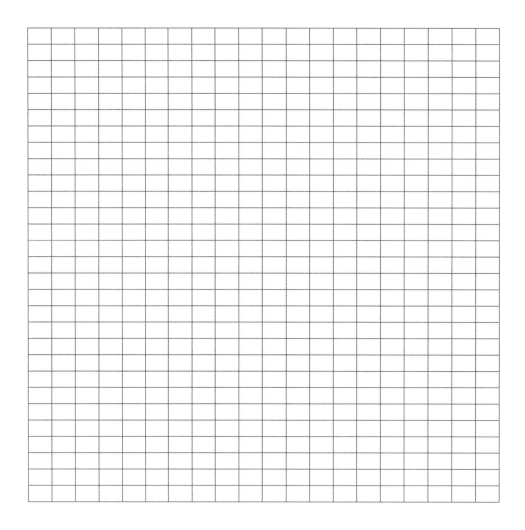

CONCLUSION AND CONNECTIONS

1. Was your initial hypothesis correct? Please restate your hypothesis and identify whether you were correct or incorrect using data to support your answer.

2. If you could do the experiment again, what would you do differently?

3. What do you think the strength of candy would be that has been heated to 170°C? Explain how you arrived at your answer.

4. Based on your findings, which of the sugar structures is easiest to package and ship around the world? Explain using specific data to support your answer.

EXPERIMENT 15:
Strong Sugar Science: Teacher Pages

DEVELOPING AN EXPERIMENT TO FIND THE RELATIONSHIP AMONG HEAT, SUGAR STRUCTURE, AND TENSILE STRENGTH FOR CANDY

This experiment uses the scientific method skills in a guided inquiry of sugar structure for different classes of candy. The lab is structured to help students use their problem-solving skills to create an experiment that relates sugar structure to strength. The experiment asks students to create a hypothesis, materials list, procedure, and data table to support their inquiry. Students then run the three trials and graph their data to determine the relationship between sugar structure and strength. The conclusion asks students to focus not only on their data but also on what they would do differently next time. This final lab represents a culmination of skills obtained throughout the other lab experiences in this book.

STANDARDS ADDRESSED
National Science Education Standards: Grades 5–8

Content Standard A: Science as Inquiry
- Abilities necessary to do scientific inquiry
- Understanding about scientific inquiry

Content Standard B: Physical Science
- Properties and changes of properties in matter
- Transfer of energy

Content Standard E: Science and Technology
- Abilities of technological design
- Understanding about science and technology

Content Standard F: Science in Personal and Social Perspectives
- Personal health
- Risk and benefits
- Science and technology in society

Content Standard G: History and Nature of Science
- Science as a human endeavor
- Nature of science

National Science Education Standards: Grades 9–12

Content Standard A: Science as Inquiry
- Abilities necessary to do scientific inquiry
- Understanding about scientific inquiry

Content Standard B: Physical Science
- Structure of atoms
- Structure and properties of matter
- Chemical reactions

Content Standard E: Science and Technology
- Abilities of technological design
- Understanding about science and technology

Content Standard F: Science in Personal and Social Perspectives
- Personal and community health
- Science and technology in local, national, and global challenges

Content Standard G: History and Nature of Science
- Science as a human endeavor
- Nature of scientific knowledge
- Historical perspectives

VOCABULARY

Variable: A factor that can change or influence an outcome.

Independent variable: The factor or variable that is being tested, or the variable that scientists choose to change in the experiment. It can also be called the *experimental variable* or *manipulated variable*.

Dependent variable: The variable that describes what happens as a result of changing the independent variable. You can also look at this variable as what is being measured to find changes that occur when the independent variable is changed. This can also be called the *responding variable*.

Controlled variables: These are factors that are not being tested and therefore are held constant throughout the experiment.

Controlled experiment: An experiment in which only one factor is being changed (the independent variable), and the other variables are being held constant to create a control group to create a standard to measure the change.

Sucrose: A crystalline disaccharide of fructose and glucose, $C_{12}H_{22}O_{11}$, found in many plants but extracted as ordinary sugar mainly from sugar cane and sugar beets, widely used as a sweetener or preservative and in the manufacture of plastics and soaps. Also called *saccharose* (*The American Heritage Dictionary of the English Language* 2000).

MATERIALS NEEDED, DECODED FOR THE GROCERY STORE

Note: The materials necessary for this lab are dependent on the procedure and number of trials decided on by the students. While you are checking students' procedures, it is necessary to keep track of any additional materials and the amount of trials so you can purchase your materials accordingly.

30 ml of glucose solution (Karo syrup)
- Karo syrup is usually found in the area with maple syrup in the grocery store. Keep in mind that this supply is for only half of the lab groups (those who are assigned the creation of candy with different types of sugar). The bottles come in a variety of sizes, so look at the ml measurements on the side of the bottle and divide by 30 to find the number of lab groups each bottle will cover. In my experience, an average-size bottle covers about 40 lab trials.
- I recommend the light corn syrup, rather than the dark, but that is just an aesthetic choice.

60 ml of white sucrose, $C_{12}H_{22}O_{11}$ (sugar)
- Sugar is sold in the area of the grocery store with flour and other baking products. A 5 lb. bag will provide sugar for around 60 lab trials.

1 g of citric acid (true lemon flavoring)
- Citric acid can be purchased from a pharmacy or a grocery store under the name "true lemon." In most stores this is kept with the sugar substitutes. True lemon is a replacement lemon flavoring that is sold in packets or bottles. A bottle will contain enough citric acid for more than 25 groups.

1 g of sodium chloride, NaCl (table salt)
- Each group uses a small amount of salt in its candy procedure, so a single salt container will be more than enough for 40 lab groups.

Food coloring
- Students can add a couple of drops of food coloring if they are interested. This can be helpful in distinguishing the different sugar structures (e.g., the hard crack is red, the soft crack is blue, etc.).

1 ml of flavoring
- Students appreciate the opportunity to add a little bit of flavoring so they get different flavors that they can share and trade after the completion of the lab. Flavorings are available as extracts in the spice section of the grocery store. I usually choose whatever flavors are on sale. These can be pricey, so be thoughtful about your purchases. One small bottle will cover about eight student groups.

Additional Materials

30 ml solid fatty acid (butter)
- This is one-fourth cup of butter. This is useful for greasing the candy molds so the candy can be removed. Each stick constitutes a cup of butter, and packages of butter tend to come in four, so a box will work for 16 lab groups.

Aluminum foil
- Each lab group will need a sheet of aluminum foil to create its mold for cooling the candy. Rolls are sold in varying quantities, but a 75 yd. roll will work for 50 lab groups.

Dish soap
- This is necessary for cleanup. I ask students to use an amount about the size of a quarter for each glass container, and I have one bottle available for every four lab groups to share.

SAFETY HIGHLIGHTS

- The Bunsen burners and ring stands present a potential for students to burn themselves if used incorrectly. Please make sure students have had Bunsen burner safety training before allowing them to participate in this lab. As a teacher, you also need to be prepared with burn treatment options, such as running the burned area under cold water, if a student gets hurt.
- The liquid sugar in this lab reaches extremely high temperatures and can cause second- and third-degree burns if it touches the skin. It is very important to be with the students for the pouring process. If you have concerns about your students pouring hot liquids, I recommend doing this lab with additional adults in the room and having only adults pour the sugar. Students need to be made aware of this risk at the outset of the lab.
- If a glass stir rod breaks during mixing, you should dispose of the entire mixture. Even if the break is minor, you may have shards of glass in the mixture that are not visible.

Note that these safety highlights are in addition to the safety information detailed in the Safety Protocol section at the beginning of this book. Please refer to that section for additional information about safety when implementing this or any lab in this book.

PREPARATION

This experiment requires class time for the students to prepare the lab before they can implement it. Therefore, the materials will not need to be ready on the first day you introduce the experiment.

PROCEDURE

I recommend having students work in teams of two or three for this experiment. The final product creates between 10 and 15 pieces of candy, depending on how large students cut the pieces, which is plenty to share among a large group. There is also a significant amount of labor involved with the preparation of heating the sugar, which can be shared equally by a large group. The large group size also cuts down on the total number of lab groups per class and overall cost of supplies.

1. To begin this lab, show a few short clips from a movie that focuses on candy. There are lots of options, but I recommend the scene from *Willy Wonka and the Chocolate Factory* where the characters are eating by the chocolate river. There are two versions of this film. I prefer the older version of the movie, but the students typically enjoy watching both. Ask the students what is so enticing about the scene(s). It's really the candy. It is impressive that the

majority of the candy in the film is all made from the basic ingredient of sucrose. Sucrose is an amazing substance that can take many different shapes with its molecules to forming a multitude of candies with different qualities. This leads students into the Background section of the lab.

2. Students are going to be designing this experiment all the way through using their skills in the scientific method. The lab details the expectations of students and highlights checkpoints when they will need to check in with you. This helps you oversee that they are on the right track, and also helps you plan for the quantity and types of supplies that will be necessary for them to implement their experiments.

3. The process of designing the experiment can take students anywhere from three 45-minute periods to one week. I recommend giving students checkpoints that need to be completed each day. This helps them focus on completing small tasks rather than feeling overwhelmed by the enormity of the lab experience. Students who are not able to complete the checkpoint in class are asked to complete that section for homework.

4. A great technology tool to use with this project is online documents such as Google Docs. By having them work on a single shared document, all students are able to contribute to the lab creation whether they are all together or at home. It also alleviates problems that can arise with large lab groups such as partners being sick and having all the documents with them. The online documents require students to have access to computers with the internet.

5. Students can use Bunsen burners or hot plates to achieve the heating step with the mixture. If you have younger students, I recommend hot plates on medium high heat. The older students may use the Bunsen burners, but depending on the size of your group, hot plates may be the safer choice.

6. Students need to be constantly stirring the sugar while it is heating until the sugar substance goes clear (showing all sugar is dissolved). The sugar will start off thick, and get thinner and turn clear as it heats. If the sugar starts to turn a dark shade of brown, that means it is burning and needs to be removed from the heat immediately. At one point as the sugar heats, it starts to bubble up and increase in volume. You can stir only the top layer to get the solution to calm back down.

7. Make sure the students are stirring with the glass stir rods and not the thermometers. Using thermometers to stir can cause them to break and ruin the final product.

8. When the students put the flavoring into the hot sugar, it will often pop back at them because of the temperature differential. It can help to have students wait 60 seconds before adding the vanilla.

9. Upon pouring out the sugar, students need to immediately place their beakers, thermometers, and glass stir rods in hot water. Cold water will cause

the glass to crack because of the temperature differential. Run these items under hot water immediately for one to two minutes and then allow the items to soak in hot water to prevent sugar from cooling on the beaker.

10. After students have completed their testing, they are welcome to eat the sugar creations (as long as the test they designed does not make this product inedible).

DATA ANALYSIS ANSWER KEY

Data analysis for this lab involves creating a graph. If students are struggling with the calculations, I recommend using a sample data set and going through the calculations as a class on the board. Then students can use the same skills and apply them directly to their data.

1. *Create a graph that shows the relationship between the structure of the sugar and the strength. Remember to include all elements of a scientific graph (title, labeled axes, units, etc.).*

   Students will need to create a graph that shows the relationship between sugar and strength. Because students create this procedure, all the graphs and data will most likely be different. Look for all elements of the graph to be completed, as well as having the sugar temperature on the *x*-axis and the unit for strength measurement on the *y*-axis.

CONCLUSION AND CONNECTIONS ANSWER KEY

This section of the lab offers a great opportunity to engage the entire class in discussion to clarify the main ideas of the lab and allow the students an opportunity to make their own connections between science and cooking. I ask that students answer the Data Analysis questions and attempt to answer the Conclusion and Connections questions, with the understanding that we will spend time the next day discussing the last section.

1. *Was your initial hypothesis correct? Please restate your hypothesis and identify whether you were correct or incorrect using data to support your answer.*

   Student hypotheses will vary for this experiment. No matter what they find, it is important that their answers use data to support the proposed relationship between sugar and strength.

2. *If you could do the experiment again, what would you do differently?*

This is an ideal opportunity for students to look at the process of analyzing errors and revising their experiment. This highlights the cyclical flow of scientific research and is a great topic of discussion that emphasizes why scientists are never "done" with researching and exploring the natural world around them.

3. *What do you think the strength of candy would be that has been heated to 170°C? Explain how you arrived at your answer.*

This question asks students to use the graph they created in the Data Analysis section to extrapolate data about how strong sugar structures would be if they had tested sugar that was in the caramel stage. Students are asked to use their data to create a model and prediction.

4. *Based on your findings, which of the sugar structures is easiest to package and ship around the world? Explain using specific data to support your answer.*

Again, individual students will answer differently based on their data and conclusion about the relationship between sugar strength and structure. Students should choose the candy structure that was the strongest according to their data, as that would be the most likely to withstand the pressures of being shipped around the world.

CROSS-CURRICULAR NOTE: MATH

This is an ideal lab to partner with the math teacher and ask students to create a line of best fit or point-slope equation to describe the relationship between sugar structure and strength. Students can explore how that line helps them to describe the relationship between the two variables.

CROSS-CURRICULAR NOTE: LITERACY

Invite students to think about why it is necessary to record all their steps, data, and results in this experiment. Share the story of scientist Stanley Pons from the University of Utah, who in 1989 along with his mentor teacher Martin Fleischman claimed to have created a device that allowed fusion to occur at room temperature. When the scientists' results could not be replicated, their fame became ridicule. This historical account provides a clear example as to why students should document their efforts in a laboratory setting.

320

OPTIONAL EXTENSIONS

Middle School

1. Take this experiment one step further to full inquiry by allowing students to determine their own question for the investigation. They could test items like time to dissolve in your mouth, how the type of sugar impacts the sugar structures, and so on.

2. Have students compare their results by testing the strength of store-bought candies that meet the sugar structure requirements for this lab. Students can see how well the manufactured candy holds up when compared with their creations.

High School

1. Ask students to compare the structural design of the sugar crystallization to bridge designs. Ask, "What similarities exist in both structures, and how do those similarities give both the bridge and sugar candy improved strength?" Students can do a study of angles and how angles of construction impact the stability of a structure.

2. Students can consider how thermal energy impacts the structure of other molecules. Encourage students to look at building materials such as concrete, steel, and iron. Ask how these materials react to thermal energy, and how those reactions are taken into account when the materials are used in engineering.

REFERENCES

About.com. Candy: Candy temperature guide: How to test the temperature of sugar syrup. *http://candy.about.com/od/candybasics/a/candytemp.htm*

American Heritage Dictionary of the English Language. 2000. Boston: Houghton Mifflin.

American Heritage Science Dictionary. 2005. Boston: Houghton Mifflin.

Food Network. n.d. Cinnamon rolls recipe. *www.foodnetwork.com/recipes/diners-drive-ins-and-dives/cinnamon-rolls-recipe/index.html*

Princeton University. 2006. WordNet 3.0. Princeton, NJ: Princeton University Press. *http://wordnet.princeton.edu*

ADDITIONAL RESOURCES

About.com. Chemistry: How to create an endothermic chemical reaction (safe). *http://chemistry.about.com/cs/howtos/ht/endothermic.htm*

Albino, G., et al. 2009. Yeast fermentation. *www.science-projects.com/Fermentation/yeast.htm*

Algren, N. 1992. *America eats.* Iowa City: University of Iowa Press.

Allrecipes.com. Butterscotch candy. *http://allrecipes.com/Recipe/butterscotch-candy/Detail.aspx*

Allrecipes.com. Proofing yeast. *http://allrecipes.com/HowTo/proofing-yeast/Detail.aspx*

American Heritage. 1964. *The American Heritage cookbook and illustrated history of American eating and drinking.* New York: American Heritage.

Apicus. 1958. *The Roman cookery book*, B. Flower, and E. Rosenbaum (translators). London: Harrap.

Aresty, E. B. 1964. *The delectable paste.* New York: Simon and Schuster.

Ask Yahoo! Where did the whole "give an apple to the teacher" thing come from? *http://ask.yahoo.com/20060420.html*

Blackstone, N. B. 1974. *Biography of Reverend William Blackstone, the pioneer of Boston and his ancestors and descendents.* Homestead, FL: N. B. Blackstone.

Boizot, P. 1976. *The pizza express cookbook.* London: Elm Tree Books.

Breadtopia. Make your own sourdough starter. *www.breadtopia.com/make-your-own-sourdough-starter*

Burns, M. 1978. *Good for me! All about food in 32 bites.* Boston: Little, Brown.

Callen, A. T. 1981. *The wonderful world of pizzas, quiches, and savory pies.* New York: Crown.

Chem4Kids.com. Acids and bases are everywhere. *www.chem4kids.com/files/react_acidbase.html*

Editors of American Heritage. 1964. *The American Heritage cookbook.* Rockville, MD: American Heritage.

eHow. How to make a wet mount microscope slide. *www.ehow.com/how_2080620_make-wet-mount-microscope-slide.html#ixzz0uiFlRop9*

Elkort, M. 1991. *The secret life of food: A feast of food and drink history, folklore, and fact.* Los Angeles: Jeremy P. Tarcher.

Exploratorium. The accidental scientist. Science of candy: Science of sugar. *www.exploratorium.edu/cooking/candy/sugar.html*

Fankhauser, D. B. 2005. American mozzarella: Microwave á la Joyce. *http://biology.clc.uc.edu/Fankhauser/Cheese/mozzarella_joyces.html*

Free Dictionary. Gluten. *www.thefreedictionary.com/Gluten*

Fussell, B. 1992. *The story of corn.* New York: Knopf.

Hazen, M. n.d. *Johnny Appleseed.* Ashland County Chapter of the Ohio Genealogical Society. *http://ashlandohiogenealogy.org/johnnyappleseed.html*

ilovebacteria.com. How does JELL-O work? *http://ilovebacteria.com/jelly.htm*

Kaboose. Homemade ice cream in a bag. *http://crafts.kaboose.com/ice-cream-in-a-bag.html*

Love, L. 1980. *The complete book of pizza.* Evanston, IL: Sassafras Press.

McClintock, T. C. 1967. Henderson Luelling, Seth Lewelling, and the birth of the Pacific Coast fruit industry. *Oregon Historical Quarterly* 68 (2): 153–174.

McDonald, L. 2007. What are good sources of protein? *www.bodyrecomposition.com/nutrition/what-are-good-sources-of-protein-speed-of-digestion-pt1.html*

Men's Total Fitness. Casein protein: The slow-digesting protein. *www.mens-total-fitness.com/casein-protein.html*

Metzger, L. n.d. The role of calcium, phosphate, lactose, and salt/moisture in cheese pH. *www.cpdmp.cornell.edu/CPDMP/Pages/Workshops/Syracuse04/ Role_of_Calcium.pdf*

Mozzarella Company. Mozzarella history. *www.mozzco.com/mozzhisty.html*

Oakley, H. 1980. *The buying guide for fresh fruits, vegetables, herbs, and nuts.* 7th ed. Hagerstown, MD: Blue Goose.

Panati, C. 1987. *Panati's extraordinary origins of everyday things.* New York: Harper and Row.

Red Star Original. The science of yeast. *www.redstaryeast.com/science_of_yeast/ information_for_educators.php*

Root, W. 1980. *Food: An authoritative and visual history and dictionary of the foods of the world.* New York: Smithmark.

Russell, S. P. 1970. *Peanuts, popcorn, ice cream, candy, and soda pop, and how they began.* Nashville, TN: Abingdon Press.

Sanger, M. B. 1976. *Escoffier, master chef.* New York: Farrar Straus Giroux.

Simmons, A. 1984. *The first American cookbook.* New York: Dover.

Sugar facts. 15 fascinating sugar facts. *www.sugarfacts.org*

Summers, V. 2009. Kitchen chemistry: What is pectin? How does it work? *www. associatedcontent.com/article/1750322/kitchen_chemistry_what_is_pectin_how_ pg2.html?cat=22*

Trager, J. 1980. *The foodbook.* New York: Avon.

Trager, J. 1995. *The food chronology: A food lover's compendium of events and anecdotes from prehistory to the present.* New York: Henry Holt.

USDA national nutrient database for standard reference. 2010. *www.nal.usda. gov/fnic/foodcomp/search*

Wilcox, E. W. 2002. *Buckeye cookery and practical housekeeping.* Carlisle, MA: Applewood Books.

Williams, B. 1976. *Cornzapoppin'! Popcorn recipes and party ideas for all occasions.* New York: Holt, Rinehart and Winston.

Wynne, P. 1975. *Apples: History, folklore, horticulture and gastronomy.* New York: Hawthorn Books.

ABOUT THE AUTHOR

Sarah Young is an eighth-grade physical science teacher at Rowland Hall Middle School in Salt Lake City, Utah. She earned a bachelor's degree in Environmental, Population, and Organism Biology from the University of Colorado at Boulder in May 2004. Upon completing her bachelor's degree, she pursued her master's degree in Education at Lesley University in Cambridge, Massachusetts. Sarah earned her degree in Secondary Science Education in May 2005, while concurrently gaining a year of direct school experience under the direction of master mentor teachers at Brookwood School in Manchester, Massachusetts. Aside from her work in the classroom, Sarah continues to be involved in the academic realm as an adjunct professor at Westminster College where she teaches master's students in secondary science methods. Sarah has published in NSTA's *Science Scope*, presented at local and national conferences, and participated in several professional development institutes. She is passionate about science education for all students and strives to help them find their "inner scientist."

ACKNOWLEDGMENTS

There are a lot of words in a book, and it was not without help that I was able to complete this collection of lab activities. Although there are *many* people who have supported my journey throughout science education, there are a few individuals who specifically contributed to this work. In acknowledgment of their help, I would like to profusely thank the following people who made this book possible.

First, thank you to all the amazing people in the Education Department at the Thomas Jefferson National Accelerator in Newport News, Virginia. The Academies Creating Teacher Scientists program with the Department of Energy took a chance on a girl from Utah in the summer of 2009, and helped me aspire to not only improve myself as a teacher but also share my work with others. Thank you to all the administration, my "BFF" ACTS science camp teachers, and of course the "Boss of Table 5" for all your help and proofreading support.

Second, thank you to the sassy English teacher down the hall. You inspire me to be a better educator. I will always admire your passion and drive, and will continue to work hard to become a better writer and remove those prepositional phrases from the ends of my sentences. I truly would not have attempted this project without your encouragement, so thank you for taking time to help a new teacher.

Finally, thank you to my family for giving their support and time to help me complete this project. A special thank you to my sweet Jake for sharing his Mom with other children and families. You always keep me smiling and laughing, for which I will always be grateful.

INDEX